Get the eBook FREE!

(PDF, ePub, Kindle, and liveBook all included)

We believe that once you buy a book from us, you should be able to read it in any format we have available. To get electronic versions of this book at no additional cost to you, purchase and then register this book at the Manning website.

Go to https://www.manning.com/freebook and follow the instructions to complete your pBook registration.

That's it!
Thanks from Manning!

Praise for *Data Without Labels*

A must read for learning unsupervised learning and GenAI.

—Khuram Pervez, EGA

A practical guide for beginners as well as practitioners.

—Amaresh Rajasekharan, IBM

The absolute resource for all important questions about data without labels.

—Arne Peter Raulf, German Aerospace Center

Comprehensive and detailed guide to mastering unsupervised learning and generative AI.

—Krishna Chaitanya Anipindi, Hexagon

Explores new ways to uncover patterns, generate insights, and push machine learning beyond labeled data.

—Stephen Tobayiwa, Unite Services GmbH

A concise guide covering both theory and implementation.

—Deepika Sinha, Head of AI/ML/Gen AI

Data Without Labels

PRACTICAL UNSUPERVISED MACHINE LEARNING

VAIBHAV VERDHAN

FOREWORD BY RAVI GOPALAKRISHNAN

MANNING

SHELTER ISLAND

For online information and ordering of this and other Manning books, please visit
www.manning.com. The publisher offers discounts on this book when ordered in quantity.
For more information, please contact

> Special Sales Department
> Manning Publications Co.
> 20 Baldwin Road
> PO Box 761
> Shelter Island, NY 11964
> Email: orders@manning.com

Manning Publications Co.
20 Baldwin Road
PO Box 761
Shelter Island, NY 11964

Development editor:	Ian Hough
Technical editor:	Davide Dev Vento
Review editor:	Kishor Rit
Production editor:	Kathy Rossland
Copy editor:	Kari Lucke
Proofreader:	Mike Beady
Technical proofreader:	Frances Buontempo
Typesetter and cover designer:	Marija Tudor

ISBN 9781617298721
Printed in the United States of America

To Yashi, Pakhi, Rudra, and Shiva

brief contents

contents

foreword

In today's dynamic landscape of AI and machine learning, the ability to extract meaningful insights from unlabeled data is transforming industries and driving innovation. As an AI leader and practitioner with experience across multiple sectors—and currently heading the Data Science and AI team at a major pharmaceutical company—I have witnessed first-hand how groundbreaking ideas reshape entire industries.

In our work in oncology and biopharma, we use AI to empower life sciences companies to educate healthcare professionals and target key stakeholders with precision—ensuring that the right therapy reaches the right patient at the right time. In regulated industries, where precision and compliance are paramount, innovative approaches that extract actionable insights from raw, unlabeled data are not just beneficial but essential.

Data Without Labels is organized into three comprehensive parts that chart a clear course from theory to application, as detailed in the table of contents. Part 1 lays the groundwork with core unsupervised learning techniques, covering clustering, dimensionality reduction, and anomaly detection to equip readers with essential tools for interpreting raw data. Part 2 advances into sophisticated methodologies, introducing self-supervised and contrastive learning approaches that overcome the limitations imposed by scarce labeled data. Part 3 bridges theory and practice, delving into deep learning essentials—from neural network building blocks, activation functions, and autoencoders with practical TensorFlow and Keras code to cutting-edge generative models, including generative adversarial networks, BERT, and large language models like GPT. This final section illustrates how these tools can be applied to real-world challenges, guiding practitioners in deploying AI-driven strategies that ensure optimal outcomes while maintaining regulatory compliance.

I am honored to support and endorse this remarkable work. May it inspire you to explore new frontiers in AI and drive innovative solutions that lead to better outcomes for patients and the broader healthcare community.

—RAVI GOPALAKRISHNAN, VICE PRESIDENT
DATA SCIENCE & AI, ASTRAZENECA

preface

Data is the new oil, electricity, and power. The amount of data available has exploded in the past 10 to 15 years. AI-based solutions are harnessing the datasets, and hence AI has made unprecedented progress in the past decade. It has transformed our lives—the way we buy, plan, travel, respond, and connect. With the introduction of cloud computing, massive computational power became readily available. One of the most powerful additions has been large language models like ChatGPT, which revolution-ized the entire ecosystem. Across all business domains, including retail, telecommuni-cations, banking, financial services, insurance, healthcare, manufacturing, and aviation—and cutting through the functions of marketing, CRM, production, supply chains, pricing, quality—data-based AI tools are proving their tremendous value. Pre-dictive algorithms, optimization solutions, and classification tools have improved effi-ciency, reduced operations cost, enhanced profit, and opened new doors to humankind. We can research for new drugs faster and more efficiently, create better and safer manufacturing processes, enhance the effectiveness of business teams, and generate superior and more mature business solutions.

As an ardent follower of AI, I have witnessed both the unwavering excitement and the complexity of navigating this complicated landscape, which is a combination of technology, engineering, research, and human interest. Throughout the process of writing this book, I have often been reminded of the complexities and nuances of understanding AI. The answers are not simple, and, honestly, the more I explored the topic, the more I came to appreciate the layers and shades that shape the way we learn, act, and understand.

This book has been a journey—a journey of discovery, reflection, challenge, and certainly arduous work. A simple thought was the inception: a curiosity about unsupervised learning solutions by harnessing deep learning and generative AI. And during this journey, the curiosity evolved into something that I hope will inspire, inform, and perhaps challenge readers. This book is a culmination of hours of brainstorming sessions, discussions and research, and thought and grit, woven together with the intention of offering something tangible as well as valuable to readers.

I've made a conscious effort to present convoluted ideas in a manner that is both approachable as well as technically thorough. The goal is not just to help you comprehend deep learning or generative AI but to help you develop a much more in-depth understanding of how these solutions are created, the mathematics behind them, and how they can be adapted to solve a range of problems.

acknowledgments

This book is possible due to support from Manning Publications: a big thank you to Manning. I owe a deep debt of gratitude to many individuals who have helped me in shaping the book. To my mentors, colleagues, and friends—thank you for your insights, patience, and unwavering support throughout this journey. I want to thank the Manning team for making this book possible, particularly Andy Waldron, the acquisitions editor who believed in this book and got it started; Ian Hough, the development editor who saw the book through the writing process; Ravi Gopalakrishnan for his excellent foreword; and Davide Dev Vento, the technical editor who provided great technical insights throughout. Davide has been a senior advanced physicist and high-performance computing specialist at Quantinuum since 2022. He specializes in computational physics, high-performance computing, parallel computing, optimization, and tuning.

Thanks also to the rest of the team working in the background to get this book published. To all the reviewers: Alessandro Buggin, Amaresh Rajasekharan, Arne Peter Raulf, Bob Liu, Clifford Thurber, Gary Bake, Joel Holmes, Juan Jimenez, Keith Kim, Krishna Chaitanya Anipindi, Lara Thompson, Leonardo Gomes da Silva, Michael Aydinbas, Monica Guimaraes, Obiamaka Agbaneje, Oliver Korten, Ondřej Krajíček, Paul Adamson, Radhakrishna Maddukuru, Ramakanth Gidijala, Richard Vaughan, Rohit Mishra, Sergio Govoni, Simon Tschoeke, Simone Sguazza, Sruti S., Stephen Tobayiwa, Subhash Talluri, Todd Cook, and Vishwesh Ravi Shrimali, your suggestions helped make this a better book.

I am grateful to my family—my wife Yashi and my lovely kids Pakhi and Rudra for bearing with me and giving me the time and space to bring this book into being.

Finally, I extend my thanks to you, the reader, for taking the time to engage with this book. Your interest in the field of AI is what is driving the continued growth in this field. I hope this book serves you well in this journey.

about this book

As you read through the chapters, I urge you to not just absorb the material but to actively experiment with the concepts and techniques presented. One of the best techniques to learn is getting your hands dirty; there are numerous practical exercises and challenges to reinforce your understanding. Whether you are reading the book in its entirety or only the portions that pique your interest, I hope you find something meaningful in these pages.

Who should read this book

This book serves as both an introduction to unsupervised learning, deep learning, and generative AI for newcomers and a comprehensive reference for experienced professionals. It is intended for those interested in the latest trends, methodologies, and best practices in unsupervised learning, including students and researchers who wish to explore unsupervised learning algorithms in depth. Data science professionals seeking insights and solutions to common challenges and managers aiming to communicate effectively with teams and clients will find value here. Additionally, curious individuals looking to learn about unsupervised learning algorithms and enhance their Python skills through case studies will benefit.

The book assumes a basic knowledge of software engineering but provides explanations and references for foundational material when needed. Familiarity with object-oriented programming languages like C++, Java, and Objective-C is advisable, as well as experience with Python, which is used throughout the book. A basic understanding of mathematics and geometry will aid in visualizing results, and knowledge of data-related use cases will assist in relating to business scenarios. Above all, an open mindset for learning is essential.

How this book is organized: A road map

The book is organized into three parts, each covering a key area of unsupervised learning.

In part 1, we explore the basic principles, mathematical foundations, and core algorithms around clustering and dimensionality reduction techniques.

As the book progresses into part 2, we dive into more advanced topics such as dealing with text data, advanced clustering, and advanced dimensionality reduction algorithms.

Part 3 (perhaps the most complex) is focused on deep learning and generative AI solutions. In this book, we aim to bridge the gap between theoretical knowledge and practical application, and hence we give emphasis to pragmatic case studies, examples, and exercises. It is complemented by developing solutions with Python using AI algorithms. All the datasets and Python code books are checked in at the GitHub location.

All the very best for the upcoming journey. We hope it is as enriching and exciting for you as it has been for us.

About the code

This book contains many examples of source code both in numbered listings and in line with normal text. In both cases, source code is formatted in a `fixed-width font` `like this` to separate it from ordinary text. Sometimes code is also **in bold** to highlight code that has changed from previous steps in the chapter, such as when a new feature adds to an existing line of code.

In many cases, the original source code has been reformatted; we've added line breaks and reworked indentation to accommodate the available page space in the book. In rare cases, even this was not enough, and listings include line-continuation markers (➡). Additionally, comments in the source code have often been removed from the listings when the code is described in the text. Code annotations accompany many of the listings, highlighting important concepts.

You can get executable snippets of code from the liveBook (online) version of this book at https://livebook.manning.com/book/data-without-labels. The complete code for the examples in the book is available for download from the Manning website at https://www.manning.com/books/data-without-labels, and from GitHub at https://github.com/vverdhan/DataWithoutLabels.

liveBook discussion forum

Purchase of *Data Without Labels* includes free access to liveBook, Manning's online reading platform. Using liveBook's exclusive discussion features, you can attach comments to the book globally or to specific sections or paragraphs. It's a snap to make notes for yourself, ask and answer technical questions, and receive help from the author and other users. To access the forum, go to https://livebook.manning.com/book/data-without-labels/discussion.

Manning's commitment to our readers is to provide a venue where a meaningful dialogue between individual readers and between readers and the author can take place. It is not a commitment to any specific amount of participation on the part of the author, whose contribution to the forum remains voluntary (and unpaid). We suggest you try asking the author some challenging questions lest his interest stray! The forum and the archives of previous discussions will be accessible from the publisher's website as long as the book is in print.

about the author

VAIBHAV VERDHAN is a seasoned data science and AI professional, and he has worked across geographies and domains. He is an industry leader and a regular speaker at conferences and summits. He loves to work on machine learning and AI problems and mentor students/professionals on data science and machine learning solutions. Currently, he resides in London with his family.

about the cover illustration

The figure on the cover of *Data Without Labels* is "Paysan des Environs de Berne," or "Peasant from the surroundings of Bern," taken from a collection by Jacques Grasset de Saint-Sauveur, published in 1788. Each illustration is finely drawn and colored by hand.

In those days, it was easy to identify where people lived and what their trade or station in life was just by their dress. Manning celebrates the inventiveness and initiative of the computer business with book covers based on the rich diversity of regional culture centuries ago, brought back to life by pictures from collections such as this one.

Part 1

Basics

Welcome to part 1.

Machine learning and AI are not magic. Neither are they a secret art that can be understood only by a select few. At their core, they are simply a way for us to help the algorithms assimilate historical datasets and generate insights for us. These insights help us to initiate better, faster, and more influential business effects We give clear, logical instructions that guide the algorithms to do what we want.

But, like any art, learning machine learning and AI take practice. It's not about memorizing Python or R or a programming language syntax or learning some commands to run the code or cut-paste the code. It's about solving pragmatic business problems, thinking about the business objectives critically, and breaking down those complex tasks meticulously into smaller and manageable steps and hence achieving the business objective.

This book isn't just about writing code; it's about learning how to think like a data scientist.

If you've never studied unsupervised learning or you've never written a single line of Python code, that's perfectly fine. It is much easier than you think. We start with simple unsupervised learning algorithms.

All the very best on this journey. Let's start with the basics, one step at a time.

1

Introduction to machine learning

This chapter covers

- An introduction to data, types of datasets, quality, and sources
- Machine learning and types of machine learning algorithms
- An overview of different types of algorithms

There are only patterns, patterns on top of patterns, patterns that affect other patterns. Patterns hidden by patterns. Patterns within patterns.

—Chuck Palahniuk

There is a saying going around: "Data is the new electricity." Data is indeed transforming our world, much like electricity has; nobody can deny that. But like electricity, we must remember that data must be properly harnessed to utilize its value. We have to clean the data and analyze and visualize it, and only then can we develop insights from it. The fields of data science, machine learning (ML), and AI are helping us to better harness data and extract trends and patterns so we can make more insightful and balanced decisions in our activities and business.

3

In this book, we unravel the puzzles of data and see how we can find the patterns hidden within. We will be studying a branch of ML referred to as *unsupervised learning*. Unsupervised learning solutions are one of the most influential approaches and are changing the face of the industry. They are utilized in banking and finance, retail, insurance, manufacturing, aviation, medical sciences, telecom, and almost every other sector.

Throughout the book, we discuss concepts of ML with a focus on unsupervised learning—the building blocks of algorithms, their nuts and bolts, background processes, and mathematical foundation. We will examine concepts, study best practices, analyze common errors and pitfalls, and use a case study–based approach that complements the learning. At the same time, we develop actual Python code for solving such problems. All the codes are accompanied by step-by-step explanations and comments.

By the time you finish this book, you will have a very good understanding of unsupervised technique-based ML, various algorithms, the mathematics and statistical foundation on which the algorithm rests, business use cases, Python implementation, and best practices.

This first chapter is designed to introduce the concepts of ML. We'll begin by discussing the concepts fundamental to all data analysis and ML: data itself, how it is managed, and what constitutes good-quality data. We'll then move on to discuss data analysis in the context of ML and deep learning, consider different types of ML algorithms, and wrap up by considering the technical toolkit recommended for getting hands-on with the content in this book. Welcome to the first chapter and all the very best!

1.1   *Technical toolkit*

The following tools are used for different facets of the project:

- *Data engineering*—Hadoop, Spark, Scala, Java, C++, SQL, Redshift, Azure, PySpark
- *Data analysis*—SQL, R, Python, Excel
- *ML*—SQL, R, Python, Excel, Weka, Julia, MATLAB, SPSS, SAS
- *Visualization*—Tableau, Power BI, Qlik, COGNOS
- *Model deployment*—Docker, Flask, Amazon S3
- *Cloud services*—Azure, AWS, GCP

In this book, we are going to use Python. You are advised to install the latest version of Python on your system. At least version 3.5+ is advisable, though the latest version as of this writing is 3.13. We will also use Jupyter Notebook, so installing Anaconda on your system is advisable.

> **NOTE** All the codes and datasets will be checked in at the GitHub repository: https://github.com/vverdhan/DataWithoutLabels. You are expected to replicate them and try to reproduce the results.

1.2   Data, data types, data management, and quality

We begin by introducing the protagonist of this book: *data*. Data can be thought of as facts and statistics that are collected for performing any kind of analysis or study. But data also has its own traits, attributes, quality measures, and management principles. It is stored, exported, loaded, transformed, and measured. In that sense, data is a tangible "thing" in its own regard, and it must be handled properly to correctly utilize it. To do that, we must properly understand data.

Let's start with the fundamentals: the definition of data. Once we've defined data, we will proceed to discuss different types of data, their respective examples, and the attributes of data that make it useful and of good quality.

1.2.1   What is data?

Data is ubiquitous. You make a phone call using a mobile network; as you do, you are generating data. You book a flight ticket and hotel for an upcoming vacation; data is being created. Our day-to-day activity-generated data might include performing a bank transaction, surfing social media, or shopping websites online. That data is transformed from one form to another, stored, cleaned, managed, and analyzed. So what actually is it?

Formally put, data is a collection of facts, observations, measures, text, numbers, images, and videos. A dataset might be clean (i.e., organized to be free from errors, inconsistencies, and irrelevant information) or unclean, be ordered (e.g., alphabetically) or unordered, or have mixed data types or all one type. As mentioned, data in itself is not useful until we clean it, arrange it, analyze it, and draw insights from it. We can visualize the transition from raw to more useful forms in figure 1.1.

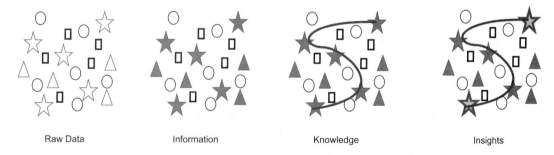

Raw Data   Information   Knowledge   Insights

Figure 1.1   How we can transform raw data to become information, knowledge, and, finally, insights that can be used in business to drive decisions and actions

Raw data is converted to information when we can find distinctions in it. When we relate the terms and "connect the dots," the same piece of information becomes knowledge. Insight is the stage where we can find the major centers and significant points. An insight should be actionable, succinct, and direct. For example, if a customer retention team of a telecom operator is told that customers who do not make a call for nine days have a 30% higher chance of churn than those who make calls, this will be a useful insight that they can work on and try to resolve. Similarly, if a line technician in a manufacturing plant is informed that using mold X results in 60% more defects than using mold Y, they will refrain from using the poorly performing mold in the future. An insight is quite useful for a business team because they can consider it and take corrective measures.

1.2.2   Various types of data

As we've discussed, data is generated by much of our day-to-day activity. We can broadly classify that data into different *types*, as shown in figure 1.2.

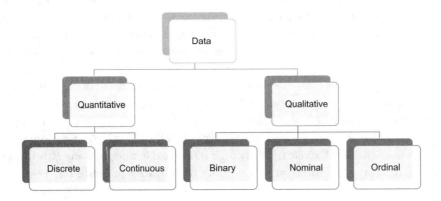

Figure 1.2   The divisions and subdivisions of data

Data can be divided into quantitative and qualitative categories, which are further subclassified:

- *Qualitative data* is the data type that cannot be measured or weighed—for example, taste, color, odor, fitness, name, etc. They can only be observed subjectively. Formally put, when we categorize something or make a classification for it, the data generated is qualitative in nature. Examples are colors in a rainbow, cities in a country, quality of a product, gender, etc. They are also called *categorical* variables. Qualitative data can be further subcategorized into binary, nominal, and ordinal datasets:
  - *Binary* data, as the name suggests, has only two classes that are mutually exclusive to each other. Examples are yes/no, dry/wet, hard/soft, good/bad, true/false, etc.
  - *Nominal* data can be described as the type of data that, though categorized, does not have any sequence or order. Examples are distinct languages that

are spoken in a country, colors in a rainbow, types of services available to a customer, cities in a country, etc.

– *Ordinal* data is similar to nominal data, except we can order it in a sequence. Examples are fast/medium/slow, positive/neutral/negative, etc.

- *Quantitative* data is all the types of data points that can be measured, weighed, scaled, recorded, etc. Examples are height, revenue, number of customers, demand quantity, area, volume, etc. They are the most common form of data and allow mathematical and statistical operations. Quantitative data is further subcategorized as discrete and continuous:

  – *Discrete* data is precise, to the point, and represented as integers. For example, the number of passengers in a plane or the population of a city cannot be in decimals.

  – *Continuous* data points can take any value, usually in a range. For example, height can take decimal values or the price of a product need not be an integer.

Any data point will generally will fall into one of these classes, based on its properties. There is one more logical grouping that can be done using source and usage, which makes a lot of sense while solving business problems. This grouping allows us to design solutions customized to the data type.

Depending on the source and usage, we can also think of data in two broad classes: structured and unstructured data. A dataset that can be represented in a row-column structure easily is a *structured* dataset. For example, transactions made by five customers in a retail store can be stored, as shown in table 1.1.

Table 1.1   An example of a structured dataset with attributes like amount, date, city, items, etc.

Customer ID	Transaction date	Amount ($)	No. of items	Payment mode	City
1001	01-June-2024	100	5	Cash	New Delhi
1002	02-June-2024	101	6	Card	New York
1003	03-June-2024	102	7	Card	London
1004	04-June-2024	103	8	Cash	Dublin
1005	05-June-2024	104	9	Cash	Tokyo

In table 1.1, for each unique customer ID, we have the transaction date, the amount spent in dollars, the number of items purchased, the mode of payment, and the city in which the transaction was made. Such a data type can be extended to employee details, call records, banking transactions, etc.

NOTE   Most of the data used in analysis and model building is structured. Structured data is easier to store, analyze, and visualize in the form of graphs and charts.

Many algorithms and techniques cater to structured data—in normal real-world language, we refer to structured data primarily. Unstructured data is not easily sorted into a row-column structure. It can be text, audio, image, or video. Figure 1.3 shows examples of unstructured data and their respective sources, as well as the primary types of unstructured data: text, images, audio, and video along with their examples.

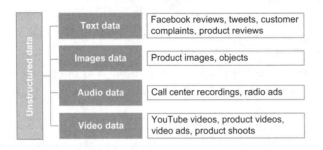

Figure 1.3 **Unstructured data, along with its various types and examples. This data is usually complex to analyze and generally requires deep learning-based algorithms.**

Computers and processors understand only binary numbers. So these unstructured data points still need to be represented as numbers so that we can perform mathematical and statistical calculations on them. For example, an image is made up of pixels. If it is a colored image, each pixel will have RGB (red, green, blue) values and each RGB can take a value (0–255). Hence, we will be able to represent an image as a matrix on which further mathematical calculations can be made. Text, audio, and video can be represented similarly.

> **NOTE** In general, deep learning-based solutions like convolutional neural networks (CNN) and recurrent neural networks (RNN) are used for unstructured data. We are going to work on text and explore CNN and RNN at a later stage in the book.

Unstructured data can be understood through an example: consider a picture of a vacuum cleaner, as shown in figure 1.4. A portion of the image can be represented as a matrix and will look like the matrix seen in the figure. This example is only for illustration purposes and doesn't show actual values.

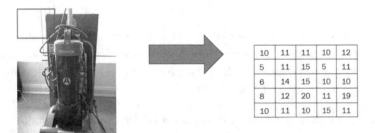

Figure 1.4 **An example of how unstructured data can be represented as a matrix to analyze. The matrix on the right is only an illustration and not the actual numbers.**

Similarly, we can have representations of text, audio, or video data. Due to the size and large number of dimensions typically present in such data, this kind of unstructured data is complex to process and model, and hence, in general, deep learning-based models serve that purpose.

In addition to the broad types of data we've discussed so far, we can have more categories like ratios or scales, which can be used to define the relationship of one variable with another. All these data points (whether structured or unstructured) are defined by the way they are generated in real life.

All of these data points have to be captured, stored, and managed. There are quite a few tools available for managing data, which we will discuss in due course. But before that, let's examine one of the most crucial but often less talked about subjects: *data quality*.

1.2.3   *Data quality*

"Garbage in, garbage out"—this principle summarizes the importance of good-quality data. If the data is dirty or incorrect and lacks any business relationship between variables, we will not be able to solve the business problem at hand. But what is the meaning of "good quality"? Imagine you want to predict rainfall this year based on last year's daily rainfall measurements. A good-quality dataset for this task would be as complete as possible (very few missing days of rainfall measurements). It would be relevant and valid (e.g., covering the same local area as where you are making your predictions), the measurements would be accurate, and the data would be readily available for you to access and use without permission problems. A bad dataset, in contrast, might have lots of "holes" in the data, might have been taken in an area distant from the site you wish to study (making it less relevant), or might be difficult to access. As you can no doubt gather, good-quality data facilitates good-quality outputs, while bad data quality actively hinders your work and will likely result in a poor outcome. The major components of data quality are shown in figure 1.5. Let's explore them one by one.

Figure 1.5   Data quality is of paramount importance; attributes of good-quality data are shown.

The major attributes of good-quality data are

- *Completeness*—We would expect our dataset to be proper and not missing any values. For example, if we are working on sales data for a year, good data will have all the values for all 12 months. Then it will be a complete data source. The completeness of a dataset ensures that we are not missing an important variable or data point.

- *Validity*—The validity of data is its conformance to the properties, characteristics, and variations that are present and being analyzed in our use case. Validity indicates if the observation and measurement we have captured are reliable and valid. For example, if the scope of the study is for 2015–2019, then using 2014 data will be invalid.

- *Accuracy*—Accuracy is an attribute focusing on the correctness of data. If we have inaccurate data, we will generate inaccurate insights, and actions will be faulty. It is a good practice to start the project by generating key performance indicators (KPIs) and comparing them with the numbers reported by the business to check the authenticity of the data available to us.

- *Representativeness*—This is one of the most important attributes of the data and often the most undermined. Representation of data means that the data in use truly captures the business need and is not biased. If the dataset is biased or is not representative enough, the model generated will not be able to make predictions on the new and unseen data, and the entire effort will go down the drain.

- *Availability*—Nonavailability of data is a challenge we face often. Data might not be available for the business problem, and then we face a dilemma on whether to continue the use case. Sometimes we face operational challenges and do not have access to the database or permission problems, or data might not be available at all for a particular variable since it is not captured. In such cases, we have to work with the data available and use surrogate variables. For example, imagine we are working on a demand generation problem. We want to predict how many customers can be expected during the upcoming sales season for a particular store. But we do not record the number of customers visiting for a few months. We can then use revenue as a surrogate field and synthesize the missing data points.

- *Consistency*—Here we check whether the data points are consistent across systems and interfaces. It should not be the case that one system is reporting a different revenue figure while another system is showing a completely different value. When faced with such a problem, we generate the respective KPIs as per the data available and seek guidance from the business team.

- *Timeliness*—Timeliness simply means that we have all the data that is required at this point. If the dataset is not available now but might become available in the future, then it might be prudent to wait.

- *Integrity*—The data tables and variables we have are interlinked and interrelated to each other. For example, an employee's details can be spread over multiple tables that are linked to each other using the employee's ID. Data integrity addresses this requirement and ensures that all such relations between the tables and respective entities are consistent.

The quality of data is of paramount importance. In pragmatic day-to-day business, often we do *not* get good-quality data. Due to multiple challenges, good, clean data that is accessible, consistent, representative, and complete is seldom found.

Degradation in quality can be due to challenges during data capturing and collection, exporting or loading, transformations done, etc. A few of the possibilities are as follows:

- We can get integers as names, or special characters like "#$!&" in a few columns, or null values, blanks, or not a number (NaN) as some of the values.
- There may be duplicates in the records.
- Outliers may occur. This is a nuisance we deal with quite a lot. For example, let's say that the average daily transactions are 1,000 for an online retailer. One fine day, due to a server problem, there were no transactions done. It is an outlier situation. Or, one fine day, the number of transactions was 1,000,000. It is again an example of an outlier. Outliers can bias the algorithms we create.
- There may be seasonal variations and movements concerning the time of the day and days of the week—all of them should be representative enough in the dataset.
- Inconsistencies in the date format can lead to multiple challenges when we try to merge multiple data sources. For example, source 1 might be using DD/MM/YYYY while another might be using MM/DD/YYYY. This is taken care of during the data loading step itself.

All these aberrations and quality problems should be addressed and cleaned thoroughly. We will be solving these data problems throughout the book and sharing the best practices to be followed.

NOTE   The quality of your raw data and the rigor shown during the cleaning process directly affect the quality of your final analysis and the maturity of your solution.

We have now defined the major attributes of data. We next study the broad process and techniques used for data engineering and management.

1.2.4   *Data engineering and management*

A strong data engineering process and mature data management practice are prerequisites for a successful ML model solution. Whether you come from a data engineering or data science background, each goes hand in hand; a data engineer would be well served by understanding the basics of data science, and vice versa. Figure 1.6 provides a high-level overview of what the engineering process and management practice might look like. The end-to-end journey of data is described—right from the process of data capturing, data pipeline, and data loading to the point it is ready for analysis.

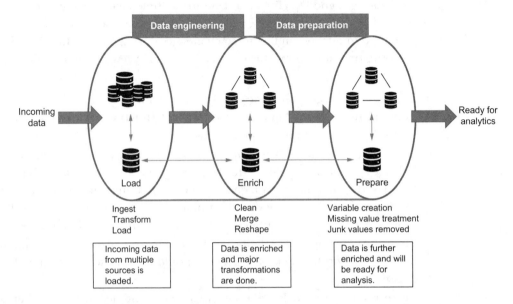

Figure 1.6   Data engineering paves the way for data analysis. It involves data loading, transformation, enrichment, cleaning, preparation, etc., which leads to the creation of data ready for analysis.

In the data engineering step, data is cleansed, conformed, reshaped, transformed, and ingested. Generally, we have a server where the final data is hosted and is ready for access. The most used process is the creation of an export, transform, load (ETL) process. Then we make the data ready for analysis. We create new variables, treat null values, enrich the data with methods, and then finally proceed to the analysis/model-building stage.

Many times, we find that terms like data analysis, data science, machine learning, data mining, artificial intelligence, business intelligence, big data, etc., are used quite interchangeably in business. It is a good idea to clarify them, which is the topic of the next section. There are plenty of tools available for each respective function that we are discussing. We will also understand the role of software engineering in this entire journey.

1.3   *Data analysis, ML, AI, and business intelligence*

ML and AI are relatively new fields, and as such, there is little standardization and differentiation in the scope of their work. This has resulted in unclear definitions and demarcation of these fields. We examine these fields—where they overlap, where they differ, and how one empowers the other. Each of the functions empowers and complements the other, as visualized in figure 1.7.

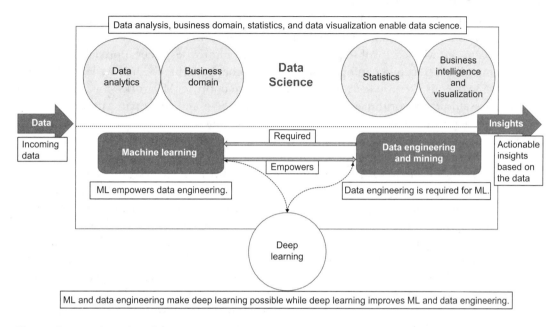

Figure 1.7 How the various fields are interlinked with each other and how they are dependent on each other

After the business problem has been defined and scoped properly, we start with the technical process. Data mining and data engineering start the whole process by providing the data required for analysis. It also exports, transforms, cleans, and loads the data so that it can be consumed by all of the respective functions. Business intelligence and visualizations use this data to generate reports and dashboards. Data analytics generates insights and trends using data. Data science stands on the pillars of data analysis, statistics, business intelligence, data visualization, ML, and data mining. ML creates statistical and mathematical models, and AI further pushes the capabilities.

ML uses traditional coding. The coding is performed in traditional languages (such as Python), and hence, all the logic and rules of computer science and software engineering are valid in ML too. ML helps us make sense of data that we are otherwise not able to comprehend. The most fascinating advantage of ML is its ability to work on very complex and high-dimensional data points like video, audio, image, text, or complex datasets generated by sensors. It allows us to think beyond the obvious. Now AI can achieve feats that were previously thought impossible. This level of pattern recognition and learning has resulted in technological breakthroughs such as self-driving cars, chatbots conversing like humans, speech-to-text conversion and translation to another language, automated grading of essays, photo captioning, etc. With the advent of generative AI, using large language models like ChatGPT, we can create images, videos, and text based on the prompt given by the user. And that is just the start!

1.4   *Nuts and bolts of ML*

Consider this: if a child has to be taught how to open a door, we show them the exact steps quite a few times. The child tries to open it but fails. They try again and fail again. But with each subsequent try, the child improvises their approach. And, after some time, the child can open the door. Another example is when we learn to drive: we make mistakes, we learn from them, and we improve. ML works similarly, wherein the statistical algorithm looks at the historical data and finds patterns and insights. The algorithm uncovers relationships and anomalies, trends and deviations, similarities and differences—and then shares actionable results with us.

Formally put, ML can be called a branch or a study of computer algorithms that works on historical data to generate insights and helps in making data-driven decisions. The algorithms are based on statistical and mathematical foundations and hence have a sound logical explanation. ML algorithms require coding, which can be done in any of the languages and tools available such as Python, R, SPSS, SAS, MATLAB, Weka, Julia, Java, etc. It also requires a domain understanding of the business.

Whenever you are doing some online shopping for clothing and the website recommends accessories that go along with it or you are booking an airplane ticket and the travel operator shows you a customized deal as per your needs and plan, most of the time, ML is working in the background. It has learned your preferences and compared them with your historical trends. It is also looking for similarities you have with other customers who behave almost the same. Based on all that analysis, the algorithm is making an intelligent recommendation to you. Quite fascinating, right?

Why exactly is ML so good at finding patterns? We humans can analyze only two or maybe three dimensions simultaneously; for example, we can pick up a pattern between two or three interacting variables. But what if there are 50 different variables all interacting? We wouldn't have a chance. An ML algorithm can work on 50, 60, or maybe 100s of dimensions simultaneously. It can work on any type of data, structured or unstructured, and it can help in the automation of tasks. Hence, it generates patterns and insights quite difficult for a human mind to visualize.

ML, like any other project, requires a team of experts who work closely with each other and complement each other's skill sets. As shown in figure 1.8, an ML project requires the following roles:

- *Business team*—Business stakeholders and subject matter experts define the business problem for the project. They own the solution, have a clear understanding of the ask, and have a clear measurable goal in sight. They course-correct the team in case of confusion and serve as experts who have a deep understanding of the business processes and operations. They are marketing managers, product owners, process engineers, quality experts, risk analysts, portfolio leads, etc. It is imperative that business stakeholders are closely knit into the team from day one. They help in course correction of the overall direction.

- *Operations team*—This team comprises the scrum master, project manager, business analysts, etc. The role of the team can be compared to a typical project management team, which tracks the progress, maintains the records, reports the day-to-day activities, and keeps the entire project on track. They create user stories and act as a bridge between the business team and the data team.

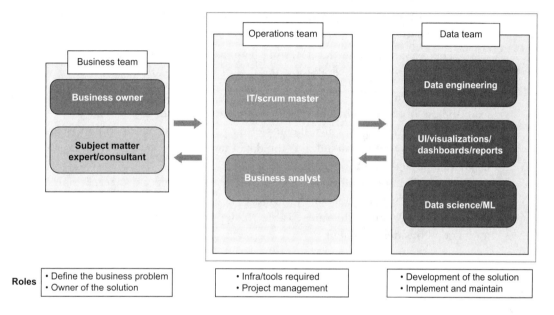

Figure 1.8   Team required for a data science project and the respective interactions of them with each other—truly a team effort

- *Data team*—The core team that creates the solution, does the coding, and generates the output in the form of a model, dashboard, report, and insights is the data team. It comprises three main pillars: the data engineering team, the UI/visualization team, and the data science team. Their functions are as follows:
  - The data engineering team is responsible for building, maintaining, integrating, and ingesting all the data points. They do a periodic data refresh and act as a prime custodian of data. They use ETL, SQL, AWS, Kafka, PySpark, etc.
  - The UI/visualization team builds dashboards, reports, interactive modules, and web applications. They use SQL, Tableau, Qlik, Power BI, and others.
  - The data science team is responsible for all the data analysis and model-building tasks. They discover patterns and insights, test hypotheses, and generate the final output that is to be finally consumed by all. The final output can be an ML model that will be used to solve the business problem. In situations where an ML model is not possible, the team might generate actionable

insights that can be useful for the business. This team requires SQL, Python, R, SAS, SPSS, etc., to complete their job.

– The DevOps team is generally a part of the data engineering team, or they can exist as a separate entity. They focus on the operationalization of the ML model. Remember: if your ML model is not being used, it is just a shiny piece of software sitting on a shelf. The UI/UX team will lead the development of the final product layer where the ML-based outputs will be surfaced to the end user. User experience is often ignored, and without an interactive and engaging user experience, ML will not be used to its full potential.

The team sometimes has a testing team as well to assess the functionality, various use cases, and overall look and feel of the application.

Having discussed the typical team structure for a data science project, we will now examine the broad steps involved in a data science project.

A data science project runs like any other project that has deadlines, stages, testing, phases, etc. The raw material is the data that passes through various phases to be cleaned, analyzed, and modeled.

Figure 1.9 shows an illustration of a data science project's stages. It starts with a business problem definition of the project. The business problem must be concise, clear, measurable, and achievable. Table 1.2 depicts an example of a bad (ill-defined) and a good business problem.

Data science project steps

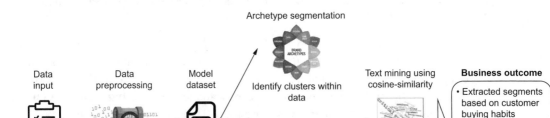

Figure 1.9 A data science project is like any other project, having stages and deadlines, dependencies, and processes.

Table 1.2 Examples of how to define a business problem to make it clear, concise, and measurable

Examples	
Ill-defined business problems	**Good business problems**
Increase the production	Optimize the various cost heads (A, B, C, and D) and identify the most optimal combination to decrease the cost by 1.2% in the next six months
Decrease the cost	
Increase the revenue by 80% in one month	From the various factors of defects in the process (X, Y, Z), identify the most significant factors to reduce the defect % by 1.8% in the next three months
Automate the entire process	

Then we move to the data discovery phase, during which we list all the data sources and host them. All the various datasets, like customer details, purchase histories, social media data, portfolios, etc., are identified and accessed. The data tables that are to be used are finalized in this step, and most of the time, we create a database for us to work, test, and learn.

We then go ahead with data preprocessing. It involves cleaning data like the removal of null values, outliers, duplicates, junk values, etc. The previous step and this one can take 60% to 70% of the project time.

We create a few reports and generate initial insights during the exploratory data analysis phase. These insights are discussed with the business stakeholders, and they guide course correction.

The data is now ready for modeling. Quite a few versions of the solution are tested. Then, depending on the requirements, we choose the best version. Generally, parameters like accuracy and statistical measures like precision and recall drive the selection of the model. We will be exploring the process of choosing the best model and terms like precision and recall in later chapters of the book. Once we choose the final model, we are ready to deploy the model in the production environment, where it will work on unseen data.

These are the broad steps in an ML project. Like any other project, there is a code repository, best practices, coding standards, common errors, pitfalls, etc., which we will discuss throughout the book.

1.5 *Types of ML algorithms*

ML models affect decision-making and follow a statistical approach to solve a business problem. They work on historical data and find patterns and trends in it. The raw material is the historical data, which is analyzed and modeled to generate a predictive algorithm. The historical data available and the sort of problem that needs to be solved informs the ML approach that should be taken. ML algorithms can be split broadly into four classes: supervised learning, unsupervised learning, semisupervised learning, and reinforcement learning, as depicted in figure 1.10. We will examine each of the four types in detail, with a focus on unsupervised learning—the topic of this book.

You might have heard about generative AI (GenAI) in the news. GenAI-based solutions generally start with unsupervised and may include supervised or reinforcement learning to specialize the model for certain tasks. We will discuss GenAI further throughout the book.

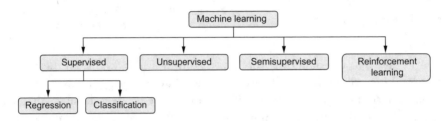

Figure 1.10 **ML algorithms can be classified as supervised learning algorithms, unsupervised learning algorithms, semisupervised learning algorithms, and reinforcement learning algorithms.**

1.5.1 *Supervised learning*

Formally put, supervised models are statistical models that use both the input data and the desired output to predict the future. The output is the value that we wish to predict and is referred to as the *target variable,* and the data used to make that prediction is called *training data.* The target variable is sometimes referred to as the *label.* The various attributes or variables present in the data are called *independent variables.* Each of the historical data points or a *training example* contains these independent variables and the corresponding target variable. Supervised learning algorithms make a prediction for unseen future data. The accuracy of the solution depends on the training done and patterns learned from the labeled historical data. An example is described in the next section.

Supervised learning problems are used in demand prediction, credit card fraud detection, customer churn prediction, premium estimation, etc. They are heavily used across domains like retail, telecom, banking and finance, aviation, insurance, and more and for functions like marketing, CRM, quality, supply chain, pricing, and so on.

Supervised learning algorithms can be further broken into regression algorithms and classification algorithms. Let's consider each of these in turn.

REGRESSION ALGORITHMS

Regression algorithms are supervised learning algorithms—that is, they require target variables that need to be predicted. These algorithms are used to predict the values of a *continuous variable.* Examples include revenue, amount of rainfall, number of transactions, production yield, and so on. In supervised classification problems, we predict a categorical variable like whether it will rain (yes/no), whether the credit card transaction is fraudulent or genuine, and so on. This is the main difference between classification and regression problems.

Let us understand the regression problem with an example. Say we assume that the weight of a person is only dependent on height and not on other parameters like gender, ethnicity, diet, etc. In such a case, we want to predict the weight of a person based on height. The dataset and the graph plotted for the same data will look like figure 1.11.

A regression model will be able to find the inherent patterns in the data and fit a mathematical equation describing the relationship. It can then take height as an input and predict the weight. Here, height is the independent variable, and weight is the dependent variable or the target variable or the label we want to predict.

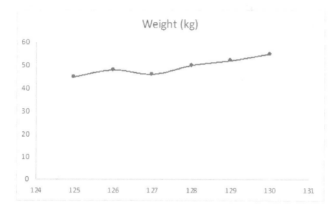

Height (cm)	Weight (cm)
125	45
126	46
127	48
128	50
129	52
130	55

Figure 1.11   Data and plot of relationship between height and weight that is used for regression problem

There are quite a few algorithms available for regression problems. Some of the major ones are as follows (although this list is certainly not exhaustive):

- Linear regression
- Decision tree
- Random forest
- k-nearest neighbor
- Boosting algorithm
- Neural network

We can use any of the algorithms to solve this problem. We will explore more by using linear regression to solve a problem.

The linear regression algorithm models the relationship between dependent variables and target variables by assuming a linear relationship between them. The linear regression algorithm would result in a mathematical equation for the problem, shown in equation 1.1:

$$\text{Weight} = \beta_0 * \text{height} + \beta_1 \tag{1.1}$$

Generally put, linear regression is used to fit a mathematical equation depicting the relationship between dependent and independent variables, shown as equation 1.2:

$$Y = \beta_0 + \beta_1 x_1 + \beta_2 x_2 + \ldots + \varepsilon \tag{1.2}$$

Here, Y is the target variable that we want to predict; x_1 is the first independent variable; x_2 is the second independent variable; ε is the error term in the equation; and β_0 is the intercept of the equation.

A simple visualization for a linear regression problem is shown in figure 1.12. Here we have the x and Y variables where x is the independent variable and Y is the target variable. The objective of the linear regression problem is to find the *line of best fit,* which can explain the randomness present in the data.

Line of best fit

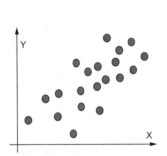
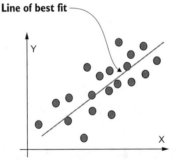

Figure 1.12 Raw data that needs to be modeled (left). Using regression, a line of best fit is identified (right).

Equation 1.2 is used to make predictions for the unseen data. There are variations in linear regression too, like simple linear regression, multiple linear regression, nonlinear regression, etc. Depending on the data at hand, we choose the correct algorithm. A complex dataset might require a nonlinear relationship between the various variables.

The next type of regression algorithm we shall explore is tree-based solutions. For tree-based algorithms like decision trees, random forests, etc., the algorithm will start from the top and then, like an `if/else` block, will split iteratively to create nodes and subnodes until we reach a terminal node (see figure 1.13). In the decision tree diagram, we start from the top with the root node, and then we perform splitting until we reach the endpoint, which is the terminal node.

Decision trees are simple to comprehend and implement, and they are fast to train. Their usability lies in the fact that they are intuitive enough to understand without much technical background.

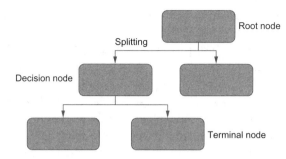

Figure 1.13 A decision tree has a root node, and after splitting, we get a decision node and a terminal node, which is the final node and cannot be split further.

There are other famous regression algorithms like k-nearest neighbor, gradient boosting, and deep learning–based solutions. Different regression algorithms are best suited to specific contexts.

To understand the effect of regression use cases, let's consider a few business-relevant use cases that are implemented in the industry:

- An airport operations team is assessing staffing requirements and wants to estimate the amount of passenger traffic expected. The estimate will help the team prepare a plan regarding future resource requirements and will help in the optimization of the resources required. Regression algorithms can help in predicting the number of passengers.
- A retailer wants to understand the expected demand for the upcoming sales season so it can plan the inventory. This will result in cost savings and avoid stock-outs. Regression algorithms can help in such planning.
- A manufacturing plant wishes to improve the yield from the existing use of various molds and raw materials. The regression solutions can suggest the best combination of molds and predict the expected yield.
- A bank offers credit cards to its customers. Consider how the credit limit offered to new customers is calculated. Based on the attributes of customers like age, occupation, income, and previous transaction history, regression algorithms can help in suggesting credit limits at a customer level.
- An insurance company wants to come up with a premium table for its customers using historical claims. The risk can be assessed based on the historical data around driver details, car information, etc. Regression can surely help with such problems.

Regression problems form the foundation of supervised learning problems and are quite heavily used in the industry. Along with classification algorithms, they serve as a go-to solution for most of the predictive problems used in real-world business.

CLASSIFICATION ALGORITHMS
Classification algorithms are used to predict the values of a categorical variable, which is the dependent variable. This target variable can be binary (yes/no, good/bad, fraud/genuine, pass/fail, etc.) or multiclass (such as positive/negative/neutral or

yes/no/don't know). Classification algorithms will ascertain whether the target event will happen by generating a probability score for the target variable.

After the model has been trained on historical data, a classification algorithm will generate a probability score for the unseen dataset, which can be used to make the final decision. Depending on the number of classes present in the target variable, our business decision will vary. Let's have a look at a use case for classification problems.

Consider this: a telecom operator is facing a problem with its decreasing subscriber base. The number of existing subscribers is shrinking, and the telecom operator would like to arrest this churn of subscribers. For this purpose, an ML model is envisioned.

In this case, the historical data or the training data available for model building might look like table 1.3. These data points are only for illustration purposes and are not exhaustive. There can be many other significant variables available.

Table 1.3   Example of a structured dataset for a telecom operator showing multiple data attributes

ID	Revenue ($)	Duration of service (years)	Avg. cost	Monthly usage (days)	Churned (Y/N)
1001	100	1.1	0.10	10	Y
1002	200	4.1	0.09	25	N
1003	300	5.2	0.05	28	N
1004	200	0.9	0.25	11	Y
1005	100	0.5	0.45	12	Y

In the example in table 1.3, the dataset comprises the past usage data of subscribers. The last column (Churned) depicts if that subscriber churned out of the system or not. For example, subscriber 1001 churned while 1002 did not. Hence, the business problem is to build an ML model based on this historical data and predict if a new unseen customer will churn or not.

Here, the churned status (yes/no) is the target variable. It is also referred to as the dependent variable. The other attributes like revenue, duration, average cost, monthly usage, etc., are independent variables that are used to create the ML model. The historical data is called the training data. Before the training of the model, the trained supervised learning model will generate prediction probabilities for a new customer.

There are quite a few algorithms available for classification problems; the major ones are as follows:

- Logistic regression
- Decision tree
- Random forest
- k-nearest neighbor
- Naïve Bayes
- Support vector machine

- Boosting algorithms
- Neural networks

One of the most popular classification algorithms is logistic regression. Logistic regression uses a logit function to model the classification problem. If we are solving for a binary classification problem, it will be binary logistic regression or multiple logistic regression. Similar to linear regression, logistic regression also fits an equation, albeit it uses a sigmoid function to generate the probability score for the event to happen.

A sigmoid function is a mathematical function that has a characteristic S-shaped curve or a sigmoid curve. The mathematical equation of a sigmoid function is shown in equation 3.1:

$$S(x) = 1/(1 + e^{-x}) \qquad\qquad\qquad (1.3)$$

which can be rewritten as equation 1.4

$$S(x) = e^x/(e^x + 1) \qquad\qquad\qquad (1.4)$$

Logistic regression uses the sigmoid function. The equation used in the logistic regression problem is shown in equation 1.5:

$$\log (p/1 - p) = \beta_0 + \beta_1 \, x_1 \qquad\qquad\qquad (1.5)$$

where p is the probability of the event happening; β_0 is the intercept term; β_1 is the coefficient for the independent variable x_1; $\log(p/1 - p)$ is called the logit; and $(p/1 - p)$ is the odds. As depicted in figure 1.14, if we try to fit a linear regression equation for the probability function, it will not do a good job. We want to obtain the probability scores (i.e., a value between 0 and 1). The linear regression will not only return values between 0 and 1 but also probability scores that are greater than 1 or less than 0. Hence, we have a sigmoid function at right in the figure, which generates probability scores for us between 0 and 1 only.

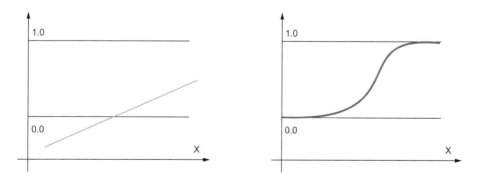

Figure 1.14   A linear regression model will not be able to do justice (left); hence, we have logistic regression for classification. Linear regression can generate probability scores more than 1 or less than 0 too, which is mathematically incorrect, whereas the sigmoid function generates probability scores between 0 and 1 only (right).

The logistic regression algorithm is one of the most widely used techniques for classification problems. It is easy to train and deploy and is often the benchmark algorithm whenever we start any supervised classification learning project.

Tree-based algorithms like decision trees and random forests can also be used for classification problems. The other algorithms are also used as per the requirements.

1.5.2 Unsupervised algorithms

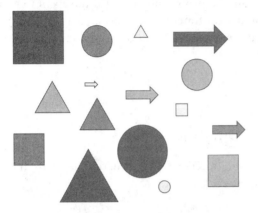

Imagine you are given some paper labels, as shown in figure 1.15. The task is to arrange them by similarity. Now, there are multiple approaches to that problem. You can use color, shape, or size. Here, we do not have any label to guide this arrangement. This is what makes unsupervised algorithms different.

Formally put, unsupervised learning only takes the input data and then finds patterns in it without referencing the target variable. An unsupervised learning algorithm therefore reacts based on the presence or lack of patterns in the dataset.

Figure 1.15 Example of various shapes that can be grouped together using different parameters

Unsupervised learning is hence used for pattern detection, exploring the insights in the dataset and understanding the structure of it, segmentation, and anomaly detection.

We can understand unsupervised learning algorithms by looking at figure 1.16. The figure on the left shows the raw data points represented in a vector space diagram. On the right is the clustering, which will be done using an unsupervised learning algorithm.

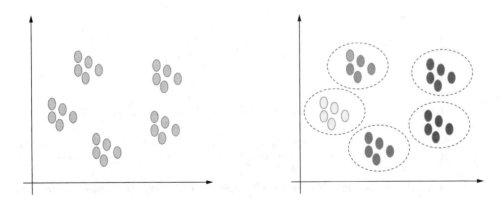

Figure 1.16 An unsupervised learning algorithm finds patterns in the data on the left and results in clusters on the right.

Some use cases for unsupervised algorithms are as follows:

- A retail group wants to understand its customers better. The task is to improve the customer's stickiness, revenue, number of visits, basket size, etc. Customer segmentation using unsupervised learning can be done here. Depending on the customer's attributes like revenue, number of visits, last visit date, age since joining, demographic attributes, etc., the segmentation will result in clusters that can be targeted personally. The result will be improved customer experience, increased customer lifetime value, etc.

- A network provider needs to create an anomaly detection system. The historical data will serve as the anomalies data. The unsupervised learning algorithm will be able to find patterns, and the outliers will be given out by the algorithm. The distinguished anomalies will be the ones that need to be addressed.

- A medical product company wishes to find if there are any underlying patterns in the image data of its patients. If there are any patterns and factors, those patients can be treated better, and maybe they require a different approach. Unsupervised learning can help with the image data, which will help address the patients' needs better.

- A digital marketing company wants to understand the "unknowns" in the incoming customer data like social media interactions, page clicks, comments, stars, etc. This understanding will help improve customers' recommendations and overall purchasing experience.

Unsupervised learning algorithms offer flexibility and performance when it comes to finding patterns. They are usable for all kinds of data—the core topic of this book—including structured data, text, or images.

The major unsupervised learning algorithms are

- Clustering algorithms
- k-means clustering
- Hierarchical clustering
- DBSCAN clustering
- Spectral clustering
- Principal component analysis
- Singular value decomposition
- Association rules
- t-distributed stochastic neighbor embedding
- Autoencoders

We cover all these algorithms in detail in the coming chapters. We will examine the mathematical concepts, the hidden processes, Python implementation, and the best practices throughout the book. Let's first understand the basic process by means of a case study.

A retailer wants to develop a deeper understanding of its consumer base and then wants to offer personalized recommendations, promotions, discounts, offers, etc. The entire customer dataset should be segmented using attributes like persona, previous purchase, response, external data, and so on (see figure 1.17).

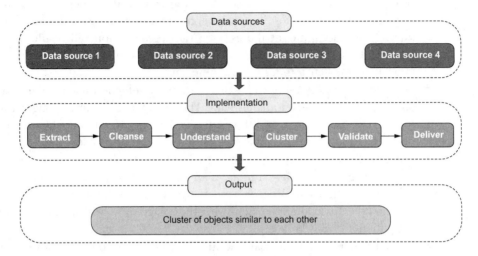

Figure 1.17   Steps in an unsupervised learning algorithm from data sources to the final solution ready for deployment

For the use case, the steps in an unsupervised learning project are as follows:

1 We start the project by defining the business problem. We wish to understand the customer base better. A customer segmentation approach can be a good solution. We want segments that are distinguishable using mathematical KPIs.

2 This is the data discovery phase. All the various datasets, like customer details, purchase histories, social media data, portfolios, etc., are identified and accessed. The data tables to be used are finalized in this step. Then, all the data tables are generally loaded into a common database, which we will use to analyze, test, and learn.

3 Now we have access to the data. The next step is to clean it and make it usable. We treat all the null values, NaN, junk values, duplicates, etc.

4 Once the data is clean and ready to be used, we perform an exploratory data analysis of it. Usually, during exploratory analysis, we identify patterns, cyclicity, aberrations, max-min range, standard deviation, etc. The outputs of the exploratory data analysis stage will be insights and understandings. We will also generate a few graphs and charts, as shown in figure 1.18.

5 We begin with the unsupervised approach now. We want to implement clustering methods, and hence we can try a few clustering methods like k-means, hierarchical clustering, etc. The clustering algorithms will result in homogeneous segments of customers based on their various attributes.

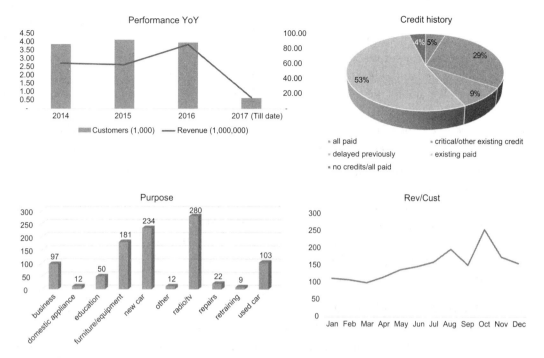

Figure 1.18 Examples of the graphs and charts from the exploratory data analysis of the data

In the case study, we will be working on the past two to three years of data, which is the training data. Since we are using an unsupervised approach, there is no target variable here. The algorithm will merge the customer segments that behave alike using their transactional patterns, their demographic patterns, and their purchase preferences. It will look like the results in figure 1.19.

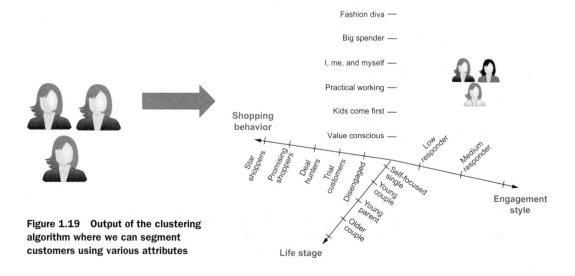

Figure 1.19 Output of the clustering algorithm where we can segment customers using various attributes

6 We now check how the various algorithms have performed; in other words, we will compare the accuracy of each algorithm. The final clustering algorithm chosen will result in homogeneous segments of customers, which can be targeted and offered customized offers.

7 We discuss the results with the business stakeholders and make iterations based on the feedback.

8 We deploy the solution in the production environment and are ready to work on new unseen datasets.

These are the broad steps in an unsupervised problem. Algorithm creation and selection are tedious tasks. We will be studying these in detail later in the book.

GenAI most often starts with an unsupervised stage. This stage enables the model to learn patterns, structures, and relationships without explicit labels. It is sometimes referred to as the pretraining stage. Once the model has been pretrained, we move to the supervised stage. Here, the pretrained model is tailored to a specific task or domain using a labeled dataset.

1.5.3 *Semisupervised algorithms*

Semisupervised learning is a middle path of the supervised and unsupervised approaches. The primary reason for a semisupervised approach is the lack of availability of a complete *labeled* dataset for training. Formally put, the semisupervised approach uses both supervised and unsupervised approaches: supervised to classify the data points and unsupervised to group them together.

In semisupervised learning, we train initially on a smaller number of labeled data points available using a supervised algorithm. Then we use it to label or *pseudo-label* new data points. The two datasets (labeled and pseudo-labeled) are combined, and we use this dataset for further analysis.

Semisupervised algorithms are used in cases where the dataset is partially available, like images in the medical industry. If we are creating a cancer detection solution by analyzing the images of patients, we will likely not have enough sample sets of training images. Here, the semisupervised approach can be helpful.

1.5.4 *Reinforcement learning*

Imagine you are playing a game of chess with a computer, and it goes like this:

- *Round 1*—You win after 5 moves.
- *Round 2*—You win after 8 moves.
- *Round 3*—You win after 14 moves.
- *Round 4*—You win after 21 moves.
- *Round 5*—The computer wins!

What is happening here is the algorithm is training itself iteratively depending on each interaction and then correcting/improving itself.

Formally, reinforcement learning solutions are self-sustained solutions that train themselves using a sequence of trial and error. One sequence follows the other. The heart of reinforcement learning is reward signals. If the action is positive, the reward is positive, indicating to continue. If the action is negative, the reward will penalize the activity. Hence, the solution will always correct itself and move ahead, thereby improving itself iteratively.

Self-driving cars are the best examples of reinforcement learning algorithms. They detect when they should turn left or right, when to move, and when to stop. Modern video games also employ reinforcement learning algorithms. Reinforcement learning allows us to break the barriers of technology and imagine things that were earlier thought impossible.

With this, we have covered the different types of ML algorithms. Together, they are harnessing the true power of data and creating a long-lasting effect on our lives. But the heart of the solutions is the technology, which we have not discussed yet. We now move to the technology stack required to make these solutions tick.

Exercise 1.1

Use these questions to check your understanding:

1 Why is ML so powerful that it is being used very heavily now?
2 What are the different types of ML algorithms, and how are they different from each other?
3 What are the steps in an ML project?
4 What is the role of data engineering, and why is it important?
5 What are the various tools available for ML?

1.6 Concluding thoughts

A common question is: Which is better, R or Python? Both are fantastic languages. Both are heavily used. But after the introduction of TensorFlow, Keras's libraries on AI, the balance has slightly tilted in favor of Python.

You've now taken your first step in the journey toward learning unsupervised machine learning techniques. It is time to wrap up.

ML and AI are indeed pathbreaking. They are changing the way we travel, order food, plan, buy, see a doctor, order prescriptions—they are making a dent everywhere. ML is indeed a powerful capability that is paving the path for the future and is proving much better than existing technology stacks when it comes to pattern identification, anomaly detection, customizations, and automation of tasks. Autonomous driving, cancer detection, fraud identification, facial recognition, image captioning, and chatbots are only a few examples where ML and AI are outperforming traditional technologies. And now is the best time to enter this field. This sector is attracting investments from almost all business functions. The field has created thousands of job opportunities across the spectrum.

At the same time, the field lacks trained professionals: data analysts, data engineers, visualization experts, data scientists, and data practitioners. They are all rare breeds now. The field requires a regular supply of budding talents who will become the leaders of tomorrow and will make data-driven decisions. We have only scratched the surface of understanding the power of data—there are still miles to be covered.

In the following chapter, we will dive deeper into the unsupervised learning concepts of clustering. The mathematical and statistical foundations, a pragmatic case study, and Python implementation are discussed. The discussion includes the simpler clustering algorithms: k-means clustering, hierarchical clustering, and DBSCAN. In the later chapters of the book, we will study more complex clustering topics like Gaussian mixture modeling clustering, time series clustering, fuzzy clustering, etc.

Summary

- Data can be conceptualized as an interconnected set of facts and statistics necessary for analysis, characterized by unique traits and governed by specific management principles.
- Real-world activities such as mobile calls, online transactions, and social media interactions continually generate data, underscoring its omnipresence in modern life.
- Raw data requires cleaning, organization, and analysis to be converted effectively into information and insights that can drive business decisions and actions.
- Data can be broadly classified into structured datasets, which follow a clear row-column format, and unstructured datasets, like text and images, which require more advanced analysis techniques.
- To analyze unstructured data, we typically transform it into numerical representations, often utilizing deep learning models such as CNNs and RNNs.
- A clear, concise, achievable, and measurable business problem is a vital step to ensure the success of a data science project.
- High-quality data is essential for reliable analysis and is characterized by attributes such as completeness, validity, accuracy, representativeness, availability, consistency, timeliness, and integrity.
- Effective data engineering and management are crucial for preparing data for analysis involving techniques like ETL processes and data cleaning.
- The role of UI/UX is of paramount importance to ensure adoption and usage by the end consumers; otherwise, ML will just be a shiny piece sitting on a shelf.
- Interconnected fields like data analysis, ML, AI, and business intelligence each play a critical role in processing and deriving insights from data.
- Supervised learning is an ML approach that uses existing data to predict future outcomes, common in tasks like demand prediction and fraud detection.
- Supervised learning is divided into regression and classification tasks, each with numerous available algorithms to model quantitative or categorical outcomes, respectively.

- Unsupervised learning algorithms discover patterns and relationships in data independently of predefined target variables, useful in activities like segmentation and anomaly detection.

- Variants of unsupervised learning algorithms include clustering techniques and methods for reducing data dimensionality, offering flexibility and performance in pattern recognition.

- Semisupervised learning bridges supervised and unsupervised methods and is effective when dealing with datasets that are partially labeled.

- Reinforcement learning involves systems that learn by trial and error, rewarding desired outcomes, and are applied in dynamic decision-making tasks, such as autonomous vehicle navigation.

- Technological solutions are at the heart of modern data-driven strategies, and understanding the technological stack is essential to maximize the effect and benefits of data solutions.

Clustering techniques 2

This chapter covers

- Clustering techniques and salient use cases in the industry
- Simple k-means, hierarchical, and density-based spatial clustering algorithms
- Implementation of algorithms in Python
- A case study on cluster analysis

> *Simplicity is the ultimate sophistication.*
>
> —Leonardo da Vinci

Nature loves simplicity and teaches us to follow the same path. Most of the time, our decisions are simple choices. Simple solutions are easier to comprehend, less time-consuming, and painless to maintain and ponder over. The machine learning world is no different. An elegant machine learning solution is not the one that is the most complicated algorithm available but the one that solves the business problem. A robust machine learning solution is easy enough to readily decipher and pragmatic enough to implement. Clustering solutions are generally easier to understand.

In the previous chapter, we defined unsupervised learning and discussed the various unsupervised algorithms available. We will cover each of those algorithms as we work through this book; in this second chapter, we focus on the first of these: clustering algorithms.

We will define clustering first and then study the different types of clustering techniques. We will examine the mathematical foundation, accuracy measurements, and pros and cons of each algorithm. We will implement three of these algorithms using Python code on a dataset to complement theoretical knowledge. The chapter ends with the various use cases of clustering techniques in the pragmatic business scenario to prepare for the actual business world. This technique is followed throughout the book—we study the concepts first, implement the actual code to enhance the Python skills, and then dive into real-world business problems.

We study basic clustering algorithms in this chapter, which are k-means clustering, hierarchical clustering, and density-based spatial clustering of applications with noise (DBSCAN) clustering. These clustering algorithms are generally the starting points whenever we want to study clustering. In the later chapters of the book, we will explore more complex algorithms like spectrum clustering, Gaussian mixture models, time series clustering, fuzzy clustering, and others. If you have a good understanding of k-means clustering, hierarchical clustering, and DBSCAN, you can skip to the next chapter. Still, it is advisable to read this chapter once—you might find something useful to refresh your concepts!

Let's first understand what we mean by clustering. Good luck on your journey to master unsupervised learning–based clustering techniques!

2.1 Technical toolkit

We use the latest version of Python in this chapter. A basic understanding of Python and code execution is expected. You are advised to refresh your knowledge of object-oriented programming and Python.

Throughout the book, we use Jupyter Notebook to execute the code. Jupyter offers flexibility in execution and debugging. It is quite user-friendly and is platform or operating-system agnostic. So, if you are using Windows, macOS, or Linux, Jupyter should work just fine.

All the datasets and code files are checked into the GitHub repository at https://mng.bz/lYq2. You need to install the following Python libraries to execute the code: `numpy`, `pandas`, `matplotlib`, `scipy`, and `sklearn`. CPU is good enough for execution, but if you face some computing lags and would like to speed up the execution, switch to GPU or Google Collaboratory (Colab). Google Colab offers free computation for machine learning solutions. I recommend studying more about Google Colab and how to use it for training machine learning algorithms.

2.2   *Clustering*

Consider this scenario: a group of children is asked to group the items in a room into different segments. Each child can use their own logic. Some might group the objects based on weight; other children might use material or color; while yet others might use all three: weight, material, and color. There are many permutations, and they depend on the parameters used for grouping. Here, a child is segmenting or clustering objects based on the chosen logic.

Formally put, *clustering* is used to group objects with similar attributes in the same segments and objects with different attributes in different segments. The resultant clusters share similarities within themselves while they are more heterogeneous between each other. We can understand this better by looking at figure 2.1.

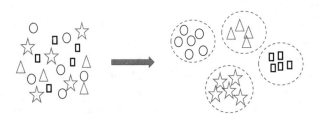

Figure 2.1   Clustering is grouping objects with similar attributes into logical segments. The grouping is based on a similar trait shared by different observations, and hence they are gathered into a group. We are using shape as a variable for clustering here.

Cluster analysis is not one individual algorithm or solution; rather it is used as a problem-solving mechanism in practical business scenarios. It is a class of algorithms under unsupervised learning and an iterative process following a logical approach and qualitative business inputs. It results in the generation of a thorough understanding of the data and the logical patterns in it, pattern discovery, and information retrieval. As an unsupervised approach, clustering does not need a target variable. It performs segmenting by analyzing underlying patterns in the dataset, which are generally multidimensional and, hence, difficult to analyze with traditional methods.

Ideally, we want the clustering algorithms to have the following attributes:

- The output clusters should be easy to explain and comprehend, usable, and make business sense. The number of clusters should not be too few or too many. For example, it is not ideal to have only two clusters, and the division is not clear and decisive. On the other hand, if we have 20 clusters, handling them will become a challenge.
- The algorithm should not be too sensitive to outliers or missing values or the noise in the dataset. Generally put, a good solution will be able to handle multiple data types.
- It is advisable for a data analyst/scientist to have a good grip on the business domain, although a good clustering solution may allow analysts with less domain understanding to train the clustering algorithm.

- The algorithm should be independent of the order of the input parameters. If the order matters, the clustering is biased on the order and hence will add more confusion to the process.
- As we generate new datasets continuously, the clusters should be scalable to newer training examples and should not be a time-consuming process.

As one could imagine, the clustering output will depend on the attributes used for grouping. In figure 2.2, there can be two logical groupings for the same dataset, and both are equally valid. Hence, it is prudent that the attributes or *variables* for clustering are chosen wisely, and often that decision depends on the business problem at hand.

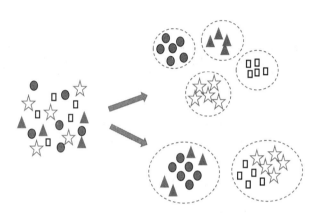

Figure 2.2   Using different attributes for clustering results in different clusters for the same dataset. Hence, choosing the correct set of attributes defines the final set of results we will achieve.

Along with the attributes used in clustering, the actual technique used also makes a big difference. There are quite a few (in fact, more than 80) clustering techniques. For the interested audience, we provide a list of all the clustering algorithms in the appendix.

Clustering can be achieved using a variety of algorithms. These algorithms use different methodologies to define similarity between objects—for example, density-based clustering, centroid-based clustering, distribution-based methods, and others. Multiple techniques, such as Euclidean distance, Manhattan distance, etc., are available to measure the distance between objects. The choice of distance measurement leads to different similarity scores. We will study these similarity measurement parameters in a later section.

At a high level, we can identify two broad clustering methods: *hard clustering* and *soft clustering* (see figure 2.3). When the decision is quite clear that an object belongs to a certain class or cluster, it is referred to as hard clustering. In hard clustering, an algorithm is quite sure of an object's class. On the other hand, soft clustering assigns a likelihood score for an object belonging to a particular cluster. So, a soft clustering method will not put an object into a cluster; rather, an object can belong to multiple clusters. Soft clustering sometimes is also called *fuzzy* clustering.

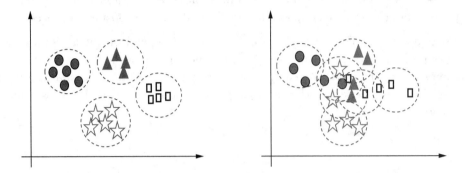

Figure 2.3   Hard clustering has distinct clusters, whereas in the case of soft clustering, a data point can belong to multiple clusters, and we get a likelihood score for a data point to belong to a cluster. The figure on the left is hard clustering, and the one on the right is soft clustering.

We can broadly classify the clustering techniques as shown in table 2.1. The methods described are not the only ones available. We can have graph-based models, overlapping clustering, subspace models, etc.

Table 2.1   Classification of clustering methodologies, brief descriptions, and examples

Serial no.	Clustering methodology	Brief description of the method	Example
1	Centroid-based clustering	Distance from a defined centroid	k-means
2	Density-based models	Data points are connected in dense regions in a vector space	DBSCAN, OPTICS
3	Connectivity-based clustering	Distance connectivity is the modus operandi	Hierarchical clustering, balanced iterative reducing and clustering using hierarchies
4	Distribution models	Modeling is based on statistical distributions	Gaussian mixture models
5	Deep learning models	Unsupervised neural network based	Self-organizing maps

Note: This list is not exhaustive.

Generally, the six most popular algorithms used in clustering in the industry are as follows:

- k-means clustering (with variants like k-medians, k-medoids)
- Agglomerative clustering or hierarchical clustering

- DBSCAN
- Spectral clustering
- Gaussian mixture models
- Balanced iterative reducing and clustering using hierarchies

Multiple other algorithms are available, like Chinese whisper, canopy clustering, SUB-CLU, FLAME, and others. We will study the first three algorithms in this chapter and some of the advanced ones in subsequent chapters in the book.

> **Exercise 2.1**
>
> Use these questions to check your understanding:
>
> 1 DBSCAN clustering is a centroid-based clustering technique. True or False?
> 2 Clustering is a supervised learning technique with a fixed target variable. True or False?
> 3 What is the difference between hard clustering and soft clustering?

2.3   *Centroid-based clustering*

Centroid-based algorithms measure the similarity of the objects based on their distance to the centroid of the clusters (for more information on centroids, see the appendix). The distance is measured between a specific data point to the centroid for the cluster. The smaller the distance, the higher the similarity. We can understand the concept by looking at figure 2.4. The figure on the right side represents the respective centroids for each of the group of clusters.

> **TIP**   To get more clarity on the concept of centroid and other mathematical concepts, refer to the appendix.

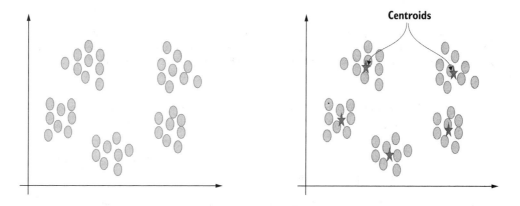

Figure 2.4   Centroid-based clustering methods create a centroid for the respective clusters, and the similarity is measured based on the distance from the centroid. In this case, we have five centroids; hence, we have five distinct clusters.

In clustering, distance plays a central role as many algorithms use it as a metric to measure the similarity. In centroid-based clustering, distance is measured between points and between centroids. There are multiple ways to measure the distance. The most widely used are as follows:

- *Euclidean distance*—This is the most common distance metric used. It represents the straight-line distance between the two points in space and is the shortest path between the two points. For example, if we want to calculate the distance between points P_1 and P_2 where coordinates are (x_1, y_1) for P_1 and (x_2, y_2) for P_2, Euclidean distance is given by equation 2.1. The geometric representation is shown in figure 2.5:

$$\text{Distance} = \sqrt{(y_2 - y_1)^2 + (x_2 - x_1)^2} \qquad \textbf{(2.1)}$$

- *Chebyshev distance*—Named after Russian mathematician Pafnuty Chebyshev, this is defined as the distance between two points such that their differences are maximum value along any coordinate dimension. Mathematically, we can represent Chebyshev distance in equation 2.2 and as shown in figure 2.5:

$$\text{Chebyshev distance} = \max\left(|y_2 - y_1|, |x_2 - x_1|\right) \qquad \textbf{(2.2)}$$

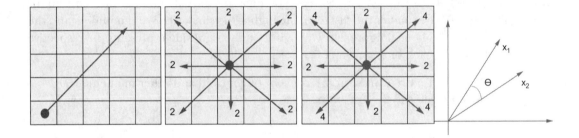

Figure 2.5 Euclidean distance, Chebyshev distance, Manhattan distance, and cosine distance are the primary distance metrics used. Note how the distance is different for two points using these metrics. In Euclidean distance, the direct distance is measured between two points, as shown by the first figure on the left.

- *Manhattan distance*—This is a very easy concept. It simply calculates the distance between two points in a grid-like path, and the distance is hence measured along the axes at right angles. Hence, sometimes it is also referred to as city block distance or the taxicab metric. Mathematically, we can represent the Manhattan distance in equation 2.3 and as shown in figure 2.5:

$$\text{Manhattan distance} = \left(|y_2 - y_1| + |x_2 - x_1|\right) \qquad \textbf{(2.3)}$$

Manhattan distance is in L1 norm form while Euclidean distance is in L2 norm form. Refer to the appendix to study the L1 norm and L2 norm in detail. If we have a high number of dimensions or variables in the dataset, Manhattan distance is a better choice than Euclidean distance. This is due to the *curse of dimensionality*, which we will study in chapter 3.

- *Cosine distance*—Cosine distance is used to measure the similarity between two points in a vector-space diagram. In trigonometry, the cosine of 0 is 1 and the cosine of 90^0 is 0. Hence, if two points are similar to each other, the angle between them will be zero; hence, cosine will be 1, which means the two points are very similar to each other and vice versa. Mathematically, cosine similarity is shown in equation 2.4. If we want to measure the cosine between two vectors *A* and *B*, then cosine is

$$\text{Cosine distance} = (A \cdot B) \ / \ (\|A\| \ \|B\|) \tag{2.4}$$

TIP If you want to refresh your knowledge on the concepts of vector factorization, refer to the appendix.

Other distance-measuring metrics, such as Hamming distance, Jaccard distance, and others, are available. Mostly, we use Euclidean distance in our pragmatic business problems, but other distance metrics are also used sometimes.

NOTE These distance metrics are true for other clustering algorithms too. I recommend testing the Python codes in the book with different distance metrics and comparing the performance.

Now that we understand the various distance metrics, we proceed to study k-means clustering, which is the most widely used algorithm.

2.3.1 *K-means clustering*

K-means clustering is an easy and straightforward approach. It is arguably the most widely used clustering method to segment data points and create nonoverlapping clusters. We have to specify the number of clusters *k* we wish to create as an input, and the algorithm will associate each observation to exactly one of the k clusters.

NOTE K-means clustering is sometimes confused with the k-nearest neighbor (KNN) classifier. Although there is some relationship between the two, KNN is used for classification and regression problems.

K-means clustering is quite an elegant approach and starts with some initial cluster centers and then iterates to assign each observation to the closest center. In the process, the centers are recalculated as the mean of points in the cluster. Let's study the approach used in a step-by-step fashion by using the diagram in figure 2.6. For the sake of simplicity, we are assuming that there are three clusters in the dataset. The steps are as follows:

1 Let's assume that we have all the data points, as shown in step 1.
2 The three centers are initialized randomly, as shown by three squares: blue, red, and green. This input of three is the final number of clusters we wish to have.

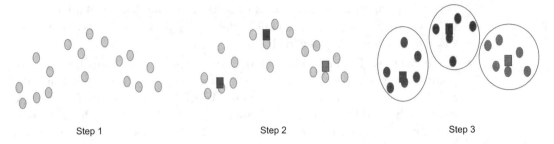

Step 1   Step 2   Step 3

Figure 2.6   Step 1 represents the raw dataset. In step 2, the algorithm initiates three random centroids as we have given the input of the number of clusters as three. In step 3, all the neighboring points of the centroids are assigned to the same cluster.

3   The distance of all the data points is calculated to the centers, and the points are assigned to the nearest center. Note that the points have attained blue, red, and green colors as they are nearest to those respective centers. (The colors are not distinguishable in the print version; hence we have grouped them together.)

4   The three centers are readjusted in this step. The centers are recalculated as the mean of the points in that cluster, as shown in figure 2.7. We can see that in step 4, the three squares have changed their respective positions as compared to step 3.

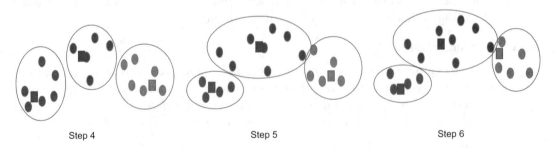

Step 4   Step 5   Step 6

Figure 2.7   The centroids are recalculated in step 4. In step 5, the data points are again reassigned new centers. In step 6, the centroids are again readjusted as per the new calculations.

5   The distance of all the data points is recalculated to the new centers and the points are reassigned to the nearest centers again. Note that two blue data points have become red while a red point has become green in this step.

6   The centers are again readjusted as they were in step 4.

7   The data points are again assigned a new cluster, as shown in figure 2.8.

8   The process will continue until convergence is achieved. In other words, the process continues until there is no more reassignment of the data points; hence, we cannot improve the clustering further, and the final clustering is achieved.

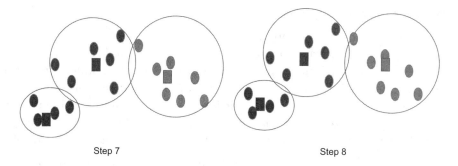

Step 7   Step 8

Figure 2.8 The centroids are recalculated, and this process continues until we can no longer improve the clustering. Then the process stops, as shown in step 8.

The objective of k-means clustering is to ensure that the within-cluster variation is as small as possible while the difference between clusters is as big as possible. In other words, the members of the same cluster are most similar to each other, while members in different clusters are dissimilar. Once the results no longer change, we can conclude that a local optimum has been reached, and clustering can stop. Hence, the final clusters are homogeneous within themselves while heterogeneous with each other.

It is imperative to note two points here:

- K-means clustering initializes the centers randomly; hence it finds a local optimum solution rather than a global optimum solution. Thus it is advisable to iterate the solution multiple times and choose the best output from all the results. By iteration, we mean to repeat the process multiple times, as in each of the iterations, the centroid chosen randomly will be different.
- We have to input the number of final clusters k we wish to have, and it changes the output drastically. A very small value of k relative to the data size will result in redundant clusters as they will not be of any use. In other words, if we have a very small value of k relative to big-sized data, data points with different characteristics will be cobbled together in a few groups. Having a very high value of k will create clusters that are different from each other minutely.

  Moreover, having a very high number of clusters will be difficult to manage and refresh in the long run. Let's study an example. If a telecom operator has 1 million subscribers, and if we take the number of clusters as two or three, the resultant cluster size will be very large. This can also lead to different customers classified in the same segment. On the other hand, if we take the number of clusters as 50 or 60, due to the sheer number of clusters, the output becomes unmanageable to use, analyze, and maintain.

With different values of k, we get different results; hence, it is necessary that we understand how we can choose the optimum number of clusters for a dataset. Now let's examine the process to measure the accuracy of clustering solutions.

2.3.2   *Measuring the accuracy of clustering*

One objective of clustering is to find the cleanest clusters. Theoretically (though not ideally), if we have the same number of clusters as the number of observations, the results will be completely accurate. In other words, if we have 1 million customers, the purest clustering will have 1 million clusters, wherein each customer is in a separate cluster. But it is not the best approach and is not a pragmatic solution either. Clustering intends to create a group of similar observations in one cluster, and we use the same principle to measure the accuracy of our solution. Other options include the following:

- *Within the cluster sum of squares (WCSS) or cohesion*—This index measures the variability of the data points with respect to the distance they are from the centroid of the cluster. This metric is the average distance of each data point from the cluster's centroid, which is repeated for each data point. If the value is too large, it shows there is a large data spread, whereas the smaller value indicates that the data points are quite similar and homogeneous and hence the cluster is compact.

   Sometimes, this intracluster distance is also referred to as *inertia* for that cluster. It is simply the summation of all the distances. The lower the value of inertia, the better the cluster is.

- *Intercluster sum of squares*—This metric is used to measure the distance between centroids of all the clusters. To get it, we measure the distance between centroids of all the clusters and divide it by the number of clusters to get the average value. The bigger it is, the better the clustering is, indicating that clusters are heterogeneous and distinguishable from each other, as represented in figure 2.9.

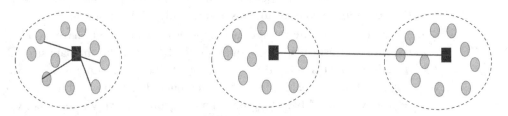

Figure 2.9   Intracluster vs. intercluster distance. Both are used to measure the purity of the final clusters and the performance of the clustering solution.

- *Silhouette value*—This is one of the metrics used to measure the success of clustering. It ranges from –1 to +1, and a higher value is better. It measures how a data point is similar to other data points in its own cluster as compared to other clusters. As a first step, for each observation we calculate the average distance from all the data points in the same cluster; let's call it x_i. Then we calculate the average distance from all the data points in the nearest cluster; let's call it y_i. We will then calculate the coefficient by equation 2.5:

$$\text{Silhouette coefficient} = (y_i - x_i) / \max(y_i, x_i) \qquad \textbf{(2.5)}$$

If the value of coefficient is −1, it means that the observation is in the wrong cluster. If it is 0, the observation is very close to the neighboring clusters. If the value of coefficient is +1, it means that the observation is at a distance from the neighboring clusters. Hence, we would expect to get the highest value for the coefficient to have a good clustering solution.

- *Dunn index*—This can also be used to measure the efficacy of the clustering. It uses the inter- and intradistance measurements defined in the previous intercluster sum of squares silhouette value sections and is given by equation 2.6:

$$\text{Dunn index} = \min \text{ (intercluster distance)} / \max \text{ (intracluster distance)} \quad \textbf{(2.6)}$$

Clearly, we would strive to maximize the value of Dunn index. To achieve it, the numerator should be as big as possible, implying that clusters are at a distance from each other, while the denominator should be as low as possible, signifying that the clusters are quite robust and close-packed.

2.3.3   *Finding the optimum value of k*

Choosing the optimum number of clusters is not easy. As I said earlier, the finest clustering is when the number of clusters equals the number of observations, but as we studied in the last section, it is not practically possible. Hence, we should provide the number of clusters k as an input to the algorithm.

Perhaps the most widely used method for finding the optimum value of k is the *elbow method*. In this method, we calculate within the cluster sum of squares or WCSS for different values of k. The process is the same as discussed in the last section. Then, WCSS is plotted on a graph against different values of k. Wherever we observe a kink or elbow, as shown in figure 2.10, we find the optimum number of clusters for the dataset. Notice the sharp edge.

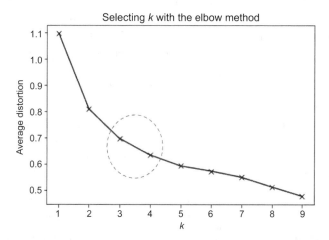

Figure 2.10   The elbow method to find the optimal number of clusters. The circle shows the kink. However, the final number of clusters is dependent on business logic, and often we merge/split clusters based on this. The ease of maintaining the clusters also plays a crucial role.

Exercise 2.2

Answer these questions to check your understanding:

1 K-means clustering does not require the number of clusters as an input. True or False?
2 KNN and k-means clustering are the same thing. True or False?
3 Describe one possible process to find the optimal value of *k*.

But this does not mean that it is the final number of clusters we suggest for the business problem. Based on the number of observations falling in each of the clusters, a few clusters might be combined or broken into subclusters. We also consider the computation cost required to create the clusters. The higher the number of clusters, the greater the computation cost and the time required. We can also find the optimum number of clusters using the silhouette coefficient we discussed earlier.

NOTE   It is imperative that the business logic of merging a few clusters or breaking a few clusters is explored. Ultimately, the solution has to be implemented in real-world business scenarios.

With this, we have examined the nuts and bolts of k-means clustering—the mathematical concepts and the process, the various distance metrics, and determining the best value of *k*.

2.3.4   *Pros and cons of k-means clustering*

The k-means algorithm is quite a popular and widely implemented clustering solution. The solution offers the following advantages:

- It is simple to comprehend and relatively easier to implement as compared to other algorithms. The distance measurement calculation makes it quite intuitive to understand even by users from nonstatistics backgrounds.
- If the number of dimensions is large, the k-means algorithm is faster than other clustering algorithms and creates tighter clusters. Hence, it is preferred if the number of dimensions is quite high.
- It quickly adapts to new observations and can generalize very well to clusters of various shapes and sizes.
- The solution produces results through a series of iterations of recalculations. Most of the time, the Euclidean distance metric is used, which makes it less computationally expensive. It also ensures that the algorithm surely converges and produces results.

K-means is widely used for real-life business problems. Though there are clear advantages of k-means clustering, we do face certain challenges with the algorithm:

- Choosing the optimum number of clusters is not easy. We should provide it as an input. With different values of *k*, the results will be completely different. The process of choosing the best value of *k* is explored in the previous section.

- The solution is dependent on the initial values of centroids. Since the centroids are initialized randomly, the output will be different with each iteration. Hence, it is advisable to run multiple versions of the solution and choose the best one.

- The algorithm is quite sensitive to outliers. Outliers can mess up the final results, and hence it is imperative that we treat outliers before starting with clustering. We can also implement other variants of the k-means algorithm, like k-modes clustering, to deal with the problem of outliers. We discuss dealing with outliers in section 11.4.4 of chapter 11. You can refer to it if you want to know how to deal with outliers.

- Since the basic principle of k-means clustering is to calculate the distance, the solution is not directly applicable to categorical variables. In other words, we cannot use categorical variables directly since we can calculate the distance between numeric values but cannot perform mathematical calculations on categorical variables. To resolve this, we can convert categorical variables to numeric ones using one-hot encoding. We discuss dealing with categorical variables in section 11.4.2 of chapter 11. You can refer to it if you want to know how to deal with categorical variables.

Despite these problems, k-means clustering is one of the most used clustering solutions due to its simplicity and ease of implementation. There are different implementations of k-means algorithms like k-median, k-medoids, etc., which are sometimes used to resolve the problems faced:

- As the name suggests, *k-median clustering* is based on the medians of the dataset as compared to the centroid in k-means. This increases the amount of computation time as the median can be found only after the data has been sorted. But at the same time, k-means is sensitive to outliers whereas k-median is less affected by them.

- *K-medoids clustering* is one of the variants of the k-means algorithm. Medoids are similar to means, except they are always from the same dataset and are implemented when it is difficult to get means, like with images. A medoid can be thought of as the most central point in a cluster that is least dissimilar to all the other members in the cluster. K-medoids choose the actual observations as the centers as compared to k-means, where the centroids may not even be part of the data. It is less sensitive to outliers as compared to the k-means clustering algorithm.

There are other versions too, including k-means++, mini-batch k-means, and others. Generally, in the industry, k-means is used for most of the clustering solutions. You can explore other options like k-means++, mini-batch k-means, etc., if the results are not desirable or if the computation is taking a lot of time. Moreover, having different distance measurement metrics may produce different results for the k-means algorithm.

This section concludes our discussion on the k-means clustering algorithm. It is time to hit the lab and develop actual Python code!

2.3.5   *K-means clustering implementation using Python*

We will now create a Python solution for k-means clustering. In this case, we are using the dataset from the link at GitHub at https://mng.bz/lYq2. This dataset has information about the features of four models of cars. Based on the features of the car, we are going to group them into different clusters:

1 Import the libraries and the dataset into a dataframe. Here, `vehicles.csv` is the input data file. If the data file is not in the same folder as the Jupyter notebook, you would have to provide the complete path to the file. `dropna` is used to remove the missing values, if any:

```
import pandas as pd
vehicle_df = pd.read_csv('vehicle.csv').dropna()
```

2 Perform some initial checks on the data, like shape, info, top five rows, distribution of classes, etc. This is to ensure that we have loaded the complete dataset and there is no corruption while loading the dataset. The `Shape` command will give the number of rows and columns in the data, `info` will describe all the variables and their respective types, and `head` will display the first five rows. The `value_counts` displays the distribution for the `class` variable. Or, in other words, `value_counts` returns the count of the unique values:

```
vehicle_df.shape
vehicle_df.info()
vehicle_df.head()
pd.value_counts(vehicle_df['class'])
```

3 Generate two plots for the variable `class`. The dataset has more examples from car while for `bus` and `van` it is balanced data. I used the `matplotlib` library to plot these graphs. The outputs of the plots are as follows (see figure 2.11):

```
import matplotlib.pyplot as plt
%matplotlib inline
pd.value_counts(vehicle_df["class"]).plot(kind='bar')
pd.value_counts(vehicle_df['class']).hist(bins=300)
```

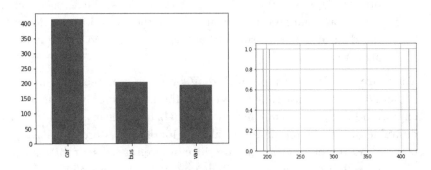

Figure 2.11   Two plots for the variable `class`

4 Check for any missing data points in the dataset. There are no missing data points in our dataset, as we have already dealt with them:

```
vehicle_df.isna().sum()
```

NOTE We cover the methods to deal with missing values in section 11.4.3 of chapter 11 as dropping the missing values is generally not the best approach.

5 Standardize the dataset. It is a good practice to standardize the dataset for clustering. It is important, as the different dimensions might be on a different scale, and one dimension may dominate the computation of distance if its values are naturally much larger than other dimensions. This is done using the `Standard-Scaler()` function. Refer to the appendix to examine different scaling techniques:

```
vehicle_df_1 = vehicle_df.drop('class', axis=1)
from scipy.stats import zscore
vehicle_df_1_z = vehicle_df_1.apply(zscore)
from sklearn.preprocessing import StandardScaler
import umpy as np
sc = StandardScaler()
X_standard = sc.fit_transform(vehicle_df_1)
```

6 Have a quick look at the dataset by generating a scatter plot. The plot displays the distribution of all the data points we have created as `X_standard` in the last step (see figure 2.12):

```
plt.scatter(X_standard[:,0], X_standard[:,1])
plt.show()
```

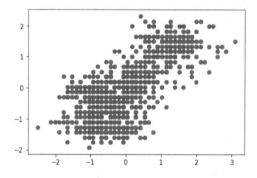

Figure 2.12   A scatter plot of the dataset

7 Perform k-means clustering. First, we have to select the optimum number of clusters using the elbow method. From the `sklearn` library, we import `KMeans`. In a `for` loop, we iterate for the values of clusters from 1 to 10. In other words, the algorithm will create between 1 and 10 clusters and will then generate the results for us to choose the optimal value of *k*.

In the following code snippet, the model object contains the output of the k-means algorithm, which is then fit on the `X_standard` generated in the last step. Here, Euclidean distance has been used as a distance metric (see figure 2.13):

```
from sklearn.cluster import KMeans
from scipy.spatial.distance import cdist
clusters=range(1,10)
meanDistortions=[]
for k in clusters:
    model=KMeans(n_clusters=k)
    model.fit(X_standard)
    prediction=model.predict(X_standard)
    meanDistortions.append(sum(np.min(cdist(X_standard,
        model.cluster_centers_, 'euclidean'), axis=1)) / X_standard
                                                          .shape[0])
plt.plot(clusters, meanDistortions, 'bx-')
plt.xlabel('k')
plt.ylabel('Average distortion')
plt.title('Selecting k with the Elbow Method')
```

Selecting the values of *k* with the elbow method for k-means clustering

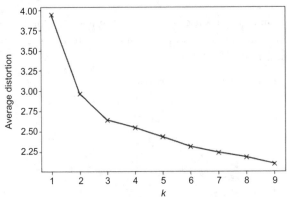

Figure 2.13   **K-means clustering**

8   As we can observe, the optimal number of clusters is three. It is the point where we can observe a sharp kink in the graph. We will continue with k-means clustering with the number of clusters as three. While there is nothing special about the number 3 here, it is best suited for this dataset. `random_state` is a parameter that is used to determine random numbers for centroid initialization. We set it to a value to make randomness deterministic. If you want to repeat the same results again, use the same random state number. It acts like a seed number:

```
kmeans = KMeans(n_clusters=3, n_init = 15, random_state=2345)
kmeans.fit(X_standard)
```

9 Get the `centroids` for the clusters:

```
centroids = kmeans.cluster_centers_
centroids
```

10 Now we use the `centroids` so that they can be profiled by the `columns`:

```
centroid_df = pd.DataFrame(centroids, columns = list(X_standard) )
```

11 We will now create a `dataframe` only for the purpose of creating the `labels`, and then we convert it into categorical variables:

```
dataframe_labels = pd.DataFrame(kmeans.labels_ , columns =
    list(['labels']))
dataframe_labels['labels'] =
    dataframe_labels['labels'].astype('category')
```

12 In this step, we join the two `dataframes`:

```
dataframe_labeled = vehicle_df_1.join(dataframe_labels)
```

13 A `groupby` is done to create a data frame required for the analysis:

```
dataframe_analysis = (dataframe_labeled.groupby(['labels'] ,
    axis=0)).head(1234)
dataframe_labeled['labels'].value_counts()
```

14 Now we create a visualization for the clusters we have defined. This is done using the `mpl_toolkits` library. The logic is simple to understand. The data points are colored as per the respective labels. The rest of the steps are related to the display of the plot by adjusting the label, title, ticks, etc. Since it is not possible to plot all 18 variables in the plot, we have chosen 3 variables to show in the plot (see figure 2.14):

```
from mpl_toolkits.mplot3d import Axes3D
fig = plt.figure(figsize=(8, 6))
ax = Axes3D(fig, rect=[0, 0, .95, 1], elev=20, azim=60)
kmeans.fit(vehicle_df_1_z)
labels = kmeans.labels_
ax.scatter(vehicle_df_1_z.iloc[:, 0], vehicle_df_1_z.iloc[:, 1],
    vehicle_df_1_z.iloc[:, 3],c=labels.astype(np.float),
    edgecolor='k')
ax.w_xaxis.set_ticklabels([])
ax.w_yaxis.set_ticklabels([])
ax.w_zaxis.set_ticklabels([])
ax.set_xlabel('Length')
ax.set_ylabel('Height')
ax.set_zlabel('Weight')
ax.set_title('3D plot of KMeans Clustering on vehicles dataset')
```

We can also test the preceding code with multiple other values of *k*. We have created the code with different values of *k*. In the interest of space, we have put the code for testing with different values of *k* at the GitHub location.

3D plot of k-means clustering on vehicles dataset

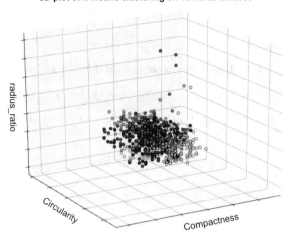

Figure 2.14   K-means clustering for the vehicles dataset

NOTE   Exploratory data analysis holds the key to a robust machine learning solution and a successful project. In the subsequent chapters, we will create detailed exploratory data analyses for datasets.

In the preceding example, we first did a small exploratory analysis of the dataset. This was followed by identifying the optimum number of clusters, which in this case comes out to be three. Then we implemented k-means clustering. You are expected to iterate the k-means solution with different initializations and compare the results, iterate with different values of k, and visualize to analyze the movements of data points.

Centroid-based clustering is one of the most recommended solutions due to its less complicated logic, ease of implementation, flexibility, and trouble-free maintenance. Whenever we require clustering as a solution, mostly we start with creating a k-means clustering solution that acts as a benchmark. The algorithm is highly popular and generally one of the first solutions utilized for clustering. Then we test and iterate with other algorithms.

2.4   *Connectivity-based clustering*

"Birds of a feather flock together" is the principle followed in connectivity-based clusters. The core concept is that objects that are connected with each other are similar to each other. Hence, based on the connectivity between these objects, they are grouped into clusters. An example of such a representation is shown in figure 2.15, where we can iteratively group observations. As an example, we are initiating with all things, dividing into living and nonliving, and so on. Such representation is known as a *dendrogram*. Since there is a tree-like structure, connectivity-based clustering is sometimes referred to as hierarchical clustering.

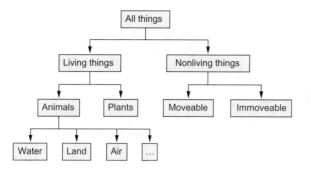

Figure 2.15 **Hierarchical clustering utilizes grouping similar objects iteratively. Such representation is known as a dendrogram.**

Hierarchical clustering fits nicely into human intuition and, hence, is easy to comprehend. Unlike k-means clustering, in hierarchical clustering we do not have to input the number of final clusters, but the method does require a termination condition (i.e., when the clustering should stop). At the same time, hierarchical clustering does not suggest the optimum number of clusters. From the hierarchy/dendrogram generated, we have to choose the best number of clusters ourselves. We will explore this more when we create the Python code for it in subsequent sections.

Figure 2.16 shows an example of hierarchical clustering. Here, the first node is the root, which is then iteratively split into nodes and subnodes. Whenever a node cannot be split further, it is called a terminal node or *leaf*.

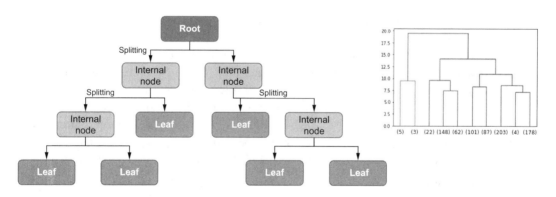

Figure 2.16 **Hierarchical clustering has a root that splits into nodes and subnodes. A node that cannot be split further is called the leaf. In the bottom-up approach, a merging of the leaves will take place.**

Since there is more than one process or logic to merge the observations into clusters, we can generate a large number of dendrograms, which is given by equation 2.7:

$$\text{Number of dendrograms} = (2n-3)! / [2^{(n-2)} (n-2)!] \qquad \textbf{(2.7)}$$

where n is the number of observations or the leaves. So, if we have only two observations, we can have only one dendrogram. If we have 5 observations, we can have 105 dendrograms. Hence, based on the number of observations, we can generate a lot of dendrograms.

Hierarchical clustering can be further classified based on the process used to create the grouping of observations, which we explore next.

2.4.1 *Types of hierarchical clustering*

Based on the grouping strategy, hierarchical clustering can be subdivided into two types: *agglomerative* clustering and *divisive* clustering (see table 2.2).

Table 2.2   Different types of hierarchical clustering

Serial no.	Agglomerative clustering	Divisive clustering
1	Bottom-up approach.	Top-down approach.
2	Each observation creates its own cluster and then merging takes place as the algorithm goes up.	We start with one cluster and then observations are iteratively split to create a tree-like structure.
3	Greedy approach is followed to merge (the greedy approach is described below).	Greedy approach is followed to split.
4	An observation will find the best pair to merge and the process completes when all the observations have merged with each other.	All the observations are taken at the start and then, based on division conditions, splitting takes place until all the observations are exhausted or the termination condition is met.

Let's explore the meaning of the greedy approach first. The greedy approach or greedy algorithm is any algorithm that makes the best choice at each step without considering the effect on future states. In other words, we live in the moment and choose the best option from the available choices at that moment. The current choice is independent of the future choices, and the algorithm will solve the subproblems later. The greedy approach may not provide the most optimal solution but generally provides a locally optimal solution that is close to the best solution in a reasonable amount of time. Hierarchical clustering follows this greedy approach while merging or splitting at a node.

We next examine the steps followed in the hierarchical clustering approach:

1 As shown in figure 2.17, let us say we have five observations in our dataset: 1, 2, 3, 4, and 5.

2 In this step, observations 1 and 2 are grouped into one and 4 and 5 are grouped into one; 3 is not grouped in any one.

3 In this step, we group the output of 4,5 in the last step and observation 3 into one cluster.

4 The output from step 3 is grouped with the output of 1,2 as a single cluster.

In this approach, from left to right, we have an agglomerative approach, and from right to left, a divisive approach is represented. In an agglomerative approach, we merge the observations, while in a divisive approach, we split the observations. We can

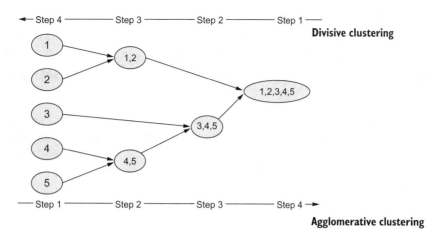

Figure 2.17 Steps followed in hierarchical clustering. From left to right, we have agglomerative clustering (merging of the nodes), while from right to left, we have divisive clustering (splitting of the nodes).

use both agglomerative and divisive approaches for hierarchical clustering. Divisive clustering is an exhaustive approach and sometimes might take more time than the other.

Similar to k-means clustering, the distance metric used to measure plays a significant role here. We are aware of and understand how to measure the distance between data points, but there are multiple methods to define that distance, which we study next.

2.4.2 Linkage criterion for distance measurement

We can use Euclidean distance, Manhattan distance, Chebyshev distance, and others to measure the distance between two observations. At the same time, we can employ various methods to define that distance. Based on this input criterion, the resultant clusters will be different. The various methods to define the distance metric are as follows:

- *Nearest neighbors or single linkages* use the distance between the two nearest points in different clusters. The distance between the closest neighbors in distinct clusters is calculated, and this is used to determine the next split/merging. It is done by an exhaustive search among all the pairs.
- *Farthest neighbor or complete linkage* is the opposite of the nearest neighbor approach. Here, instead of taking the nearest neighbors, we concentrate on the most distant neighbors in different clusters. In other words, the distance between the clusters is calculated by the greatest distance between two objects.
- *Group average linkage* calculates the average of the distances between all the possible pairs of objects in two different clusters.
- The *Ward linkage* method aims to minimize the variability of the clusters that are getting merged into one.

We can use these options of distance metrics while we are developing the actual code for hierarchical clustering and compare the accuracies to determine the best distance metrics for the dataset. During algorithm training, the algorithm merges the observations, which will minimize the linkage criteria chosen. We can visualize the various linkages in figure 2.18.

> **NOTE** Such inputs to the algorithm are referred to as hyperparameters. These are the values we feed to the algorithm to generate the results as per our requirement, and they act as our control on the algorithm. An example of a hyperparameter is k in k-means clustering.

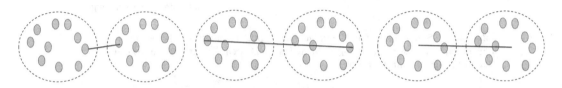

Figure 2.18   Single linkage is for closest neighbors (left); complete linkage is for farthest neighbors (center); and group average is for the average of the distance between clusters (right).

With this, we have understood the working mechanisms in hierarchical clustering. But we have still not addressed the mechanism to determine the optimum number of clusters using hierarchical clustering, which we examine next.

2.4.3   *Optimal number of clusters*

Recall that in k-means clustering, we have to give the number of clusters as an input to the algorithm. We use the elbow method to determine the optimum number of clusters. In the case of hierarchical clustering, we do not have to specify the number of clusters to the algorithm, but we still have to identify the number of final clusters we wish to have. We use a dendrogram to answer that question.

Let us assume that we have 10 data points in total at the bottom of the chart, as shown in figure 2.19. The clusters are merged iteratively until we get the one final cluster at the top. The height of the dendrogram at which two clusters get merged with each other represents the respective distance between the said clusters in the vector-space diagram.

From a dendrogram, the number of clusters is given by the number of vertical lines being cut by a horizontal line. The *optimum* number of clusters is given by the number of vertical lines in the dendrogram cut by a horizontal line such that it intersects the tallest of the vertical lines. Or if the cut is shifted from one end of the vertical line to another, the length covered is the maximum. A dendrogram utilizes branches of clusters to show how closely various data points are related to each other. In a

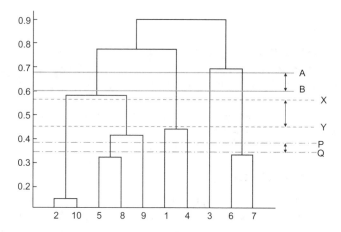

Figure 2.19 Dendrogram to identify the optimum number of clusters. The distance between X and Y is more than between A and B and between P and Q; hence, we choose that as the cut to create clusters and the number of clusters chosen is five. The x-axis represents the clusters, while the y-axis represents the distance (dissimilarity) between two clusters.

dendrogram, clusters that are located at the same height level are more closely related than clusters that are located at different height levels.

In the example shown in figure 2.19, we have shown three potential cuts: AB, PQ, and XY. If we take a cut above AB, it will result in two very broad clusters, while below PQ will result in nine clusters that will become difficult to analyze further.

Here, the distance between X and Y is more than between A and B and between P and Q. So we can conclude that the distance between X and Y is the maximum, and hence, we can finalize that as the best cut. This cut intersects at five distinct points; hence, we should have five clusters. The height of the cut in the dendrogram is similar to the value of k in k-means clustering. In k-means clustering, k determines the number of clusters. In hierarchical clustering, the best cut determines the number of clusters we wish to have.

Similar to k-means clustering, the final number of clusters is not dependent on the choice from the algorithm only. Business acumen and pragmatic logic play a vital role in determining the final number of clusters. Recall that one of the important attributes of clusters is their usability, which we discussed in section 2.2.

Sometimes we also use cophenetic correlation coefficient to measure how well the dendrogram represents the actual pairwise distance between the points. It compares the cophenetic distance, which is the height at which two points merged first in the dendrogram, with the original dissimilarity between the points.

There is one more index known as the Calinski-Haranasz index. It measures the ratio of between-cluster dispersion to within-cluster dispersion. A higher value means better clustering, and hence we choose the optimal number of clusters to maximize this index.

2.4.4   *Pros and cons of hierarchical clustering*

Hierarchical clustering is a strong clustering technique and is quite popular, too. Similar to k-means, it also uses distance as a metric to measure similarity. At the same time, there are a few challenges with the algorithm. The advantages of hierarchical clustering are as follows:

- Perhaps the biggest advantage of hierarchical clustering is the reproducibility of results. Recall in k-means clustering, the process starts with random initialization of centroids giving different results. In hierarchical clustering, we can reproduce the results.
- In hierarchical clustering, we do not have to input the number of clusters to segment the data.
- The implementation is easy to implement and comprehend. Since it follows a tree-like structure, it is explainable to users from nontechnical backgrounds.
- The dendrogram generated can be interpreted to give a very good understanding of the data with a visualization.

At the same time, we do face some challenges with hierarchical clustering algorithms, which are as follows:

- The biggest challenge we face with hierarchical clustering is the time taken to converge. The time complexity for k-means is linear, while for hierarchical clustering it is quadratic. For example, if we have "n" data points, then for k-means clustering the time complexity will be $O(n)$, while for hierarchical clustering it is $O(n^3)$.

TIP   Refer to the appendix if you want to study $O(n)$.

- Since the time complexity is $O(n^3)$, it is a time-consuming task. Moreover, the memory required to compute is at least $O(n^2)$, making hierarchical clustering quite a time-consuming and memory-intensive process. And this is the problem even if the dataset is medium. The computation required might not be a challenge if we are using high-end processors, but it surely can be a concern for regular computers.
- The interpretation of dendrograms at times can be subjective; hence due diligence is required while interpreting dendrograms. The key to interpreting a

dendrogram is to focus on the height at which any two data points are connected. It can be subjective, as different analysts can decipher different cuts and try to prove their methodology. Hence, it is advisable to interpret the results in the light of mathematics and marry the results with real-world business problems.

- Hierarchical clustering cannot undo the previous steps it has done. Even if we feel that a connection made is not proper and should be rolled back, there is no mechanism to remove the connection.

- The algorithm is very sensitive to outliers and messy datasets. The presence of outliers, NULL, missing values, duplicates, etc., makes a dataset messy. Hence the resultant output might not be proper or what we expected.

But despite all the challenges, hierarchical clustering is one of the most widely used clustering algorithms. Generally, we create both k-means clustering and hierarchical clustering for the same dataset to compare the results of the two. If the number of clusters suggested and the distribution of respective clusters look similar, we get more confident about the clustering methodology used.

We have covered the theoretical background of hierarchical clustering. It is time to take action and jump into Python for coding.

2.4.5   *Hierarchical clustering case study using Python*

We will now create a Python solution for hierarchical clustering using the same dataset we used for k-means clustering:

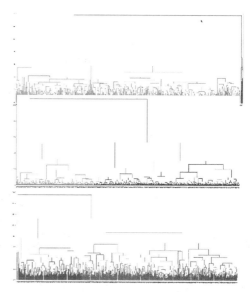

1 Load the required libraries and dataset. For this, follow steps 1 to 6 we followed for the k-means algorithm.

2 Next, we create hierarchical clustering using three linkage methods: average, ward, and complete. Then the clusters will be plotted. The input to the method is the X_Standard variable, the linkage method used, and the distance metric. Then, using the matplotlib library, we plot the dendrogram. In the following code snippet, simply change the method from "average" to "ward" and "complete" and get the respective results (see figure 2.20):

Figure 2.20   Hierarchical clustering using average, ward, and complete linking methods (top to bottom, respectively)

```
from scipy.cluster.hierarchy import dendrogram, linkage
Z_df_average = linkage(X_standard, 'average', metric='euclidean')
Z_df_average.shape
```

```
plt.figure(figsize=(30, 12))
dendrogram(Z_df_average)
plt.show()
```

3 We now want to choose the number of clusters we wish to have. For this purpose, let's re-create the dendrogram by subsetting the last 10 merged clusters. We have chosen 10 as it is generally an optimal choice; I advise you to test with other values too (see figure 2.21):

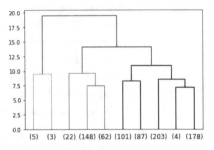

```
dendrogram(
    Z_df_complete,
    truncate_mode='lastp',   p=10,)
plt.show()
```

Figure 2.21   A dendrogram subsetting the last 10 merged clusters

4 We observe that the most optimal distance is 10.

5 Cluster the data into different groups. By using the logic described in the last section, the number of optimal clusters is going to be four:

```
from scipy.cluster.hierarchy import fcluster
hier_clusters = fcluster(Z_df_complete, max_distance,
    criterion='distance')
hier_clusters
len(set(hier_clusters))
```

6 Plot the distinct clusters using the `matplotlib` library. In the print version of the book, you will not see different colors. The output of the Python code will have the colors; I advise that you run the code to appreciate the output. The same output is available in the GitHub repository (see figure 2.22):

```
plt.scatter(X_standard[:,0], X_standard[:,1], c=hier_clusters)
plt.show()
```

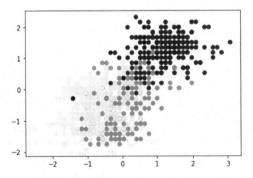

Figure 2.22   A plot of the distinct clusters using the `matplotlib` library

7 For different values of distance, the number of clusters will change, and the plot will look different. We are showing different results for distances of 5, 15, and 20 and different numbers of clusters generated for each iteration. Figure 2.23 shows that we get completely different results for different values of distances as we move from left to right. We should be cautious when we choose the value of the distance, and sometimes we might have to iterate a few times to get the best value.

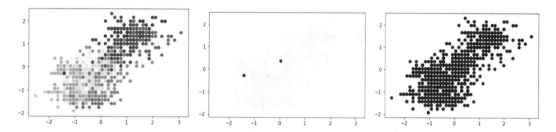

Figure 2.23   The number of clusters using different values of distance

Using hierarchical clustering, we segment the data on the left side to the one on the right side of figure 2.24. The left side represents the raw data, while on the right, we have a representation of the clustered dataset. In the print version of the book, you won't see the different colors. The output of the Python code will have the colors. The same output is available at the GitHub repository.

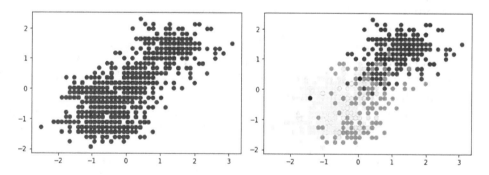

Figure 2.24   Segmenting the data using hierarchical clustering

Hierarchical clustering is a robust method and is highly recommended. Along with k-means, it creates a great foundation for clustering-based solutions. Most of the time, at least these two techniques are used when we create clustering solutions, and then we move on to iterate with other methodologies.

2.5   Density-based clustering

We have studied k-means in the earlier sections. Recall how it uses a centroid-based method to assign a cluster to each of the data points. If an observation is an outlier, the outlier point pulls the centroid toward itself and is also assigned a cluster like a normal observation. These outliers do not necessarily bring information to the cluster and can affect other data points disproportionally but are still made a part of the cluster. Moreover, getting clusters of arbitrary shapes, as shown in figure 2.25, is a challenge with the k-means algorithm. Density-based clustering methods solve the problem.

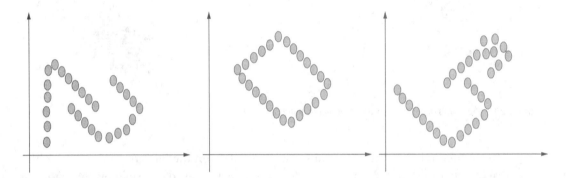

Figure 2.25   DBSCAN is highly recommended for irregular-shaped clusters. With k-means, we generally get spherical clusters; DBSCAN can resolve it.

In the density-based method, the clusters are identified as the areas that have a higher density as compared to the rest of the dataset. In other words, given a vector-space diagram where the data points are represented, a cluster is defined by adjacent regions or neighboring regions of high-density points. This cluster will be separated from other clusters by regions of low-density points. The observations in the sparse areas or separating regions are considered noise or outliers in the dataset. A few examples of density-based clustering are shown in figure 2.25.

We mentioned two terms: neighborhood and density. To understand density-based clustering, we will study these terms in the next section.

2.5.1   Neighborhood and density

Imagine we represent data observations in a vector-space, and we have a point P. We now define the neighborhood for this point P. The representation is shown in figure 2.26. For a point P we have defined an ε—neighborhoods for it that are the points equidistant from P. In a 2D space, it is represented by a circle; in a 3D space it is a sphere; and for a n-dimensional space, it is n-sphere with center P and radius ε. This defines the concept of *neighborhood*.

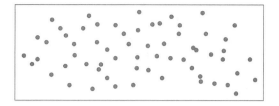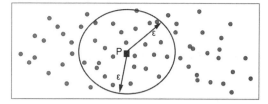

Figure 2.26 **Representation of data points in a vector-space diagram. On the right-side we have a point P, and the circle drawn is of radius ε. So, for $\varepsilon > 0$, the neighborhood of P is defined by the set of points that are at less than or equal to ε distance from the point P.**

Now let's explore the term *density*. Recall density is mass divided by volume (mass/volume). The higher the mass, the higher the density, and the lower the mass, the lower the density. Conversely, the lower the volume, the higher the density, and vice versa.

In the previous context, mass is the number of points in the neighborhood. In figure 2.26 we can observe the effect of ε on the number of data points or the mass. When it comes to volume, in the case of 2D space, volume is πr^2, while for a sphere that is 3D, it is $4/3\ \pi r^3$. For spheres of n-dimensions, we can calculate the respective volume as per the number of dimensions, which will be π times a numerical constant raised to the number of dimensions.

So, in the two cases shown in figure 2.27, for a point P, we can get the number of points (mass) and volumes, and then we can calculate the respective densities. But the absolute values of these densities mean nothing to us; rather how they are similar (or different) from nearby areas is what's important. The points that are in the same neighborhood and have similar densities can be grouped into one cluster.

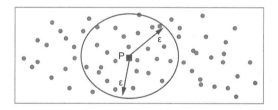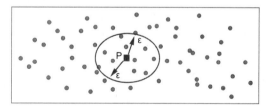

Figure 2.27 **The effect of radius ε. On the left side, the number of points is more than on the right side. So the mass of the right side is less, since it contains a smaller number of data points.**

In an ideal case scenario, we wish to have highly dense clusters with a maximum number of points. In the two cases shown in figure 2.28, we have a less dense cluster depicted on the left and a high-dense one on the right.

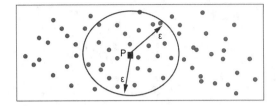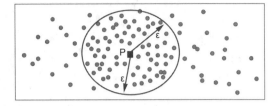

Figure 2.28 Denser clusters are preferred over less dense ones. Ideally, a dense cluster, with a maximum number of data points, is what we aim to achieve from clustering.

From the preceding discussion, we can conclude that

- If we *increase* the value of ε, we will get a *higher* volume but not necessarily a higher number of points (mass). It depends on the distribution of the data points.
- If we *decrease* the value of ε, we will get a *lower* volume but not necessarily a lower number of points (mass).

These are the fundamental points we adhere to. Hence, it is imperative that we choose clusters that have high density and cover the maximum number of neighboring points.

2.5.2   *DBSCAN clustering*

DBSCAN clustering is one of the highly recommended density-based algorithms. It clusters the data observations that are closely packed in a densely populated area but does not consider the outliers in low-density regions. Unlike k-means, we do not specify the number of clusters, and the algorithm is able to identify irregular-shaped clusters, whereas k-means generally proposes spherical-shaped clusters. Similar to hierarchical clustering, it works by connecting the data points but with the observations that satisfy the density criteria or the threshold value.

> **NOTE** DBSCAN was proposed in 1996 by Martin Ester, Hans-Peter Kriegal, Jörg Sander, and Xiaowei Xu. The algorithm was given the Test of Time award in 2014 at ACM SIGKDD. The paper can be accessed at https://mng.bz/BXvl.

DBSCAN works on the concepts of neighborhood we discussed in the last section. We will now dive deeper into the working methodology and building blocks of DBSCAN.

NUTS AND BOLTS OF DBSCAN CLUSTERING

Let's now examine the core building blocks of DBSCAN clustering. We know it is a density-based clustering algorithm, and hence the neighborhood concept is applicable here.

Say we have a few data observations that we need to cluster. We also locate a data point P. Then we can easily define two hyperparameter terms:

- The radius of the neighborhood around P, known as ε, which we discussed in the last section.

- The minimum number of points we wish to have in the neighborhood of P or, in other words, the minimum number of points that are required to create a dense region. This is referred to as minimum points (minPts). It is one of the parameters we can input by applying a threshold on minPts.

Based on these concepts, we can classify the observations into three broad categories: core points, border or reachable points, and outliers:

- *Core points*—Any data point x can be termed as a core point if at least minPts are within ε distance of it (including x itself), shown as squares in figure 2.29. They are the building blocks of our clusters and are called core points. We use the same value of radius (ε) for each point and hence the *volume* of each neighborhood remains constant. But the number of points will vary and hence the *mass* varies. Consequently, the density varies as well. Since we put a threshold using minPts, we are putting a limit on density. So we can conclude that core points fulfill the minimum density threshold requirement. It is imperative to note that we can choose different values of ε and minPts to iterate and fine-tune the clusters.
- *Border points or reachable points*—A point that is not a core point in the clusters is called a border point, shown as filled circles in figure 2.29.

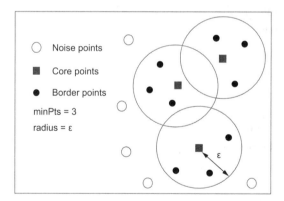

Figure 2.29   Core points are shown as squares; border points are shown as filled circles, while noise is unfilled circles. Together, these three are the building blocks for DBSCAN clustering.

A point y is directly reachable from x if y is within ε distance of core point x. A point can only be approached from a core point, and it is the primary condition or rule to be followed. Only a core point can reach a noncore point, and the opposite is not true. In other words, a noncore point can only be reached by other core points; it cannot reach anyone else. In figure 2.29, border points are represented as dark circles.

To understand the process better, we have to understand the term *density-reachable* or *connectedness*. In figure 2.30, we have two core points: X and Y. We can directly go from X to Y. Point Z is not in the neighborhood of X but is in the neighborhood of Y. So we cannot directly reach Z from X, but we can surely reach Z from X through Y or, in other words, using the neighborhood of Y, we can travel to Z from X. Conversely, we cannot go from Z to X since Z is the border point and, as described earlier, we cannot travel from a border point.

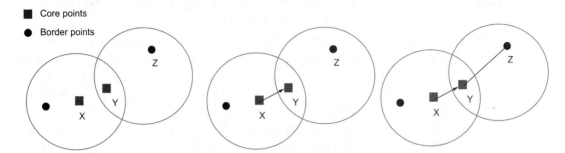

Figure 2.30   X and Y are the core points, and we can travel from X to Y. Though Z is not in the immediate neighborhood of X, we can still reach Z from X through Y. This is the core concept of density-connected points used in DBSCAN clustering.

- *Outliers*—All the other points are outliers. In other words, if it is not a core point or is not a reachable point, it is an outlier, shown as unfilled circles in figure 2.29. They are not assigned any cluster.

STEPS IN **DBSCAN** CLUSTERING

The steps in DBSCAN clustering are as follows:

1 We start with assigning values for ε and minPts required to create a cluster.
2 We start with picking a random point, let's say P, which is not yet given any label (i.e., it has not been analyzed and assigned any cluster).
3 We then analyze the neighborhood for P. If it contains a sufficient number of points (i.e., higher than minPts), then the condition is met to start a cluster. If so, we tag the point P as the *core point*. If a point cannot be recognized as a core point, we will assign it the tag of *outlier* or *noise*. We should note this point can be made a part of a different cluster later. Then we go back to step 2.
4 Once this core point P is found, we start creating the cluster by adding all directly reachable points from P and then increase this cluster size by adding more points directly reachable from P. Then we add all the points to the cluster, which can be included using the neighborhood by iterating through all these points. If we add an outlier point to the cluster, the tag of the outlier point is changed to a border point.
5 This process continues until the density cluster is complete. We then find a new unassigned point and repeat the process.
6 Once all the points have been assigned to a cluster or called an outlier, we stop our clustering process.

There are iterations in the process. Then, once the clustering concludes, we utilize business logic to either merge or split a few clusters.

Exercise 2.4

Answer these questions to check your understanding:

1 Compare and contrast the importance of DBSCAN clustering with respect to k-means clustering.
2 A noncore point can reach a core point and vice versa is also true. True or False?
3 Explain the significance of neighborhood and minPts.
4 Describe the process to find the most optimal value of *k*.

Now we are clear with the process of DBSCAN clustering. Before creating the Python solution, we will examine the advantages and disadvantages of the DBSCAN algorithm.

PROS AND CONS OF DBSCAN CLUSTERING

DBSCAN has the following advantages:

- Unlike k-means, we need not specify the number of clusters to DBSCAN.
- The algorithm is quite a robust solution for unclean datasets. Unlike other algorithms, it can deal with outliers effectively.
- We can determine irregular-shaped clusters too. Arguably, this is the biggest advantage of DBSCAN clustering.
- Only the input of radius and minPts is required by the algorithm.

DBSCAN has the following challenges:

- The differentiation in clusters is sometimes not clear using DBSCAN. Depending on the order of processing the observations, a point can change its cluster. In other words, if a border point P is accessible by more than one cluster, P can belong to either cluster, which is dependent on the order of processing the data.
- If the difference in densities among different areas of the datasets is very big, then the optimum combination of ε and minPts will be difficult to determine, and hence DBSCAN will not generate effective results.
- The distance metric used plays a highly significant role in clustering algorithms, including DBSCAN. Arguably, the most common metric used is Euclidean distance, but if the number of dimensions is quite large, then it becomes a challenge to compute.
- The algorithm is very sensitive to different values of ε and minPts. Sometimes finding the most optimum value becomes a challenge.

PYTHON SOLUTION FOR DBSCAN CLUSTERING

We will use the same dataset we have used for k-means and hierarchical clustering:

1 Load the libraries and dataset up to step 6 in the k-means algorithm.

2 Import additional libraries:

```
from sklearn.cluster import DBSCAN
from sklearn.preprocessing import StandardScaler
from sklearn.preprocessing import normalize
from sklearn.neighbors import NearestNeighbors
```

Here we fit the model with a value for minimum distance and radius:

```
db_default = DBSCAN(eps = 0.0375, min_samples = 6).fit(X_standard)
labels = db_default.labels_
```

The number of distinct clusters is 1:

```
list(set(labels))
```

3 We are not getting any results for clustering here. In other words, there will not be any logical results of clustering since we have not provided the optimal values for minPts and ε.

4 Now we will find the optimum values for ε (see figure 2.31). For this, we will calculate the distance to the nearest points for each point and then sort and plot the results. Wherever the curvature is maximum, it is the best value for ε. For minPts, generally minPts $\geq d + 1$ where d is the number of dimensions in the dataset:

```
neigh = NearestNeighbors(n_neighbors=2)
nbrs = neigh.fit(X_standard)
distances, indices = nbrs.kneighbors(X_standard)
distances = np.sort(distances, axis=0)
distances = distances[:,1]
plt.plot(distances)
```

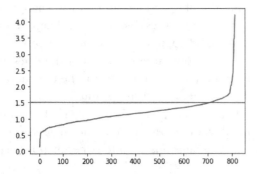

Figure 2.31   Finding the optimum value of ε

NOTE See the paper at https://iopscience.iop.org/article/10.1088/1755-1315/31/1/012012/pdf for further study on how to choose the values of radius for DBSCAN.

5 The best value is coming up as 1.5, as observed in the point of defection. We will use it and set the minPts as 5, which is generally taken as a standard:

```
db_default = DBSCAN(eps=1.5, min_samples=5)
db_default.fit(X_standard)
clusters = db_default.labels_
```

6 Now we can observe that we are getting more than one cluster:

```
list(set(clusters))
```

7 Let's plot the clusters (see figure 2.32). In the print version of the book, you will not see different colors. The output of the Python code will have the colors. The same output is available at the GitHub repository:

```
colors = ['blue', 'red', 'orange', 'green', 'purple', 'black', 'brown',
    'cyan', 'yellow', 'pink']
vectorizer = np.vectorize(lambda x: colors[x % len(colors)])
plt.scatter(X_standard[:,0], X_standard[:,1], c=vectorizer(clusters))
```

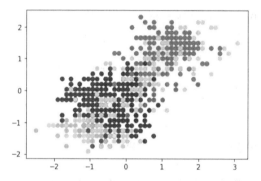

Figure 2.32 Plotting the clusters

We have thus created a solution using DBSCAN. I advise you to compare the results from all three algorithms. In real-world scenarios, we test the solution with multiple algorithms, iterate with hyperparameters, and then choose the best solution.

Density-based clustering is quite an efficient solution and, to a certain extent, is a very effective one too. It is heavily recommended if the shape of the clusters is suspected to be irregular.

With this, we conclude our discussion on DBSCAN clustering. In the next section, we solve a business use case on clustering. In the case study, the focus is less on technical concepts and more on business understanding and solution generation.

2.6 Case study using clustering

We will now define a case study that employs clustering as one of the solutions. The objective of the case study is to give you a flavor of the practical and real-life business world. This case study–based approach is also followed in job-related interviews, wherein a case is discussed during the interview stage. I highly recommend you understand how we implement machine learning solutions in pragmatic business scenarios.

A case study typically has a business problem, the dataset available, the various solutions that can be used, the challenges faced, and the final chosen solution. We also discuss the problems faced while implementing the solution in real-world business.

So let's start our case study on clustering using unsupervised learning. In the case study, we focus on the steps we take to solve the case study and not on the technical algorithms, as there can be multiple technical solutions to a particular problem.

2.6.1   *Business context*

The industry we are considering can be retail; telecom; banking, financial services, and insurance; aviation; healthcare; or any other industry that has a customer base. For any business, the objective is to generate more revenue for the business and ultimately increase the overall profit of the business. To increase revenue, the business would want to have increasingly more new customers. The business would also want the existing consumers to buy more and buy more often. So the business always strives to keep the consumers engaged and happy and to increase their transactional value with the business.

For this to happen, the business must have a thorough understanding of its consumer base; it must know their tastes, price points, category preferences, affinity, preferred marketing/communication channels, etc. Once the business has examined and understood the consumer base minutely, then

- The product team can improve the product features as per the consumer's need.
- The pricing team can improve the price of the products by aligning them to customers' preferred prices. The prices can be customized for a customer, or loyalty discounts can be offered.
- The marketing team and customer relationship team can target the consumers with a customized offer.
- The teams can win back the consumers who are going to churn or stop buying from the business, can enhance their spending, increase the stickiness, and increase the customer lifetime value.
- Overall, different teams can align their offerings as per the understanding of the consumers generated. And the end consumer will be happier, more engaged, and more loyal to the business, leading to more fruitful consumer engagement.

The business hence should dive deep into the consumers' data and generate an understanding of the base. The customer data can look like that shown in the next section.

2.6.2   Dataset for the analysis

We take as an example an apparel retailer that has a loyalty program and that saves the customer's transaction details. The various (not exhaustive) data sources are shown in figure 2.33.

CustID	Revenue	Invoices	Items	Discount%
123	100	2	10	30
124	101	3	12	0
125	102	4	15	5
126	103	2	11	40

CustID	DOB	City	Gender
123	01/01/1990	A	M
124	02/01/1990	B	F
125	03/01/1990	C	M
126	04/01/1990	D	F

ItemNo	Price	Subcategory	Category
1	10	A	P
2	11	B	Q
3	12	C	R
4	10	D	S

StoreID	StoreName	City	Area
100	XYZ	A	1000
101	PQR	B	2000
102	ABC	C	1500
103	TUV	D	2500

Figure 2.33   Data sources for an apparel retail store

We can have store details, such as store ID, store name, city, area, number of employees, etc. We can have an item hierarchies table, which has all the details of the items like price, category, etc. Then we can have customer demographic details like age, gender, city, and customer transactional history. Clearly, by joining such tables, we will be able to create a master table that will have all the details in one place.

> **NOTE**   I advise you to develop a good skill set for SQL. It is required in almost all of the domains related to data—be it data science, data engineering, or data visualization, SQL is ubiquitous.

Figure 2.34 is an example of a master table. This is not an exhaustive list of variables, and the number of variables can be much larger than the ones shown. The master table has some raw variables like Revenue, Invoices, etc., and some derived variables like Average Transaction Value, Average Basket Size, etc.

CustID	Revenue	Invoices	Items bought	Age	Gender	Avg txn value	Avg basket size	Days since last txn	City
1	1000	2	2	25	M	500	1	20	A
2	2000	4	5	26	F	500	1.25	12	B
3	3000	3	4	27	M	1000	1.33	30	C
4	4000	4	5	28	F	1000	1.25	25	D
5	5000	2	1	29	F	2500	0.5	1	E

Figure 2.34   A master table

We could also take an example of a telecom operator. In that subscriber usage, call rate, revenue, days spent on the network, data usage, etc., will be the attributes we analyze. Hence, based on the business domain at hand, the datasets will change.

Once we have the dataset, we generally create derived attributes from it. For example, the average transaction value attribute is total revenue divided by the number of invoices. We create such attributes in addition to the raw variables we already have.

2.6.3   *Suggested solutions*

There can be multiple solutions to the problem, some of which we include in the following:

- We can create a dashboard to depict the major key performance indicators. This will allow us to analyze the history and take necessary actions based on it. But the dashboard will only show the information that we already know (to some extent).
- We can perform data analysis using some of techniques we used in the solutions in the earlier sections. This will solve a part of the problem and, moreover, it is difficult to consider multiple dimensions simultaneously.
- We can create predictive models to predict if the customers are going to shop in the coming months or are going to churn in the next X days, but this will not solve the problem completely. To be clear, "churn" here means that the customer no longer shops with the retailer in the next X days. Here, duration X is defined as per the business domain. For example, for the telecom domain, X will be less than in the insurance domain. This is due to the fact that people use mobile phones every day, whereas in the insurance domain, most customers pay the premium yearly. So customer interaction is less for insurance.
- We can create customer segmentation solutions wherein we group customers based on their historical trends and attributes. This is the solution we will use to solve this business problem.

2.6.4   *Solution for the problem*

Recall figure 1.9 in chapter 1, where we discussed the steps we follow in the machine learning algorithm. Everything starts with defining the business problem and then we move on to data discovery, preprocessing, etc. For our case study here, we will utilize a similar strategy. We have already defined the business problem; data discovery is done and we have completed the exploratory data analysis and the preprocessing of the data. To create a segmentation solution using clustering, follow these steps:

1 We start with finalizing the dataset we wish to feed to the clustering algorithms. We might have created some derived variables, treated some missing values or outliers, etc. In the case study, we would want to know the minimum/maximum/average values of transactions, invoices, items bought, etc. We would be interested to know the gender and age distribution. We also would like to know the mutual relationships between these variables, such as if women customers use the online mode more than male customers. All of these questions are answered as part of this step.

TIP   A Python Jupyter notebook is checked in at the GitHub repository, which provides detailed steps and code for the exploratory data analysis and data preprocessing. Check it out!

2   We create the first solution using k-means clustering followed by hierarchical clustering. For each of the algorithms, iterations are done by changing hyperparameters. In the case study, we will choose parameters like the number of visits, total revenue, distinct categories purchased, online/offline transactions ratio, gender, age, etc., as parameters for clustering.

3   A final version of the algorithm and respective hyperparameters are chosen. The clusters are analyzed further in the light of business understanding.

4   More often, the clusters are merged or broken, depending on the size of the observations and the nature of the attributes present in them. For example, if the total customer base is 1 million, it will be really hard to take action on a cluster of size 100. At the same time, it will be equally difficult to manage a cluster of size 700,000.

5   We then analyze the clusters we finally have. The clusters distribution is checked for the variables, their distinguishing factors are understood, and we give logical names to the clusters. We can expect to see such a clustering output as shown in figure 2.35.

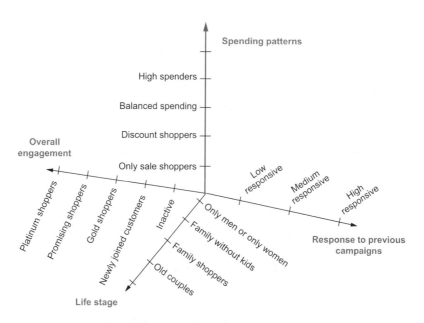

Figure 2.35   Segmentation based on a few dimensions like response, life stage, engagement, and spending patterns. The dimensions are not exhaustive, and in a real-world business problem, the number of dimensions can be higher.

In the example clusters shown, we have depicted spending patterns, responsiveness to previous campaigns, life stage, and overall engagement as a few dimensions. Respective subdivisions of each of these dimensions are also shown. The clusters will be a logical combination of these dimensions. The actual dimensions can be much higher.

The segmentation shown in figure 2.35 can be used for multiple domains and businesses. The parameters and attributes might change, the business context may be different, the extent of data available might vary—but the overall approach remains similar.

In addition to the applications we saw in the last section, let's examine a few use cases here:

- Market research utilizes clustering to segment the groups of consumers into market segments; then the groups can be analyzed better in terms of their preferences. Product placement can be improved, pricing can be made tighter, and geography selection will be more scientific.
- In the bioinformatics and medical industry, clustering can be used to group genes into distinct categories. Groups of genes can be segmented and comparisons can be assessed by analyzing the attributes of the groups.
- Clustering is used as an effective data preprocessing step before we create algorithms using supervised learning solutions. It can also be used to reduce the data size by focusing on the data points belonging to a cluster.
- Clustering is utilized for pattern detection across both structured and unstructured datasets. We have already studied the case for a structured dataset. For text data, it can be used to group similar types of documents, journals, news, etc. We can also employ clustering to work and develop solutions for images. We will study unsupervised learning solutions for text and images in later chapters.
- As the algorithms work on similarity measurements, clustering can be used to segment the incoming dataset as fraud or genuine, which can be used to reduce the number of criminal activities.

The use cases of clustering are many. We have discussed only the prominent ones. Clustering is one of the algorithms that changes the working methodologies and generates a lot of insights around the data. It is widely used across telecom; retail; banking, financial services, and insurance; aviation; and others.

At the same time, there are a few problems with the algorithm. We next examine the common problems we face with clustering.

2.7 *Common challenges faced in clustering*

Clustering is not a completely straightforward solution without any challenges. Like any other solution in the world, clustering too has its share of problems. The most common challenges we face in clustering are as follows:

- *Too much data*—Sometimes the magnitude of the data is quite big, and there are a lot of dimensions available. In such a case, it becomes difficult to manage the dataset. The computation power might be limited, and like any project, there is finite time available. To overcome the problem, we can

- Try to reduce the number of dimensions by finding the most significant variables by using a supervised learning-based regression approach or decision tree algorithm, etc.
- Reduce the number of dimensions by employing principal component analysis or singular value decomposition, etc.

- *A noisy dataset*—"Garbage in, garbage out" is a cliché that is true for clustering too. If the dataset is messy, it creates a lot of problems. The problems can include

- Missing values (i.e., NULL, NA, ?, blanks, etc.).
- Outliers present in the dataset.
- Junk values like #€¶§^ etc., present in the dataset.
- Wrong entries made in the data. For example, if a name is entered in the Revenue field, it is an incorrect entry.

We discuss the steps and the process to resolve these problems in later chapters. In this chapter, we are examining how to work with categorical variables.

- *Categorical variables*—While discussing, recall the problem where k-means was not able to use categorical variables. We solve that problem next.

  To convert categorical variables into numeric ones, we can use *one-hot encoding*. This technique adds additional columns equal to the number of distinct classes as shown in the following figure. The variable city has unique values as London and New Delhi. We can observe that two additional columns have been created with 0 or 1 filled in for the values (see figure 2.36).

CustID	City	Sales	Age		CustID	London	NewDelhi	Sales	Age
1234	London	100	25		1234	1	0	100	25
1235	NewDelhi	101	26		1235	0	1	101	26
1236	NewDelhi	102	27		1236	0	1	102	27
1237	NewDelhi	103	28		1237	0	1	103	28
1238	London	104	29		1238	1	0	104	29

Figure 2.36 Using one-hot encoding to convert categorical variables into numeric ones

Using one-hot encoding does not always ensure an effective and efficient solution. Imagine if the number of cities in this example is 100; then we will have 100 additional columns in the dataset, and most of the values will be filled in with 0. Hence, in such a situation, it is advisable to group a few values.

- *Distance metrics*—With different distance metrics, we might get different results. Though there is no "one size fits all," Euclidean distance is most often used for measuring distance.

- *Subjective interpretations*—Interpretations for the clusters are quite subjective. By using different attributes, completely different clustering can be done for the same datasets. As discussed earlier, the focus should be on solving the business problem at hand. This holds the key to choosing the hyperparameters and the final algorithm.
- *Time-consuming*—Since a lot of dimensions are dealt with simultaneously, sometimes converging the algorithm takes a lot of time.

Despite all these challenges, clustering is a widely recognized and utilized technique.

2.8 Concluding thoughts

Unsupervised learning is not an easy task. But it is certainly a very engaging one. It does not require any target variable, and the solution identifies the patterns itself, which is one of the biggest advantages of unsupervised learning algorithms. And the implementations are already having a great effect on the business world. We studied one of these solution classes called clustering in this chapter.

Clustering is an unsupervised learning solution that is useful for pattern identifications, exploratory analysis, and, of course, segmenting the data points. Organizations heavily use clustering algorithms and proceed to the next level of understanding consumer data. Better prices can be offered, more relevant offers can be suggested, consumer engagement can be improved, and overall customer experience becomes better. After all, a happy consumer is the goal of any business. Clustering can be used not only for structured data but for text data, images, videos, and audio too. Due to its capability to find patterns across multiple datasets using a large number of dimensions, clustering is the go-to solution whenever we want to analyze multiple dimensions together.

In this second chapter of this book, we introduced concepts of unsupervised-based clustering methods. We examined different types of clustering algorithms—k-means clustering, hierarchical clustering, and DBSCAN clustering—along with their mathematical concepts, respective use cases, and pros and cons with an emphasis on creating actual Python code for these datasets.

In the following chapter, we will study dimensionality reduction techniques like principal component analysis and singular value decomposition. We will discuss the building blocks for techniques, their mathematical foundation, advantages and disadvantages, and use cases and perform actual Python implementation.

2.9 Practical next steps and suggested readings

The following provides suggestions for what to do next and offers some helpful reading:

- Get the online retail data from https://mng.bz/dXqo. This dataset contains all the online transactions occurring between January 12, 2010, and September 12, 2011, for a UK-based retailer. Apply the three algorithms described in the chapter to identify which customers the company should target and why.

- Get the IRIS dataset from https://www.kaggle.com/uciml/iris. It includes three iris species with 50 samples, each having some properties of the flowers. Use k-means and DBSCAN and compare the results.
- Explore the dataset at UCI for clustering at http://archive.ics.uci.edu/ml/index.php.
- Study the following papers on k-means clustering, hierarchical clustering, and DBSCAN clustering:
  - K-means clustering

    https://mng.bz/rKqJ

    https://mng.bz/VVEy

    https://ieeexplore.ieee.org/document/1017616
  - Hierarchical clustering

    https://ieeexplore.ieee.org/document/7100308

    https://mng.bz/xKqd

    https://mng.bz/AQno
  - DBSCAN clustering

    https://arxiv.org/pdf/1810.13105.pdf

    https://ieeexplore.ieee.org/document/9356727

Summary

- Clustering is used for a variety of purposes across all industries, such as retail, telecom, finance, and pharma. Clustering solutions are implemented for customer and marketing segmentation to better understand the customer base, which further improves targeting.
- Clustering groups objects with similar attributes into segments, aiding in data understanding and pattern discovery without needing a target variable.
- Using clustering, we find the underlying patterns in a dataset and identify the natural groupings in the data.
- There can be multiple clustering techniques based on the methodology. A few examples are k-means clustering, hierarchical clustering, DBSCAN, and fuzzy clustering.
- Different clustering algorithms (k-means, hierarchical, DBSCAN) offer distinct pros and cons, and each is suitable for different data characteristics and purposes.
- Clustering is categorized into hard clustering, where objects belong to a single cluster, and soft clustering, where objects can belong to multiple clusters.
- Different clustering attributes and techniques, such as centroid-based, density-based, and distribution models, lead to varied clustering results.
- Effective clustering algorithms produce comprehensible, scalable, and independent clusters, handling outliers and multiple data types with minimal domain input.

- Distance metrics for clustering include Euclidean, Chebyshev, Manhattan, and cosine distances.
- Centroid-based clustering measures similarity based on the distance to the centroid of clusters.
- K-means clustering creates nonoverlapping clusters by specifying the number of clusters, k, and assigning data points to the nearest center iteratively.
- The elbow method is a common technique to determine the optimal number of clusters in k-means clustering.
- K-means is based on the centroid of the cluster.
- Hierarchical clustering creates clusters based on connectivity and does not require a predefined number of clusters.
- Hierarchical clustering can be agglomerative (bottom-up) or divisive (top-down) and uses linkage criteria to measure distances.
- DBSCAN identifies clusters based on point density and effectively distinguishes outliers.
- DBSCAN does not require specifying the number of clusters and is suited for irregular-shaped clusters.
- Measuring clustering accuracy involves metrics like WCSS, intercluster sum of squares, silhouette value, and the Dunn index.

Dimensionality reduction

Knowledge is a process of piling up facts; wisdom lies in their simplification.

—Martin H. Fischer

We face complex situations in life. Life throws multiple options at us, and we choose a few viable ones from them. This decision of shortlisting is based on the significance, feasibility, utility, and perceived profit from each of the options. The ones that fit the bill are then chosen. A perfect example can be selecting your vacation destination. Based on the weather, travel time, safety, food, budget, and several other options, we choose a few where we would like to spend our next vacation. In this chapter, we study precisely the same—how to reduce the number of options—albeit in the data science and machine learning world.

In the last chapter, we covered major clustering algorithms. We also went over a case study. The datasets we generate and use in such real-world examples have a lot of variables. Sometimes, there can be more than 100 variables or *dimensions* in the data. But not all of them are important. Having a lot of dimensions in the dataset is referred to as the curse of dimensionality. To perform any further analysis, we choose a few from the list of all of the dimensions or variables. In this chapter, we study the need for dimension reductions, various dimensionality techniques, and the respective pros and cons. We will dive deeper into the concepts of principal component analysis (PCA) and singular value decomposition (SVD) and their mathematical foundations and complement these with Python implementation. Also, continuing our structure from the last chapter, we will examine a real-world case study in the telecommunication sector. There are other advanced dimensionality reduction techniques like t-distributed stochastic neighbor embedding (t-SNE) and linear discriminant analysis (LDA), which we will explore in later chapters.

Clustering and dimensionality reductions are the major categories of unsupervised learning. We studied major clustering methods in the last chapter, and we discuss dimensionality reduction in this chapter. With these two solutions, we cover a lot of ground in the unsupervised learning domain. But there are many more advanced topics to be covered, which are part of the latter chapters of the book.

Let's first understand what we mean by the "curse of dimensionality."

3.1   Technical toolkit

We are using the same version of Python as in the last chapters. Jupyter Notebook will be used in this chapter too.

All the datasets and code files are available at the GitHub repository at (https:// mng.bz/ZlBR). You need to install the following Python libraries to execute the code: `numpy`, `pandas`, `matplotlib`, `scipy`, and `sklearn`. Since you have used the same packages in the last chapter, you don't need to install them again. CPU is good enough for execution, but if you face some computing problems, switch to GPU or Google Colab. Refer to the appendix if you face any problems with the installation of any of these packages.

3.2   The curse of dimensionality

Let us continue with the vacation destination example we introduced earlier. The choice of destination is dependent on several parameters: safety, availability, food, nightlife, weather, budget, health, and so on. Having too many parameters is confusing. Let us understand by a real-life example.

Consider this: a retailer wishes to launch a new range of shoes in the market, and for that, a target group of customers should be chosen. This target group will be reached through email, SMS, newsletter, etc. The business objective is to entice these customers to buy the newly launched shoes. From the entire customer base, the target group of customers can be chosen based on variables like customer age, gender, budget, preferred category, average spend, frequency of shopping, and so on. These many variables or *dimensions* make it hard to shortlist the customers based on a sound data analysis technique. We would be analyzing too many parameters simultaneously, examining the effect of each on the shopping probability of the customer, and hence it becomes too tedious and confusing of a task. It is the curse of dimensionality problem we face in real-world data science projects. We can face the curse of dimensionality in one more situation wherein the number of observations is fewer than the number of variables. Consider a dataset where the number of observations is X, while the number of variables is more than X—in such a case, we face the curse of dimensionality.

An easy method to understand any dataset is through visualization. Let's visualize a dataset in a vector-space diagram. If we have only one attribute or feature in the dataset, we can represent it in one dimension (see the left diagram in figure 3.1). For example, we might wish to capture only the height of an object using a single dimension. If we have two attributes, we need two dimensions, as shown in the middle diagram in figure 3.1, wherein to get the area of an object, we will require both length and width. If we have three attributes, for example, to calculate the volume, which requires length, width, and height, we require a 3D space, as shown in the diagram at right in figure 3.1. This requirement will continue to grow based on the number of attributes.

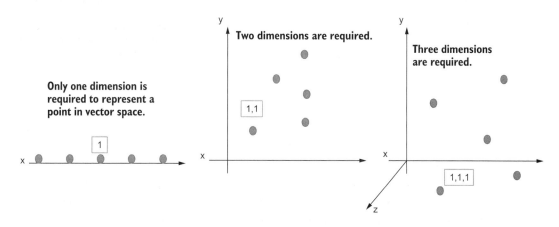

Figure 3.1   Only one dimension is required to represent the data points—for example, to represent the height of an object (left). We need two dimensions to represent a data point. Each data point can correspond to the length and width of an object, which can be used to calculate the area (middle). Three dimensions are required to show a point (right). Here, it can be length, width, and height, which are required to get the volume of an object. This process continues based on the number of dimensions present in the data.

Consider a dataset where you have an attribute for a data point—for example, gender. Then we add age and then education, address, and so on. To represent these attributes, the number of dimensions will keep on increasing. Hence, it is quite easy for us to conclude that with an increase in the number of dimensions, the amount of space required to represent increases by leaps and bounds. This is referred to as the *curse of dimensionality*. The term was introduced by Richard E. Bellman and is used to refer to the problem of having too many variables in a dataset—some of which are significant while many others may be less important.

There is another well-known theory named the *Hughes phenomenon*, shown in figure 3.2. Generally, in data science and machine learning, we wish to have as many variables as possible to train our model. The performance of the supervised learning classifier algorithm will increase to a certain limit and will peak with the most optimal number of variables. But, using the same amount of training data and with an increased number of dimensions, there is a decrease in the performance of a supervised classification algorithm. In other words, it is not advisable to have the variables in a dataset if they are not contributing to the accuracy of the solution. We should remove such variables from the dataset.

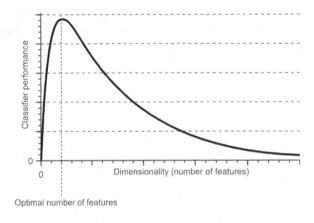

Figure 3.2   **The Hughes phenomenon shows that the performance of a machine learning model will improve initially with an increase in the number of dimensions. But a further increase leads to a decrease in the model's performance.**

An increase in the number of dimensions has the following effects on the machine learning model:

- As the model deals with an increased number of variables, the mathematical complexity increases. For example, in the case of the k-means clustering method we discussed in the last chapter, when we have a greater number of variables, the distance calculation between respective points will become complex. Hence the overall model becomes more complex.
- The dataset generated in a larger dimensional space can be much sparser as compared to a smaller number of variables. The dataset will be sparser as some of the variables will have missing values, NULLs, etc. Therefore, space is much

emptier, the dataset is less dense, and a smaller number of variables have values associated with them.

- With increased complexity in the model, the processing time required increases. The system feels the pressure to deal with so many dimensions.
- The overall solution becomes more complex to comprehend and execute. Recall chapter 1, where we discussed supervised learning algorithms. Due to the high number of dimensions, we might face the problem of overfitting in supervised learning models.

DEFINITION When a supervised learning model has good accuracy on training data but lesser accuracy on unseen data, it is referred to as *overfitting*. Overfitting is a nuisance as the very aim of machine learning models is to work well on unseen datasets, and overfitting defeats this purpose.

Let us relate things to a real-world example. Consider an insurance company offering different types of insurance policies like life insurance, vehicle insurance, health insurance, home insurance, etc. The company wishes to use data science and execute clustering use cases to enhance the customer base and the total number of policies sold. They have customer details like age, gender, profession, policy amount, historical transactions, number of policies held, annual income, type of policy, number of historical defaults, etc. At the same time, let us assume that variables like whether the customer is left-handed or right-handed, whether they wear black or brown shoes, what shampoo brand they use, the color of their hair, and their favorite restaurant are also captured. If we include all the variables in the dataset, the total number of variables in the resultant dataset will be quite high. The distance calculation will be more complex for a k-means clustering algorithm, the processing time will increase, and the overall solution will be quite complex.

It is also imperative to note that *not* all the dimensions or variables are significant. Hence, it is vital to filter out the important ones from all the variables we have. Remember, nature always prefers simpler solutions! In the case discussed previously, it is highly likely that variables like hair color and favorite restaurant, etc., will not affect the outputs. So it is in our best interest to reduce the number of dimensions to ease the complexity and reduce the computation time. At the same time, it is also vital to note that dimensionality reduction is not always desired. It depends on the type of dataset and the business problem we wish to resolve. We will explore this more when we work on the case study in subsequent sections of the chapter.

Exercise 3.1

Answer these questions to check your understanding:

1 The curse of dimensionality refers to having a lot of data. True or False?
2 Having a high number of variables will always increase the accuracy of a solution. True or False?
3 How does a large number of variables in a dataset affect the model?

We have established that having a lot of dimensions is a challenge for us. We next examine the various methods to reduce the number of dimensions.

3.3   *Dimension reduction methods*

We studied the disadvantages of having really high-dimensional data in the last section. A fewer number of dimensions might result in a simpler structure for our data, which will be computationally efficient. At the same time, we should be careful when reducing the number of variables. The output of the dimension reduction method should be complete enough to represent the original data and should not lead to any information loss. In other words, if originally we had, for example, 500 variables and we reduced it to 120 significant ones, still these 120 *should* be robust enough to capture *almost* all the information. Let us understand using a simple example.

Consider this: we wish to predict the amount of rainfall a city will receive in the next month. The rainfall prediction for that city might be dependent on temperature over a period, wind speed measurements, pressure, distance from the sea, elevation above sea level, etc. These variables make sense if we wish to predict rainfall. At the same time, variables like the number of cinema halls in the city, whether the city is the capital of the country, or the number of red cars in the city will not affect the prediction of rainfall. In such a case, if we do not use the number of cinema halls in the city to predict the amount of rainfall, it will not reduce the capability of the system. The solution, in all probability, will still be able to perform quite well. Hence, in such a case, no information will be lost by dropping such a variable, and surely we can drop it from the dataset. On the other hand, removing variables such as temperature or distance from the ocean will very likely negatively affect the prediction accuracy. This is a very simple example highlighting the need to reduce the number of variables.

The dimensions or the number of variables can be reduced by a combination of manual and algorithm-based methods. But before studying them in detail, there are a few mathematical terms and components we should be aware of, which we will discuss next.

3.3.1   *Mathematical foundation*

There are quite a few mathematical terms that one must know to develop a thorough understanding of dimensionality reduction methods. We are trying to reduce the number of dimensions of a dataset. A dataset is nothing but a matrix of values—thus, a lot of the concepts are related to matrix manipulation methods, their geometrical representation, and performing transformations on such matrices. The mathematical concepts are discussed in the appendix. You also need an understanding of eigenvalues and eigenvectors. These concepts will be reused throughout the book; they are been put in the appendix for quick reference. You are advised to go through them before proceeding.

3.4   *Manual methods of dimensionality reduction*

To tackle the curse of dimensionality, we wish to reduce the number of variables in a dataset. The reduction can be done by removing the variables from the dataset. Or a very simple solution for dimensionality reduction can be combining the variables that can be grouped logically or can be represented using a common mathematical operation.

For example, as shown in figure 3.3, the data can be from a retail store where different customers have generated different transactions. We will get the sales, the number of invoices, and the number of items bought by each customer over a period. In the table, customer 1 has generated two invoices, bought five items in total, and generated a total sale of 100.

Customer ID	Sales	Invoices	No. of items	Customer ID	ATV	ABS
1	100	2	5	1	50	2.5
2	200	2	4	2	100	2
3	300	10	12	3	30	1.2
4	400	2	10	4	200	5
5	500	5	12	5	100	2.4

Figure 3.3 In the first table, we have the sales, invoices, and number of items as the variables. In the second table, they have been combined to create new variables.

If we wish to reduce the number of variables, we might combine three variables into two variables. Here we have introduced variables average transaction value (ATV) and average basket size (ABS) wherein ATV = Sales/Invoices and ABS = Number Of Items/Invoices.

So, in the second table for customer 1, we have ATV as 50 and ABS as 2.5. Hence, the number of variables has been reduced from three to two. The process here is only an example of how we can combine various variables. It does not mean that we should replace sales with ATV as a variable.

This process can continue to reduce the number of variables. Similarly, for a telecom subscriber, say we have the minutes of mobile calls made during 30 days in a month. We can add them to create a single variable—minutes used in a month. These examples are very basic ones to start with. Using the manual process, we can employ two other commonly used methods: manual selection and using correlation coefficient.

3.4.1 *Manual feature selection*

Continuing from the rainfall prediction example we discussed in the last section, a data scientist might be able to drop a few variables. This will be based on a deep understanding of the business problem at hand and the corresponding dataset being used. However, it is an underlying assumption that the dataset is quite comprehensible for the data scientist and that they understand the business domain well. Most of the time, the business stakeholders will be able to guide on such methods. The variables must also be unique, and not much dependency should exist. As shown in figure 3.4, we can remove a few of the variables that might not be useful for predicting rainfall.

Temperature	Pressure	Elevation	Is_capital	Number of cars	Distance from the sea	Numer of malls	Number of parks
50	1.1	200	Y	1000	100	5	4
51	1.2	200	N	1200	120	4	6
52	1.1	200	Y	1100	150	5	8
54	1.2	200	N	2000	200	2	4
54	1.2	200	Y	2100	120	6	2

Temperature	Pressure	Elevation	Distance from the sea
50	1.1	200	100
51	1.2	200	120
52	1.1	200	150
54	1.2	200	200
54	1.2	200	120

Figure 3.4 In the first table, we have all the variables present in the dataset. Using business logic, some of the variables that might not be of much use have been discarded in the second table. But this is to be done with due caution; the best way is to get guidance from the business stakeholders.

Sometimes, feature selection methods are also referred to as *wrapper methods*. Here, a machine learning model is wrapped or fitted with a subset of variables. In each iteration, we will get a different set of results. The set that generates the best results is selected for the final model.

3.4.2 *Correlation coefficient*

Correlation between two variables simply means that they have a mutual relationship with each other. The change in the value of one variable will affect the value of another, which means that data points with similar values in one variable have similar values for the other variable. The variables that are highly correlated with each other supply similar information, so one of them can be dropped.

NOTE Correlation is described in detail in the appendix.

For example, for a retail store, the number of invoices generated in a day will be highly correlated with the amount of sales generated, so one of them can be dropped. Another example is students who study for a higher number of hours will have better grades than the ones who study less (mostly!).

But we should be careful in dropping the variables and not trust correlation alone. The business context of a variable should be thoroughly understood before making any decision.

NOTE It is a good idea to discuss this with the business stakeholders before dropping any variables from the study.

Correlation-based methods are sometimes called *filter methods*. Using correlation coefficients, we can filter and choose the variables that are most significant.

Exercise 3.2
Answer these questions to check your understanding:
1 We can drop a variable simply if we feel it is not required. True or False?
2 If two variables are correlated, always drop one of them. True or False?

Manual methods are easier solutions and can be executed quite efficiently. The dataset size is reduced, and we can proceed with the analysis. But manual methods are sometimes subjective and depend a lot on the business problem at hand. Many times, it is also not possible to employ manual methods for dimension reduction. In such situations, we have algorithm-based methods, which we study in the next section.

3.4.3 *Algorithm-based methods for reducing dimensions*

We examined manual methods in the last section. Continuing from there, we examine algorithm-based methods in this section. The algorithm-based techniques are based on a more mathematical base and hence prove to be more scientific methods. In real-world business problems, we use a combination of both manual and algorithm-based techniques. Manual methods are straightforward to execute as compared to algorithm-based techniques. Also, we cannot comment on the comparison of both techniques, as they are based on different foundations. But at the same time, it is imperative that you put due diligence into the implementation of algorithm-based techniques.

The major techniques used in dimensionality reductions are listed as follows. We explore some of them in this book:

- PCA
- SVD
- LDA
- Generalized discriminant analysis
- Non-negative matrix factorization
- Multidimension scaling
- Locally linear embeddings
- IsoMaps
- Autoencoders
- t-SNE

These techniques are utilized for the common end goal: transform the data from a high-dimensional space to a low-dimensional one. Some of the data transformations are linear in nature, while some are nonlinear.

We discuss PCA and SVD in detail in this chapter. In the later chapters of the book, other major techniques will be explored. PCA is perhaps the most quoted dimensionality reduction method, which is explored in the next section.

3.5 *Principal component analysis*

Consider this: you are working on a dataset that has 250 variables. It is almost impossible to visualize such a high-dimensional space. Some of the 250 variables might be correlated with each other and some of them might not be, and there is a need to reduce the number of variables without losing much information. PCA allows us to mathematically select the most important features and leave the rest. PCA does reduce the number of dimensions but also preserves the most important relationships between the variables and the important structures in the dataset. Hence, the number of variables is reduced, but the important information in the dataset is kept safe.

PCA is a projection of high-dimensional data in lower dimensions. In simpler terms, we are reducing an n-dimensional space into an m-dimensional one where $n > m$ while maintaining the nature and the essence of the original dataset. In the process, the old variables are reduced to newer ones while maintaining the crux of the original dataset. The new variables thus created are called *principal components*. The principal components are a linear combination of the raw variables. As a result of this transformation, the first principal component captures the maximum randomness or the highest variance in the dataset. The second principal component created is orthogonal to the first component.

> **NOTE**   If two straight lines are orthogonal to each other, it means they are at an angle of 90° to each other.

The process continues to the third component and so on. Orthogonality allows us to maintain that there is no correlation between subsequent principal components.

> **NOTE**   PCA utilizes linear transformation of the dataset, and such methods are sometimes referred to as feature projections. The resultant dataset or the projection is used for further analysis.

Let us understand this better using an example. In figure 3.5, we have represented the total perceived value of a home using some variables. The variables are area (sq m), number of bedrooms, number of balconies, distance from the airport, distance from the train station, and so on; we have 100+ variables.

Area (sq m)	Number of bedrooms	Number of balconies	Distance from airport	No. of schools	...and so on
100	2	2	20	2	
200	3	2	21	4	
250	4	4	16	2	
400	4	3	15	5	
450	5	4	25	4	

Figure 3.5   **The variables on which the price of a house can be estimated**

We can combine some of the variables mathematically and logically. PCA will create a new variable that is a linear combination of some of the variables, as shown in the following example. It will get the best *linear* combination of original variables so that the new variable is able to capture the maximum variance of the dataset. Equation 3.1 is only an example shown for illustration purposes wherein we are showing a new variable created by a combination of other variables.

$$\text{new\_variable} = a*\text{area} - b*\text{bedrooms} + c*\text{distance} - d*\text{schools} \tag{3.1}$$

Now let's understand the concept visually. In a vector-space diagram, we can represent the dataset, as shown in figure 3.6. The left figure represents the raw data where we can visualize the variables in an x-y diagram. As discussed earlier, we wish to create a linear combination of variables. In other words, we wish to create a mathematical equation that will be able to explain the relationship between x and y.

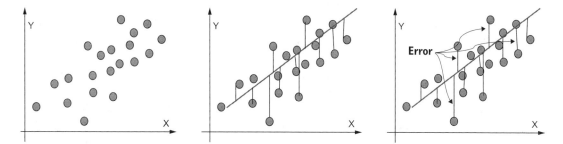

Figure 3.6 **The dataset can be represented in a vector-space diagram (left). The straight line can be called the line of best fit having the projections of all the data points on it (middle). The differences between the actual value and the projections are the error terms (right).**

The output of such a process will be a straight line as shown in the middle diagram in figure 3.6. This straight line is sometimes referred to as the *line of best fit*. Using this line of best fit, we can predict a value of y for a given value of x. These predictions are nothing but the projections of data points on a straight line.

The difference between the actual value and the projections is the error, as shown in the right diagram in figure 3.6. The total sum of these errors is called the total projection error.

There can be multiple options for this straight line, as shown in figure 3.7. These different straight lines will have different errors and different values of variances captured.

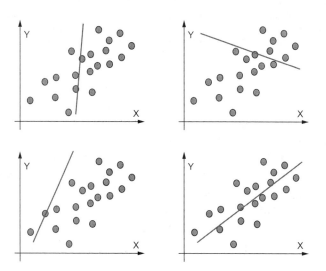

Figure 3.7 **The dataset can be captured by several lines, but not all the straight lines will be able to capture the maximum variance. The equation that gives the minimum error will be the one chosen.**

The straight line that can capture the maximum variance will be the chosen one. In other words, it gives the minimum error. It will be the *first principal component*, and the direction of maximum spread will be the *principal axis*.

The second principal component will be derived in a similar fashion. Since we know the first principal axis, we can subtract the variance along this principal axis from the total variance to get the residual variance. In other words, using the first principal component, we would capture some variance in the dataset. But there will be a portion of the total variance in the dataset that is still unexplained by the first principal component. The portion of the total variance unexplained is the residual variance. Using the second principal component, we wish to capture as much variance as we can.

Using the same process to capture the direction of maximum variance, we will get the second principal component. The second principal component can be at several angles with respect to the first one, as shown in figure 3.8. It is mathematically proven that if the second principal component is orthogonal (i.e., 90°) to the first principal component, this allows us to capture the maximum variance using the two principal components. In figure 3.8, we can observe that the two principal components are at an angle of 90° to each other.

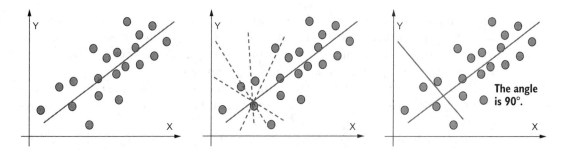

Figure 3.8   The first figure on the left is the first principal component. The second principal component can be at different angles with respect to the first principal component (middle). We should find the second principle that allows us to capture the maximum variance. To capture the maximum variance, the second principal component should be orthogonal to the first one, and thus the combined variance captured is maximized (right).

The process continues for the third and fourth principal components and so on. With more principal components, the representation in a vector space becomes difficult to visualize. You can think of a vector space diagram with more than three axes. Once all the principal components are derived, the dataset is projected onto these axes. The columns in this transformed dataset are the *principal components*. The principal components created will be fewer than the number of original variables and will capture the maximum information present in the dataset.

Before we examine the process of PCA in-depth, let's study its important characteristics:

- PCA aims to reduce the number of dimensions in the resultant dataset.

- PCA produces principal components that aim to reduce the noise in the dataset by maximizing the feature variance.
- At the same time, the principal components reduce the redundancy in the dataset. This is achieved by minimizing the covariance between the pairs of features.
- The original variables no longer exist in the newly created dataset. Instead, new variables are created using these variables.
- It is not necessary that the principal components map one-to-one with all the variables present in the dataset. They are a new combination of the existing variables. Hence, they can be a combination of several different variables in one principal component (as shown in equation 3.1).
- The new features created from the dataset do not share the same column names.
- The original variables might be correlated with each other, but the newly created variables are unrelated to each other.
- The number of newly created variables is fewer than the original number of variables. The process to select the number of principal components has been described in section 3.5.2. After all, that is the whole purpose of dimensionality reduction.
- If PCA has been used for reducing the number of variables in a training dataset, the testing/validation datasets should be reduced by using PCA.
- PCA is not synonymous with dimensionality reduction only. It can be put into use for a number of other usages beyond dimensionality reduction like feature extraction, data visualization, multicollinearity detection, preprocessing, etc. Using a PCA only for dimensionality reduction will be a misnomer for sure.

We will now examine the approach used while implementing PCA, and then we will develop a Python solution using PCA. We need not apply all the steps while we develop the codes, as the heavy lifting has already been done by the packages and libraries. The steps given here are taken care of by the packages, but still, it is imperative that you understand these steps to properly appreciate how PCA works:

1. In PCA, we start with *normalizing our dataset* as a first step. It ensures that all our variables have a common representation and become comparable. We have methods to perform the normalization in Python, which we will study when we develop the code. To explore more about normalizing the dataset, see the appendix.

2. Get the covariance in the normalized dataset. It allows us to study the relationship between the variables. We generally create a covariance matrix, as shown in the Python example in the next section.

3. We can then calculate the eigenvectors and eigenvalues of the covariance matrix. The mathematical concept of eigenvectors is given in the appendix.

4. We then sort the eigenvalues in decreasing order of eigenvalues. We choose the eigenvectors corresponding to the maximum value of eigenvalues. The

components chosen will be able to capture the maximum variance in the dataset. There are other methods to shortlist the principal components, which we will explore while we develop the Python code.

> **Exercise 3.3**
>
> Answer these questions to check your understanding:
> 1   PCA will result in the same number of variables in the dataset. True or False?
> 2   PCA will be able to capture 100% of the information in the dataset. True or False?
> 3   What is the logic of selecting principal components in PCA?

So, in essence, principal components are the linear combinations of the original variables. The weight in this linear combination is the eigenvector satisfying the error criteria of the least square method.

3.5.1   *Eigenvalue decomposition*

In the context of PCA, the eigenvector will represent the direction of the vector and the eigenvalue will be the variance that is captured along that eigenvector. See figure 3.9, where we break the original n x n matrix into components.

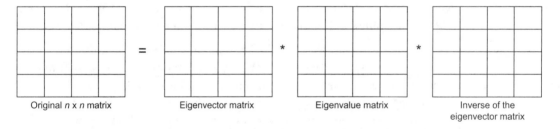

Original n x n matrix   Eigenvector matrix   Eigenvalue matrix   Inverse of the
                                                                                         eigenvector matrix

Figure 3.9   Using eigenvalue decomposition, the original matrix can be broken into an eigenvector matrix, an eigenvalue matrix, and an inverse of an eigenvector matrix. We implement PCA using this methodology.

Mathematically, we can show the relation with equation 3.2

$$A * v = \lambda * v \tag{3.2}$$

where A is a square matrix, v is the eigenvector, and λ is the eigenvalue. Here, it is important to note that the eigenvector matrix is the orthonormal matrix, and its columns are eigenvectors. The eigenvalue matrix is the diagonal matrix, and its eigenvalues are the diagonal elements. The last component is the inverse of the eigenvector matrix. Once we have the eigenvalues and the eigenvectors, we can choose the significant eigenvectors for getting the principal components.

We present PCA and SVD as two separate methods in this book. Both methods are used to reduce high-dimensional data into lower-dimensional ones and, in the process, retain the maximum information in the dataset. The difference between the two is SVD exists for any sort of matrix (rectangular or square), whereas eigen decomposition is possible only for square matrices. You will understand it better once we have covered SVD later in this chapter.

3.5.2 Python solution using PCA

We have studied the concepts of PCA and the process using eigenvalue decomposition. It is time for us to dive into Python and develop a PCA solution on a dataset. I will show you how to create eigenvectors and eigenvalues on the dataset. To implement the PCA algorithms, we will use the `sklearn` library. Libraries and packages provide a faster solution for implementing algorithms.

We use the Iris dataset for this problem. It is one of the most popular datasets used for machine learning problems. The dataset contains data of three iris species with 50 samples each and having properties of each flower, like petal length, sepal length, etc. The objective of the problem is to predict the species using the properties of the flower. The independent variables, hence, are the flower properties, whereas the variable "species" is the target variable. The dataset and the code are checked in at the GitHub repository. Here we are using the inbuilt PCA functions, which reduce the effort required to implement PCA. The steps are as follows:

1 Load all the necessary libraries. We are going to use `numpy`, `pandas`, `seaborn`, `matplotlib`, and `sklearn`. Note that we have imported PCA from `sklearn`.

NOTE The following are the standard libraries. You will find that almost all the machine learning solutions would import these libraries in the solution notebook:

```
import numpy as np
import pandas as pd
import seaborn as sns
import matplotlib.pyplot as plt
from sklearn.decomposition import PCA
from sklearn.preprocessing import StandardScaler
```

2 Load the dataset now. It is a .csv file:

```
iris_df = pd.read_csv('IRIS.csv')
```

3 We will now perform a basic check on the dataset, looking at the first five rows, the shape of the data, the spread of the variables, etc. We are not performing an extensive exploratory data analysis here as the steps are covered in chapter 2. The dataset has 150 rows and 6 columns (see figure 3.10).

```
iris_df.head()
```

```
iris_df.head()
```

	Id	SepalLengthCm	SepalWidthCm	PetalLengthCm	PetalWidthCm	Species
0	1	5.1	3.5	1.4	0.2	Iris-setosa
1	2	4.9	3.0	1.4	0.2	Iris-setosa
2	3	4.7	3.2	1.3	0.2	Iris-setosa
3	4	4.6	3.1	1.5	0.2	Iris-setosa
4	5	5.0	3.6	1.4	0.2	Iris-setosa

```
iris_df.describe()
iris_df.shape
```

```
iris_df.describe()
```

	Id	SepalLengthCm	SepalWidthCm	PetalLengthCm	PetalWidthCm
count	150.000000	150.000000	150.000000	150.000000	150.000000
mean	75.500000	5.843333	3.054000	3.758667	1.198667
std	43.445368	0.828066	0.433594	1.764420	0.763161
min	1.000000	4.300000	2.000000	1.000000	0.100000
25%	38.250000	5.100000	2.800000	1.600000	0.300000
50%	75.500000	5.800000	3.000000	4.350000	1.300000
75%	112.750000	6.400000	3.300000	5.100000	1.800000
max	150.000000	7.900000	4.400000	6.900000	2.500000

Figure 3.10   Code output

4   Here, we should break the dataset into independent variables and a target variable. X_variables here represent the independent variables, which are in columns 2–5 of the dataset while y_variable is the target variable, which is "species" in this case and is the final column in the dataset. Recall we wish to predict the species of a flower using the other properties. Hence, we have separated the target variable "species" and other independent variables:

```
X_variables = iris_df.iloc[:,1:5]
X_variables
y_variable = iris_df.iloc[:,5]
```

5   Normalize the dataset. The built-in method of StandardScalar() does the job for us quite easily.

NOTE   The StandardScalar() method normalizes the dataset for us. It subtracts the mean from the variable and divides it by the standard deviation. For more details on normalization, refer to the appendix.

We invoke the method and then use it on our dataset to get the transformed dataset. Since we are working on independent variables, we are using `X_variables` here. First, we invoke the `StandardScalar()` method. Then we use the `fit_transform` method. The `fit_transform` method first fits the transformers to *X* and *Y* and then returns a transformed version of *X*:

```
sc = StandardScaler()
transformed_df = sc.fit_transform(X_variables)
```

6   Calculate the covariance matrix and print it. The output is shown in figure 3.11. Getting the covariance matrix is straightforward using `numpy`:

```
covariance_matrix = np.cov(transformed_df.T)
covariance_matrix
```

```
array([[ 1.00671141, -0.11010327,  0.87760486,  0.82344326],
       [-0.11010327,  1.00671141, -0.42333835, -0.358937  ],
       [ 0.87760486, -0.42333835,  1.00671141,  0.96921855],
       [ 0.82344326, -0.358937  ,  0.96921855,  1.00671141]])
```

Figure 3.11   The covariance matrix

7   Calculate the eigenvalues. Inside the `numpy` library, we have the built-in functionality to calculate the eigenvalues. We will then sort the eigenvalues in descending order. To shortlist the principal components, we can choose eigenvalues greater than 1. This criterion is called *Kaiser criteria*. We are exploring other methods too.

NOTE   The eigenvalue represents how good a component is as a summary of the data. If the eigenvalue is 1, it means that the component contains the same amount of information as a single variable; hence, we choose the eigenvalue that is greater than 1.

In this code, first we get the `eigen_values` and `eigen_vectors`, and then we arrange them in descending order (see figure 3.12):

```
eigen_values, eigen_vectors = np.linalg.eig(covariance_matrix)
eigen_pairs = [(np.abs(eigen_values[i]), eigen_vectors[:,i]) for i in
    range(len(eigen_values))]
print('Eigenvalues arranged in descending order:')
for i in eigen_pairs:
    print(i[0])
```

```
Eigenvalues arranged in descending order:
2.9303537755893165
0.9274036215173417
0.1483422264816399
0.02074601399559571
```

Figure 3.12   Eigenvalues arranged in descending order

8 Invoke the PCA method from the `sklearn` library. The method is used to fit the data here. Note we have not yet determined the number of principal components we wish to use in this problem:

```
pca = PCA()
pca = pca.fit(transformed_df)
```

9 The principal components are now set. Let's have a look at the variance explained by them. We can observe that the first component captures 72.77% variation, the second captures 23.03% variation, and so on (figure 3.13):

```
explained_variance = pca.explained_variance_ratio_
explained_variance
```

```
array([0.72770452, 0.23030523, 0.03683832, 0.00515193])
```

Figure 3.13   The degree of variance of the principal components

10 We now plot the components in a bar plot for better visualization (see figure 3.14):

```
dataframe = pd.DataFrame({'var':pca.explained_variance_ratio_,
            'PC':['PC1','PC2','PC3','PC4']})
sns.barplot(x='PC',y="var",
        data=dataframe, color="b");
```

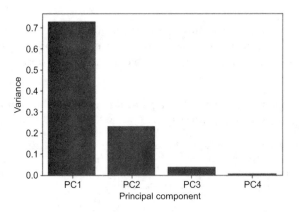

Figure 3.14   Bar plot of the principal components

11 Here we draw a scree plot to visualize the cumulative variance being explained by the principal components (see figure 3.15):

```
plt.plot(np.cumsum(pca.explained_variance_ratio_))
plt.xlabel('number of components')
```

```
plt.ylabel('cumulative explained variance')
plt.show()
```

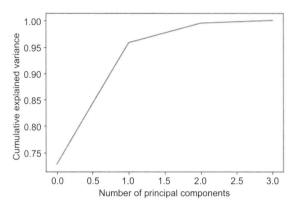

Figure 3.15   Scree plot of cumulative variance

12   In this case study, we choose the top two principal components as the final solutions, as these two capture 95.08% of the total variance in the dataset:

```
pca_2 = PCA(n_components =2 )
pca_2 = pca_2.fit(transformed_df)
pca_2d = pca_2.transform(X_variables)
```

13   We will now plot the dataset with respect to two principal components. For that, species must be tied back to the actual values of the species variable, which are Iris-setosa, Iris-versicolor, and Iris-virginica. Here, 0 is mapped to Iris-setosa, 1 is Iris-versicolor, and 2 is Iris-virginica. In the following code, first the species variable gets its values replaced by using the mapping discussed earlier:

```
iris_df['Species'] = iris_df['Species'].replace({'Iris-setosa':0, 'Iris-
versicolor':1, 'Iris-virginica':2})
```

14   We will now plot the results with respect to two principal components. The plot shows the dataset reduced to two principal components we have just created. These principal components can capture 95.08% variance of the dataset. The first principal component represents the x-axis in the plot while the second principal component represents the y-axis in the plot (see figure 3.16). The color represents the various classes of Species. The print version of the book will not show the different colors, but the output of the Python code will. The same output is also available at the GitHub repository:

```
plt.figure(figsize=(8,6))
plt.scatter(pca_2d[:,0], pca_2d[:,1],c=iris_df['Species'])
plt.show()
```

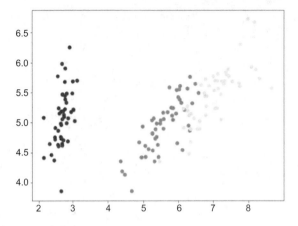

Figure 3.16   The results for two principal components

This solution has reduced the number of components from four to two and still is able to retain most of the information. Here, we have examined three approaches to select the principal components based on the Kaiser criteria, the variance captured, and the scree plot.

Let us quickly analyze what we have achieved using PCA. Figure 3.17 shows two representations of the same dataset. The one on the left is the original dataset of `X_variables`. It has four variables and 150 rows. The right is the output of PCA. It has 150 rows but only two variables. Recall we have reduced the number of dimensions from four to two. So, the number of observations has remained 150, while the number of variables has reduced from four to two.

	SepalLengthCm	SepalWidthCm	PetalLengthCm	PetalWidthCm
0	5.1	3.5	1.4	0.2
1	4.9	3.0	1.4	0.2
2	4.7	3.2	1.3	0.2
3	4.6	3.1	1.5	0.2
4	5.0	3.6	1.4	0.2
...	...	...	...	...
145	6.7	3.0	5.2	2.3
146	6.3	2.5	5.0	1.9
147	6.5	3.0	5.2	2.0
148	6.2	3.4	5.4	2.3
149	5.9	3.0	5.1	1.8

```
pca_2d[0:5]

array([[2.66923088, 5.18088722],
       [2.69643401, 4.6436453 ],
       [2.4811633 , 4.75218345],
       [2.57151243, 4.62661492],
       [2.59065822, 5.23621104]])
```

```
len(pca_2d)

150
```

150 rows × 4 columns

Figure 3.17   The figure on the left shows the original dataset, which has 150 rows and four variables. After the implementation of PCA at right, the number of variables has been reduced to two. The number of rows remains the same as 150, which is shown by the length of pca_2d.

Once we have reduced the number of components, we can continue to implement a supervised learning or an unsupervised learning solution. We can implement the preceding solution for any of the other real-world problems where we aim to reduce the number of dimensions. We explore this more in section 3.8.

With this, we have covered PCA. The GitHub repository contains a very interesting PCA decomposition with variables and a corresponding plot.

3.6 *Singular value decomposition*

PCA transforms the data linearly and generates principal components that are not correlated with each other. But the process followed in eigenvalue decomposition can only be applied to *square matrices*, whereas SVD can be implemented to any $m \times n$ matrix.

Say we have matrix A. The shape of A is $m \times n$, or it contains m rows and n columns. The transpose of A can be represented as A^T.

We can create two other matrices using A and A^T as $A\,A^T$ and A^TA. These resultant matrices $A\,A^T$ and A^TA have some special properties, which are as follows (the mathematical proof of the properties is beyond the scope of the book):

- They are symmetric and square matrices.
- Their eigenvalues are either positive or zero.
- Both $A\,A^T$ and A^TA have the same eigenvalue.
- Both $A\,A^T$ and A^TA have the same rank as the original matrix A.

The eigenvectors of $A\,A^T$ and A^TA are referred to as singular vectors of A. The square root of their eigenvalues is called singular values.

Since both matrices ($A\,A^T$ and A^TA) are symmetrical, their eigenvectors are orthonormal to each other. In other words, because they are symmetrical, the eigenvectors are perpendicular to each other and can be of unit length.

Now, with this mathematical understanding, we can define SVD. As per the SVD method, it is possible to factorize any matrix A, as shown in equation 3.3:

$$A = U * S * V^T \tag{3.3}$$

Here, A is the original matrix, U and V are the orthogonal matrices with orthonormal eigenvectors taken from $A\,A^T$ and A^TA, respectively, and S is the diagonal matrix with r elements equal to the singular values. In simple terms, SVD can be seen as an enhancement of the PCA methodology using eigenvalue decomposition.

> **NOTE** Singular values are better and numerically more robust than eigenvalues decomposition.

PCA was defined as the linear transformation of input variables using principal components. All those concepts of linear transformation, such as choosing the best components, etc., remain the same. The major process steps also remain similar, except in SVD we use a slightly different approach wherein the eigenvalue decomposition is replaced by singular vectors and singular values. It is often advisable to use SVD when we have a sparse dataset; in the case of a denser dataset, PCA can be utilized.

Exercise 3.4

Answer these questions to check your understanding:

1 SVD works on the eigenvalue decomposition technique. True or False?
2 PCA is a much more robust methodology than SVD. True or False?
3 What are singular values and singular vectors in SVD?

3.6.1   *Python solution using SVD*

In this case study, we are using the *mushrooms* dataset. This dataset contains descriptions of 23 species of grilled mushrooms. There are two classes: either the mushroom is *e*, which means it is edible, or the mushroom is *p*, meaning it is poisonous. The steps are as follows:

1 Import the libraries:

```
import numpy as np
import pandas as pd
import seaborn as sns
import matplotlib.pyplot as plt
from sklearn.preprocessing import LabelEncoder, StandardScaler
```

2 Import the dataset and check for shape, head, etc. (see figure 3.18):

```
mushrooms_df = pd.read_csv('mushrooms.csv')
mushrooms_df.shape
mushrooms_df.head()
```

class	cap-shape	cap-surface	cap-color	bruises	odor	gill-attachment	gill-spacing	gill-size	gill-color	...
p	x	s	n	t	p	f	c	n	k	...
e	x	s	y	t	a	f	c	b	k	...
e	b	s	w	t	l	f	c	b	n	...
p	x	y	w	t	p	f	c	n	n	...
e	x	s	g	f	n	f	w	b	k	...

stalk-surface-below-ring	stalk-color-above-ring	stalk-color-below-ring	veil-type	veil-color	ring-number	ring-type	spore-print-color	population
s	w	w	p	w	o	p	k	s
s	w	w	p	w	o	p	n	n
s	w	w	p	w	o	p	n	n
s	w	w	p	w	o	p	k	s
s	w	w	p	w	o	e	n	a

Figure 3.18   Code output

3 As we can observe, the values are categorical in nature in the dataset. They should be first encoded into numeric values. This is not the only approach for dealing with categorical variables. There are other techniques too, which we will explore throughout the book.

First, invoke the `LabelEncoder` and then apply it to all the columns in the dataset. The `LabelEncoder` converts the categorical variables into numeric ones using the one-hot encoding method:

```
encoder = LabelEncoder()
for col in mushrooms_df.columns:
        mushrooms_df[col] = encoder.fit_transform(mushrooms_df[col])
```

4 Have another look at the dataset. All the categorical values have been converted to numeric ones (see figure 3.19):

```
mushrooms_df.head()
```

	class	cap-shape	cap-surface	cap-color	bruises	odor	gill-attachment	gill-spacing	gill-size	gill-color	...
0	1	5	2	4	1	6	1	0	1	4	...
1	0	5	2	9	1	0	1	0	0	4	...
2	0	0	2	8	1	3	1	0	0	5	...
3	1	5	3	8	1	6	1	0	1	5	...
4	0	5	2	3	0	5	1	1	0	4	...

stalk-surface-below-ring	stalk-color-above-ring	stalk-color-below-ring	veil-type	veil-color	ring-number	ring-type	spore-print-color	population
2	7	7	0	2	1	4	2	3
2	7	7	0	2	1	4	3	2
2	7	7	0	2	1	4	3	2
2	7	7	0	2	1	4	2	3
2	7	7	0	2	1	0	3	0

**Figure 3.19
Code output**

5 The next two steps are the same as the last case study, wherein we break the dataset into `X_variables` and `y_label`. Then the dataset is normalized:

```
X_variables = mushrooms_df.iloc[:,1:23]
y_label = mushrooms_df.iloc[:, 0]
scaler = StandardScaler()
X_features = scaler.fit_transform(X_variables)
```

6 Implement the SVD. There is a method in `numpy` that implements SVD. The output is u, s, and v, where u and v are the singular vectors and s is the singular value. If you wish, you can analyze their respective shapes and dimensions:

```
u, s, v = np.linalg.svd(X_features, full_matrices=True)
```

7 We know that singular values allow us to compute variance explained by each of the singular vectors. We will now analyze the percentage variance explained by each singular vector and plot it (see figure 3.20). The results are shown to three decimal places. Then we plot the results as a histogram plot. On the x-axis, we have the singular vectors while on the y-axis we have the percent of variance explained:

```
variance_explained = np.round(s**2/np.sum(s**2), decimals=3)
variance_explained
sns.barplot(x=list(range(1,len(variance_explained)+1)),
            y=variance_explained, color="blue")
plt.xlabel('SVs', fontsize=16)
plt.ylabel('Percent of the variance explained', fontsize=15)
```

```
Text(0, 0.5, 'Percent of the variance explained')
```

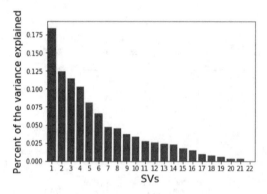

Figure 3.20   Code output

8 Create a dataframe (see figure 3.21). This new dataframe `svd_df` contains the first two singular vectors and the metadata. We then print the first five rows using the head command:

```
col_labels= ['SV'+str(i) for i in range(1,3)]
svd_df = pd.DataFrame(u[:,0:2], index=mushrooms_df["class"].tolist(),
columns=col_labels)
svd_df=svd_df.reset_index()
svd_df.rename(columns={'index':'Class'}, inplace=True)
svd_df.head()
```

	Class	SV1	SV2
0	1	0.003238	-0.006710
1	0	0.012864	0.001919
2	0	0.010474	-0.001863
3	1	0.004988	-0.005202
4	0	-0.003887	0.008522

Figure 3.21   Dataframe containing the first two singular vectors and the metadata

9   Like the last case study, we replace numeric values with actual class labels; `1` is edible while `0` is poisonous:

```
svd_df['Class'] = svd_df['Class'].replace({1:'Edible', 0:'Poison'})
```

10   We now plot the variance explained by the two components (see figure 3.22). Here, we have chosen only the first two components. You are advised to take the optimum number of components using the methods described in the last section and plot the respective scatter plots. Here, on the x-axis, we have shown the first singular vector SV1, and on the y-axis we have shown the second singular vector SV2. The print version of the book does not show the different colors, but the output of the Python code does. The same output is available at the GitHub repository too:

```
color_dict = dict({'Edible':'Black',
                   'Poison': 'Red'})
sns.scatterplot(x="SV1", y="SV2", hue="Class",
                palette=color_dict,
                data=svd_df, s=105,
                alpha=0.5)
plt.xlabel('SV 1: {0}%'.format(variance_explained[0]*100), fontsize=15)
plt.ylabel('SV 2: {0}%'.format(variance_explained[1]*100), fontsize=15)
```

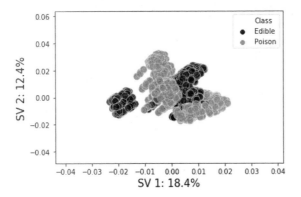

Figure 3.22 Plot of the variance explained by two components

We can observe the distribution of the two classes with respect to the two components. The two classes—`Edible` and `Poison`—are color-coded as black and red, respectively. As we have noted previously, we have chosen only two components to show the effect using a visualization plot. You should choose the optimum number of components using the methods described in the last case study and then visualize the results using different singular vectors. This solution can be used to reduce dimensions in a real-world dataset.

3.7   *Pros and cons of dimensionality reduction*

In the initial sections of the chapter, we discussed the drawbacks of the curse of dimensionality. In the last few sections, we discovered PCA and SVD and implemented them using Python. Now we will examine the advantages and challenges of these techniques. The major advantages of implementing PCA or SVD are

- A reduced number of dimensions leads to less complexity in the dataset. The correlated features are removed and transformed. Treating correlated variables manually is a tough task, which is quite manual and frustrating. Techniques like PCA and SVD do that job for us quite easily. The number of correlated features is minimized, and overall dimensions are reduced.
- Visualization of the dataset is better if the number of dimensions is fewer. It is very difficult to visualize and depict a very high-dimensional dataset.
- The accuracy of the machine learning model is improved if the correlated variables are removed. These variables do not add anything to the performance of the model.
- The training time is reduced as the dataset is less complex. Hence, less computation power and time are required.
- Overfitting is a nuisance in supervised machine learning models. It is a condition where the model behaves very well on the training dataset but not so well on the testing/validation dataset. It means that the model may not be able to perform well on real-world unseen datasets. And it defeats the entire purpose of building the machine learning model. PCA/SVD helps tackle overfitting by reducing the number of variables.

At the same time, there are a few challenges we face with dimensionality reduction techniques, which are as follows:

- The new components created by PCA/SVD are often less interpretable. They are a combination of the independent variables in the dataset and do not actually relate to the real world; hence it can be difficult to relate them to real-world scenarios.
- Numeric variables are required for PCA/SVD. Hence all the categorical variables should be represented in numeric form.
- Normalization/standardization of the dataset is required before the solution can be implemented.
- There might be information loss when we use PCA or SVD. The principal components *cannot* replace the original dataset, and hence there might be some loss of information when we implement these methods.

However, despite a few challenges, PCA and SVD are used for reducing dimensions in a dataset. They are two of the most popular methods and are quite heavily used. Note that these are linear methods; we cover nonlinear methods of dimensionality reduction in a later part of the book.

We have now covered the two most important techniques used in dimensionality reduction. We will examine more advanced techniques in the later chapters. It is time to move on to the case study.

3.8   Case study for dimension reduction

Let's explore a real-world case to relate the use of PCA and SVD in real-world business scenarios. Consider this: you are working for a telecommunication service provider. You have a subscriber base, and you wish to cluster the consumers over several parameters. The challenge is the huge number of dimensions available to be analyzed.

The objective will be to reduce the number of attributes using dimension reduction algorithms. The consumer dataset might include the following:

- Demographic details of the subscriber, which will consist of age, gender, occupation, household size, marital status, etc. (see figure 3.23).

Mobile number	Age	Gender	Marital status	Household size	City	Country	Children	...
12345678900	25	M	Married	2	New York	US	0	
98765432100	26	F	Unmarried	4	London	UK	0	
45656465210	27	U	Married	4	New Delhi	India	2	
89323242111	28	M	Unmarried	2	Dublin	Ireland	0	
31822338924	29	F	Married	5	Tokyo	Japan	3	

Note: This list is not exhaustive.

Figure 3.23   Demographic details of a subscriber like age, gender, marital status, household size, city, etc.

- Subscription details of the consumer, which might look like figure 3.24.

Mobile number	Prepaid/Postpaid	Tenure	Home broadband included	Family pack included	...
12345678900	Prepaid	1	Y	N	
98765432100	Postpaid	1.5	Y	N	
45656465210	Prepaid	1.2	N	Y	
89323242111	Prepaid	2	Y	Y	
31822338924	Postpaid	5	N	Y	

Note: This list is not exhaustive.

Figure 3.24   Subscription details of a subscriber like tenure, postpaid/prepaid connection, etc.

- Consumer usage, such as the minutes, call rates, data usages, services, etc. (see figure 3.25).

Mobile number	Minutes	SMS	Data usage	National minutes	Days on network	International minutes	National SMS	International SMS	...
12345678900	199	123	1 GB	170	24	101	104	141	
98765432100	105	119	2 GB	118	10	120	116	123	
45656465210	130	137	2.5 GB	156	23	181	182	181	
89323242111	110	161	4 GB	162	18	125	116	157	
31822338924	186	172	5 GB	139	25	177	167	138	

Note: This list is not exhaustive.

Figure 3.25   Usage of a subscriber specifies the number of minutes used, SMS sent, data used, days spent in a network, national or international usage, etc.

- Payment and transaction details of the subscribers, which could be the various transactions made, the mode of payment, frequency of payments, days since last payment made, etc. (see figure 3.26).

Mobile number	No. of transactions	Value	Mode	Frequency	...
12345678900	20	100	Cash	Monthly	
98765432100	15	150	Card	Yearly	
45656465210	25	1000	Online	Monthly	
89323242111	5	10	Voucher	Monthly	
31822338924	40	400	Cash	Weekly	

Figure 3.26   Transaction details of a subscriber showing all the details of amount, mode, etc.

- Many more attributes. So far, we have established that the number of variables involved are indeed high. Once we join all these data points, the number of dimensions in the final data can be huge (see figure 3.27).

Mobile number	Age	Gender	Marital status	Children	Mins	Data usage	SMS	Value	Frequency	Others...
12345	20	F	Unmarried	0	200	1	100	10	Monthly	...
12346	21	F	Married	1	200	2	120	15	Weekly	...
12347	22	M	Unmarried	0	210	1	140	12	Monthly	...
12348	23	M	Married	2	90	4	120	10	Quarterly	...
12349	24	F	Married	2	1000	5	110	11	Yearly	...

Figure 3.27   The final dataset is a combination of all the aforementioned datasets. It will be a big, really high-dimensional dataset to be analyzed.

We should reduce the number of attributes before we proceed to any supervised or unsupervised solution. In this chapter, we focus on dimensionality reduction techniques, and hence the steps cover that aspect of the process. In later chapters, we will examine exploratory analysis in more detail.

As a first step, we will perform a sanity check of the dataset and do the data cleaning. We will examine the number of data points, number of missing values, duplicates, junk values present, etc. This will allow us to delete any variables that might be very sparse or contain not much information. For example, if the gender is available for only 0.01% of the customer base, it might be a good idea to drop the variable. Or if all the customers state their gender is male, the variable is not adding any new information to us, and hence it can be discarded. Sometimes, using business logic, a variable might be dropped from the dataset. An example has been discussed in section 3.4. In this step, we might combine a few variables. For example, we might create a new variable as average transaction value by dividing the total amount spent by the total number of transactions. In this way, we will be able to reduce a few dimensions.

NOTE   A Python Jupyter notebook is available in the GitHub repository, where we have given a very detailed solution for the data cleaning step.

Once we are done with the basic cleaning of the data, we start with the exploratory data analysis. As a part of exploratory analysis, we examine the spread of the variable, its distribution, mean/median/mode of numeric variables, and so on. This is sometimes referred to as *univariate analysis*. This step allows us to measure the spread of the variables, understand the central tendencies, examine the distribution of different classes for categorical variables, and look for any anomalies in the values. For example, using the dataset mentioned earlier, we will be interested in analyzing the maximum/minimum/average data usage or the percentage distribution of gender or age. We would want to know the most popular method to make a transaction, and we would also be interested to know the maximum/minimum/average amount of the transactions. The list goes on.

Then we explore the relationships between variables, which is referred to as *bivariate analysis*. Crosstabs, or distribution of data, is a part of bivariate analysis. A correlation matrix is created during this step. Variables that are highly correlated are examined thoroughly. And based on business logic, one of them might be dropped. This step is useful to visualize and understand the behavior of one variable in the presence of other variables. We can examine their mutual relationships and the respective strength of the relationships. In this case study, we would answer questions such as, "Do subscribers who use more data spend more time on the network as compared to subscribers who send more SMS?", "Do the subscribers who make a transaction using the online mode generate more revenue than the ones using cash?", or "Is there a relationship between gender/age and the data usage?" Many such questions are answered during this phase of the project.

> **NOTE** A Python Jupyter notebook is available in the GitHub repository, which provides detailed steps and code for the univariate and bivariate phases. Check it out!

At this stage, we have a dataset that has a huge number of dimensions, and we want to reduce the number of dimensions. Now is a good time to implement PCA or SVD. The techniques will reduce the number of dimensions and will make the dataset ready for the next steps in the process, as shown in figure 3.28. The figure is only representative

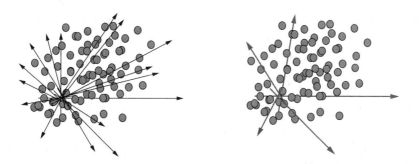

Figure 3.28 A very high-dimensional dataset will be reduced to a low-dimensional one by using principal components that capture the maximum variance in the dataset.

in nature to depict the effect of dimensionality reduction methods. Notice how the large number of black lines in the left figure is reduced to a smaller number of red lines in the right figure.

The output of dimensionality reduction methods will be a dataset with a lower number of variables. The dataset can be then used for supervised or unsupervised learning. We have already looked at the examples using Python in the earlier sections of the chapter.

This concludes our case study on telecom subscribers. The case can be extended to any other domain like retail; banking, financial services, and insurance; aviation; healthcare; manufacturing; and others.

3.9   Concluding thoughts

Data is everywhere in various forms, levels, and dimensions and with varying levels of complexity. It is often mentioned that "the more data, the better." It is indeed true to a certain extent. But with a really high number of dimensions, it becomes quite a herculean task to make sense of it. The analysis can become biased and very complex to deal with. We explored this curse of dimensionality in this chapter. We found PCA and SVD can be helpful to reduce this complexity. They make the dataset ready for the next steps.

Dimensionality reduction is not as straightforward as it looks. It is not an easy task, but it is certainly a very rewarding one. And it requires a combination of business acumen, logic, and common sense. The resultant dataset might still require some additional work. But it is a very good point for building a machine learning model.

This marks the end of the third chapter. It also ends the part 1 of the book. In this part, we have covered a few core algorithms. We started with the first chapter of the book, where we explored the fundamentals and basics of machine learning. In the second chapter, we examined three algorithms for clustering. In this third chapter, we explored PCA and SVD.

In the second part of the book, we change gears and study more advanced topics. We start with association rules in the next chapter. Then we go into advanced clustering methods of time-series clustering, fuzzy clustering, Gaussian mixture mode clustering, etc. That is followed by a chapter on advanced dimensionality reduction algorithms like t-SNE and LDA. To conclude the second part, we examine unsupervised learning on text datasets. The third part of the book is even more advanced, so still a long way to go. Stay tuned!

3.10   Practical next steps and suggested readings

The following provides suggestions for what to do next and offers some helpful reading:

- Use the vehicles dataset used in the last chapter for clustering and implement PCA and SVD on it. Compare the performance on clustering before and after implementing PCA and SVD.

- Get the datasets from https://mng.bz/2y9g. You can find many datasets. Compare the performance of PCA and SVD on these datasets.
- Go through the following papers on PCA:
  - https://mng.bz/1XKX
  - https://mng.bz/Pd0w
  - https://mng.bz/JYeo
  - https://mng.bz/wJqO
- Go through the following research papers on SVD:
  - https://mng.bz/qxqA
  - https://mng.bz/7pNm
  - https://arxiv.org/pdf/1211.7102.pdf

Summary

- The "curse of dimensionality" refers to problems arising from high-dimensional datasets with too many variables, complicating the analysis and model performance.
- High dimensions can lead to a sparse dataset, increased mathematical complexity, longer processing times, and potential overfitting in machine learning models.
- Hughes phenomenon shows that increasing variables only improves model performance up to a point, after which it declines.
- Not all dimensions are significant; some may not contribute meaningfully to a model's accuracy and should be removed to reduce complexity.
- Data visualization can help explain datasets by reducing them to fewer dimensions that still capture significant information.
- Manual dimension reduction includes dropping insignificant variables or combining them logically to reduce dataset dimensions.
- Algorithm-based methods for dimension reduction include PCA, SVD, LDA, and t-SNE, among others, which transform high-dimensional data into low-dimensional spaces.
- PCA reduces dimensions by creating principal components that capture maximum variance while minimizing redundancy and noise.
- SVD enhances PCA, handling any matrix shape and decomposing them into singular values and vectors to maintain dataset information.
- Each reduction technique requires the normalization of data and converting categorical variables to numeric forms.
- Dimensionality reduction simplifies datasets, enhancing visualization and model accuracy, reducing computation time, and mitigating overfitting risks.
- Challenges with dimensionality reduction include the loss of interpretability, information loss, and the requirement for numerical data.

- Both PCA and SVD are widely used to effectively reduce dimensions, and each is suitable for different dataset densities.
- The techniques can be applied in various industries like retail; banking, financial services, and insurance; and healthcare to simplify high-dimensional datasets for analysis.
- The reduction process involves preliminary data cleaning and exploratory data analysis and then applying dimension-reduction techniques.

Part 2

Intermediate level

Kudos on finishing the first part, and welcome to the second part.

Think of the journey in this book as your workshop, where raw concepts and fundamentals are turned into case studies and working solutions using Python. Each concept we cover, each algorithm we study, and each case study we solve here is a building block, but it's up to you to put them together in creative ways and implement them in your real-life business. This implementation should help you solve business problems in ways that are both logical and creative. The algorithms, tools, and techniques you are learning will allow you to create functional, powerful solutions—step by step.

The true art of machine learning lies not in knowing all the algorithms by heart or cramming the deepest of mathematical concepts but in knowing how to approach the problem, use the available dataset effectively and efficiently, and finally solve problems. You should not ignore the user experience while revealing the insights to the end user.

You've learned the fundamentals of unsupervised learning in the first part; it is now time to move to slightly more advanced topics. In this part, we'll dive into association rules, advanced clustering, and dimensionality reduction techniques.

Association rules

The power of association is stronger than the power of beauty; therefore, the power of association is the power of beauty.

—John Ruskin

Congratulations on finishing the first part of the book! You explored the basics of unsupervised learning and algorithms like k-means clustering, hierarchical clustering, DBSCAN, principal component analysis, and others. It is expected that you have covered the mathematical concepts in the first part and created the Python codes to solve the exercise given at the end of each chapter.

Welcome to the second part of the book where we use the concepts learned in the first part and explore slightly more complex topics. We start with association rules in this chapter.

Next time you visit a nearby grocery store, look around inside the store and notice the arrangements of various items. You would find shelves with items like milk, eggs, bread, sugar, washing powder, soaps, fruits, vegetables, cookies, and various other items neatly stacked. Have you ever wondered about the logic of these arrangements and how these items are laid out? Why are certain products kept near each other while others are quite far from one another? Obviously, the arrangement cannot be done in a random manner, and there has to be scientific reasoning behind it. Or do you wonder: How does Netflix recommend movies to you based on your movie history like a sequence? We are going to find the answers to these questions in this chapter. Like always, we study the concepts first. We go through the mathematical logic for different algorithms, the pros and cons of each, and practical implementations using Python. A business case study is provided at the end of the chapter to complement the knowledge. Welcome to the fourth chapter and all the very best!

4.1   Technical toolkit

We will continue to use the same version of Python and Jupyter Notebook we have used so far. The codes and datasets used in this chapter have been checked in at the same Github location.

You will need to install a few Python libraries for this chapter, including `apyori`, `pyECLAT`, `fpgrowth_py`, and `pyspade`. Along with this, you will need `numpy` and `pandas`. Using libraries, we can implement the algorithms very quickly. Otherwise, coding these algorithms from scratch is quite a time-consuming and painstaking task.

Let's get started with association rules.

4.2   Association rule overview

You might have heard the famous "beer and diaper story." As per this anecdote, customers (mostly young men) in a supermarket who buy diapers also buy beer in the same invoice. In other words, young men who are buying diapers for their babies have quite a high probability of buying beer in the same transaction. We will not comment on the authenticity of the story, but *association rule learning* can be attributed as the logic derived from this story.

Formally put, association rules can be used to find compelling relationships between the variables that are present in the datasets. We can use association rules for measuring the correlations and co-occurrences between the variables in a dataset. In the example given here (assuming the story is true), one could analyze the daily customer transactions. And if a relationship emerges between beer and diapers, it is a very strong insight for the supermarket, which can allow it to customize their placements of beer and diapers or tailor the marketing strategy or even alter the prices.

We can understand by a different example in a supermarket. Assume that by analyzing five invoices generated in a supermarket, we get the data as shown in table 4.1. In this example, in invoice number 1001 milk is purchased and thus has a value of 1, whereas cheese is not purchased and thus is 0.

Table 4.1 Examples of invoices generated in a supermarket

Invoice number	Milk	Eggs	Bread	Cheese
1001	1	1	1	0
1002	0	0	0	1
1003	1	1	1	0
1004	0	1	0	1
1005	1	1	0	1

So, in invoice number 1001, milk, eggs, and bread are purchased while in invoice number 1002, only cheese is purchased. Here we can see that whenever milk and eggs are purchased together, bread is always purchased in the same invoice. It is an important discovery indeed.

Now scale up this understanding to thousands of transactions made in a day. It will lead to very strong relationships that human eyes are generally oblivious to, but association rule algorithms can uncover them for us. This can lead to better product placements, better prices on the products, and much more optimized marketing spending. Such patterns will enhance the customer experience and prove quite handy to improve overall customer satisfaction.

We can visualize association rules as shown in figure 4.1. Here there are some incoming variables represented as nodes 1, 2, 3, 4, etc. These nodes are related to each other as shown by the arrows. This relationship between them gives rise to rules A and B. If we relate back to the beer/diaper story we mentioned at the start of this section, rule A can be that when a young male customer buys diapers, they also often buy beer, while rule B can be that when milk and eggs are purchased, often bread is bought too.

The example of the supermarket is sometimes referred to as *market*

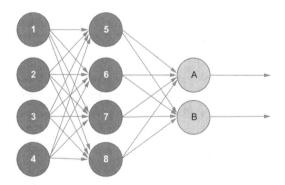

Figure 4.1 An association rule can be visualized as the relationship between various variables in the dataset. These variables are linked to each other, and significant relationships are established between them.

basket analysis. But association rules are applicable not only in grocery retail. Their utility has been proven in other sectors like bioinformatics, the medical industry, intrusion detection, etc. They can be utilized by Netflix or Spotify to analyze historical user behavior and then recommend the content the user most likely is going to like. Web developers can analyze the historical clicks and usages of the customers on their websites. By identifying the patterns, they can find out what users tend to click and which features will maximize their engagement. Medical practitioners can use association rules to better diagnose patients. The doctors can compare the probability of the symptoms in relationship with other symptoms and provide more accurate diagnoses. The use cases occur across multiple business domains and business functions.

4.3   *The building blocks of association rules*

We covered the definition of an association rule in the last section. Now let's understand the mathematical concept behind association rules. Assume that we have the following datasets in a retail store:

- Let $X = \{x_1, x_2, x_3, x_4, x_5 ...., x_n\}$ are the n items available in the retail store. For example, they can be milk, eggs, bread, cheese, apples, and so on.
- Let $Y = \{y_1, y_2, y_3, y_4, y_5 ...., y_m\}$ are the m transactions generated in that retail store. Each transaction could have all or some items from the retail store.

Obviously, each item in the transaction will be bought from the retail store only. In other words, every item in transactions in set Y will be a subset of items in set X. At the same time, each item would have a unique identifier attached to it, and each transaction would have a unique invoice number attached to it.

Now we are interested in analyzing the patterns and discovering the relationships. This will be used to generate any rule or insight. So let's define the meaning of the rule first.

Assume that we find a rule that whenever items in list P are bought, items in list Q are also bought. This rule can be written as follows:

1 The rule is P -> Q. It means that whenever items defined in P are bought, it leads to a purchase in Q too.
2 Items in P will be a subset of X or $P \subseteq X$.
3 Similarly, items in Q will be a subset of X or $Q \subseteq X$.
4 P and Q cannot have any common element or $P \cap Q = 0$

Now let's understand these mathematical concepts with a real-world example. Assume that X = {milk, bananas, eggs, cheese, apples, bread, salt, sugar, cookies, butter, cold drinks, water}. These are the total items available in the retail shop.

Y = {1001, 1002, 1003, 1004, 1005} are the five invoices generated in that retail store. The respective items purchased in each of these invoices are given in figure 4.2.

Invoice number	Milk	Bananas	Eggs	Cheese	Apples	Bread	Salt	Sugar	Cookies	Butter	Cold drinks	Water
1001	1	1	1	0	0	0	1	0	0	1	1	1
1002	0	0	0	1	0	0	1	0	0	1	0	1
1003	1	1	1	0	1	0	0	0	1	0	0	1
1004	0	1	0	1	1	1	1	0	1	0	0	0
1005	1	1	1	1	0	0	0	1	0	1	1	0

Figure 4.2   Example of five invoices generated in a retail store

Note how for each invoice, we have 0 and 1 associated for each of the items. These invoices are just for illustration purposes. In the actual invoices, the number of items can be much more. Using this dataset, let's assume we create two rules that {milk, bananas} -> {eggs} and {milk, bananas} -> {bread}.

The first rule means that whenever milk and bananas are bought together, eggs are also purchased in the same transaction. The second rule means that whenever milk and bananas are bought together, bread is also bought in the same transaction. By analyzing the dataset, we can clearly see that rule 1 is always true whereas rule 2 is not.

> **NOTE**   The items on the left side of a rule are called the *antecedent* or the LHS and the ones on the right side of a rule are called the *consequents* or the RHS.

In the real world, for any such rule to have significance, the same pattern must repeat itself across several hundreds and thousands of transactions. Only then would we conclude that the rule is indeed true and can be generalized across the entire database.

At the same time, there can be many such rules. In a retail shop where thousands of invoices are generated daily, there can be hundreds of such rules. How can we find out which rules are significant and which are not? This can be understood using the concepts of *support, confidence, lift,* and *conviction,* which we will study in the next section.

4.3.1   Support, confidence, lift, and conviction

We identified the meaning of a rule in an association rule in the last section. We also understand that there can be hundreds of rules based on the transactional dataset. In this section, we will explore how we can measure the effectiveness of such rules and shortlist the most interesting ones. This can be achieved using the concepts of support, confidence, lift, and conviction.

Recall in the last section we discussed the generalization of a rule. Support, confidence, lift, and conviction allow us to measure the level of generalization. In simple terms, using these four parameters, we can determine how useful the rule can be in our pragmatic real-world business. After all, if a rule is not useful or is not powerful enough, it is not required to be implemented. Support, confidence, lift, and conviction are the parameters to check the efficacy of the rule. We look at these concepts in detail next.

We will use the dataset in table 4.2 to understand the concepts of support, confidence, lift, and conviction. The first invoice, 1001, has milk, eggs, and bread while cheese is not purchased. Again, for the sake of this example, we have taken only four items in total.

Table 4.2   Dataset to understand the concept of support, confidence, lift, and conviction

Invoice Number	Milk	Eggs	Bread	Cheese
1001	1	1	1	0
1002	0	1	1	1
1003	1	1	1	0

Table 4.2   Dataset to understand the concept of support, confidence, lift, and conviction *(continued)*

Invoice Number	Milk	Eggs	Bread	Cheese
1004	0	1	0	1
1005	0	1	1	0

Here, for an invoice, 1 represents if an item is present in that invoice while 0 shows that the item was not purchased in that particular invoice. For example, invoice number 1001 has milk, eggs, and bread while 1002 has eggs, bread, and cheese.

SUPPORT

Support measures the frequency percentage of the items in the datasets. In simpler terms, it measures the percentage of transactions in which the items are occurring in the dataset.

Support can be denoted as follows:

$$\text{Support} = \frac{\text{(Total number of transactions in which the item of rule is present)}}{\text{(Total number of transactions present in the data base)}}$$

Refer to table 4.2. Say we are interested in the rule {milk, eggs} -> {bread}. In such a scenario, there are two transactions in which all three items (milk, eggs, and bread) are present. The total number of transactions is five. This means that the support for the rule is 2/5, which is 0.4 or 40%.

Now say we are interested in the rule {bread, eggs} -> {cheese}. In such a scenario, there is only one transaction in which all three items are present. The total number of transactions is five. This means that the support for the rule is 1/5, which is 0.2 or 20%.

> **NOTE**   The higher the support for a rule, the better it is. Generally, we put a minimum threshold to get support. A minimum threshold is generally determined in consultation with the business stakeholders.

CONFIDENCE

Confidence measures how often the rule is true; that is, it measures the percentage of transactions that contain antecedents that also contain consequents.

So if we wish to measure the confidence of the rule A -> B:

$$\text{Confidence} = \frac{\text{support}(A \cup B)}{\text{support}(A)}$$

Here, the numerator is supported when both *A* and *B* are present in the transaction, while the denominator refers to the support only for *A*.

Refer to table 4.2. Again, say we are interested in the rule {milk, eggs} -> {bread}. In such a scenario, there are two transactions in which both milk and eggs are present. Hence, the support is 2/5 = 0.4. It is the denominator. There are two transactions in which all three (milk, eggs, bread) are present. Hence, support is 2/5 = 0.4, which is the numerator. Putting in the preceding equation, the confidence for the rule {milk, eggs} -> {bread} is 0.4/0.4 = 1.

Now say we are interested in the rule {eggs, bread} -> {cheese}. In such a scenario, there are four transactions in which (eggs, bread) are present. The total number of transactions is five. This means that the support is 4/5, which is 0.8. There is only one transaction in which all three items (eggs, bread, cheese) are present. So the support is 1/5 = 0.2. Hence the confidence for the rule {eggs, bread} -> {cheese} is 0.2/0.8 = 0.25.

> **NOTE**   The higher the confidence in the rule, the better it is. Like support, we put a minimum threshold on confidence.

Sometimes this is also referred to as the *conditional probability* of A on B. It can be understood as the probability of B occurring provided A has already occurred and can be written as P(A|B). So, in the preceding examples, the probability of cheese to be bought provided eggs, bread is already bought is 25% while the probability of bread to be purchased, provided milk, eggs are already purchased is 100%.

LIFT AND CONVICTION

Lift is a very important measurement criterium for a rule. Lift for a rule A -> B can be defined as

$$\text{Lift}(A \rightarrow B) = \frac{\text{support}(A \cup B)}{\text{support}(A) * \text{support}(B)}$$

Here the numerator is supported when both A and B are present in the transaction, while the denominator refers to the support for A multiplied by the support for B.

Again, refer to table 4.2 and say we are interested in the rule {milk, eggs} -> {bread}. In such a scenario, there are two transactions in which all three (milk, eggs, bread) are present. Hence, support is again 2/5 = 0.4, which is the numerator. There are two transactions in which only (milk, eggs) are present, so the support is 2/5 = 0.4. There are four transactions in which bread is present, hence the support is 4/5 = 0.8. Putting in the preceding equation, the lift for the rule {milk, eggs} -> {bread} is 0.4/(0.4 x 0.8) = 1.25.

Then say we are interested in the rule {eggs, bread} -> {cheese}. In such a scenario, there is only one transaction in which (eggs, bread, cheese) are present. The total number of transactions is five. This means that the support is 1/5, which is 0.2. There are two transactions in which (cheese) is present. So the support is 2/5 = 0.4. There are four transactions in which (eggs, bread) are present, so the support is 4/5 = 0.8. Putting in the preceding equation, the lift for the rule {eggs, bread} -> {cheese} is 0.2/(0.4 x 0.8) = 0.625.

If the value of the lift is *equal to 1*, it means that the antecedent and precedent are independent of each other, and no rule can be drawn from it.

If the value of lift is *greater than 1*, it means that the antecedent and precedent are dependent on each other. This rule can be used for predicting the antecedent in future transactions. This is the insight we want to draw from the dataset.

If the value of lift is *less than 1*, it means that the antecedent and precedent are substitutes of each other. The presence of one can have a negative effect on the other. It is also an important insight that can be used by the business teams for strategic planning.

While we evaluate any rule using the lift, it is imperative that we apply domain knowledge to it. For example, if we evaluate the rule {eggs, bread} -> {cheese} and if we find that eggs, bread can be a substitute for cheese, we know that it is not true in real life. Hence, in such a scenario we cannot make any decision for this role. We must use domain knowledge to draw any conclusions for this rule.

At the same time, rule {milk, eggs} -> {bread} might be a rule that can be true many times. For many customers, when they purchase milk and eggs together, it is highly likely that bread will be purchased in the same transaction. Hence this rule makes much more sense for such customers. The objective is to have a strong business logic to either support or disapprove a rule identified using the algorithm.

Conviction is another important parameter, which is given by the following formula:

$$\text{Conviction}(A \rightarrow B) = \frac{1 - \text{support}(B)}{1 - \text{confidence}(A \rightarrow B)}$$

Refer to table 4.2. Again, say we are interested in the rule {eggs, bread} -> {cheese}. In such a scenario, there is only one transaction in which (cheese) is present. The total number of transactions is five. So, it means that the support is $1/5$, which is 0.2 and will be used in the numerator. We have already calculated the confidence as 0.625. Putting back in the formula, we can calculate conviction as $(1 - 0.2)/(1 - 0.625) = 2.13$

We can interpret the conviction as: the rule {eggs, bread} -> {cheese} would be incorrect 2.13 times more often if the association between {eggs, bread, cheese} was purely chosen at random.

In most of the business scenarios, lift is the measurement criteria used. There are other measurement parameters, too, like leverage, collective strength, etc. But most of the time, confidence, support, lift, and conviction are used to measure the effectiveness of any rule.

Exercise 4.1

Answer these questions to check your understanding:

1. Support measures how often the rule is present in the dataset. True or False?
2. If the lift is greater than 1, it means that the two items are independent of each other. True or False?
3. The lower the value of confidence, the better the rule. True or False?

While we evaluate any rule while analyzing the dataset, most of the time, we set a threshold for the confidence, support, lift, and conviction. It allows us to reduce the number of rules and filter out the irrelevant ones. In other words, we are interested in only the rules that are very frequent. We will study this in more detail when we create a Python solution for a dataset.

4.4 Apriori algorithm

The Apriori algorithm is one of the most popular algorithms used for association rules. It was proposed by Agrawal and Shrikant in 1994. The link to the paper is given at the end of the chapter.

Apriori is used to understand and analyze the frequent items in a transactional database. It utilizes a "bottom-up" approach where the first candidates are generated based on the frequency of the subsets. Let us understand the entire process by means of an example. We will use the same dataset we have discussed earlier (see table 4.2). The process used in the Apriori algorithm will look like figure 4.3.

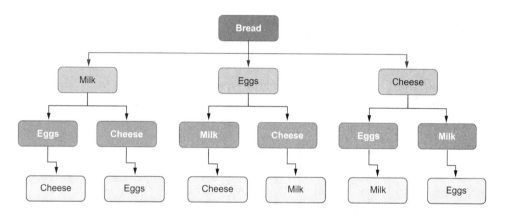

Figure 4.3   The Apriori algorithm process

Let us say we wish to analyze the relationship of bread with all the other items in the dataset. In this case, level 1 is bread, and we find its frequency of occurrence.

Then we move to the next layer, which is layer 2. Now we find the relationship of bread with each of the other items: milk, eggs, and cheese, which are at layer 2. Here again we find the respective frequencies of occurrence for all the possible combinations, which are {bread, milk}, {bread, eggs}, and {bread, cheese}. See figure 4.4.

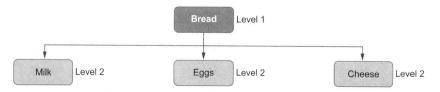

Figure 4.4   We have bread at level 1 while the other items (milk, eggs, and cheese) are kept at level 2. Bread is kept at level 1 since we wish to analyze the relationship of bread with all the other items.

After layer 2 has been analyzed, we move to the third layer and fourth layer and so on. This process continues until we reach the last layer wherein all the items have been exhausted.

As a result of this process, we can calculate the support for all the possible combinations. For example, we would know the support for

> {bread} -> {milk},
>
> {bread} -> {eggs}, and
>
> {bread} -> {cheese}.

For the next level, we would also get the support for

> {bread, milk} -> {eggs},
>
> {bread, eggs} -> {milk},
>
> {bread, milk} -> {cheese},
>
> {bread, cheese} -> {milk},
>
> {bread, cheese} -> {eggs}, and
>
> {bread, eggs} -> {cheese}.

Now, using the same process, all the possible combinations for the next level are calculated. For example, {bread, eggs, milk} -> {cheese}, {bread, eggs, cheese} -> {milk}, and so on.

When all the item sets have been exhausted, the process will stop. The complete architecture can look like figure 4.5.

Now we can easily understand that the possible number of combinations is quite high, which is one of the challenges with Apriori. But Apriori is quite a powerful algorithm and is very popular too. Now it's time to implement Apriori using Python.

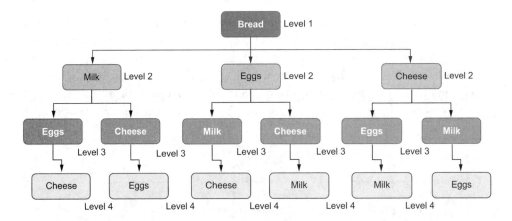

Figure 4.5   The complete architecture for the Apriori algorithm. Here we would have calculated support for all the possible combinations. The relationships between all the items are explored, and because of this entire database scan, the speed of Apriori gets hampered.

4.4.1 Python implementation

We will now proceed with Python implementation of the Apriori algorithm. The dataset and Python Jupyter Notebook are checked in at the GitHub repository. You might have to install `apyori`.

To install the libraries, simply do the following:

```
import sys
!{sys.executable} -m pip install apyori
```

The steps are as follows:

1 Import the necessary libraries for the use case. We are importing `numpy` and `pandas`. For implementing Apriori, we have a library called `apyori`, which is also imported:

```
import numpy as np
import pandas as pd
from apyori import apriori
```

2 Import the dataset `store_data.csv` file:

```
store_dataset = pd.read_csv('store_data.csv')
```

You are also advised to have a look at the dataset by opening the .csv file. It will look like the screenshot in figure 4.6. The first 25 rows are shown in the screenshot. Each row represents an invoice.

	A	B	C	D	E	F	G	H	I
1	shrimp	almonds	avocado	vegetables mix	green grapes	whole wheat flour	yams	cottage cheese	energy drink
2	burgers	meatballs	eggs						
3	chutney								
4	turkey	avocado							
5	mineral water	milk	energy bar	whole wheat rice	green tea				
6	low fat yogurt								
7	whole wheat pasta	french fries							
8	soup	light cream	shallot						
9	frozen vegetables	spaghetti	green tea						
10	french fries								
11	eggs	pet food							
12	cookies								
13	turkey	burgers	mineral water	eggs	cooking oil				
14	spaghetti	champagne	cookies						
15	mineral water	salmon							
16	mineral water								
17	shrimp	chocolate	chicken	honey	oil	cooking oil	low fat yogurt		
18	turkey	eggs							
19	turkey	fresh tuna	tomatoes	spaghetti	mineral water	black tea	salmon	eggs	chicken
20	meatballs	milk	honey	french fries	protein bar				
21	red wine	shrimp	pasta	pepper	eggs	chocolate	shampoo		
22	rice	sparkling water							
23	spaghetti	mineral water	ham	body spray	pancakes	green tea			
24	burgers	grated cheese	shrimp	pasta	avocado	honey	white wine	toothpaste	
25	eggs								
26	parmesan cheese	spaghetti	soup	avocado	milk	fresh bread			

Figure 4.6 Screenshot of the .csv file

3   Next we perform some basic checks on the data by the `.info` and `.head` commands (see figure 4.7):

```
store_dataset.info()
```

```
store_dataset.info()

<class 'pandas.core.frame.DataFrame'>
RangeIndex: 7500 entries, 0 to 7499
Data columns (total 20 columns):
shrimp               7500 non-null object
almonds              5746 non-null object
avocado              4388 non-null object
vegetables mix       3344 non-null object
green grapes         2528 non-null object
whole weat flour     1863 non-null object
yams                 1368 non-null object
cottage cheese        980 non-null object
energy drink          653 non-null object
tomato juice          394 non-null object
low fat yogurt        255 non-null object
green tea             153 non-null object
honey                  86 non-null object
salad                  46 non-null object
mineral water          24 non-null object
salmon                  7 non-null object
antioxydant juice       3 non-null object
frozen smoothie         3 non-null object
spinach                 2 non-null object
olive oil               0 non-null float64
dtypes: float64(1), object(19)
memory usage: 1.1+ MB
```

```
store_dataset.head()
```

In [7]:
```
1  store_dataset.head()
```
Out[7]:

	shrimp	almonds	avocado	vegetables mix	green grapes	whole wheat flour	yams	cottage cheese	energy drink	tomato juice	low fat yogurt	green tea	honey	salad
0	burgers	meatballs	eggs	NaN	NaN	NaN	NaN	NaN	NaN	NaN	NaN	NaN	NaN	NaN
1	chutney	NaN	NaN	NaN	NaN	NaN	NaN	NaN	NaN	NaN	NaN	NaN	NaN	NaN
2	turkey	avocado	NaN	NaN	NaN	NaN	NaN	NaN	NaN	NaN	NaN	NaN	NaN	NaN
3	mineral water	milk	energy bar	whole wheat rice	green tea	NaN	NaN	NaN	NaN	NaN	NaN	NaN	NaN	NaN
4	low fat yogurt	NaN	NaN	NaN	NaN	NaN	NaN	NaN	NaN	NaN	NaN	NaN	NaN	NaN

Figure 4.7   Output for `.info` **and** `.head` **commands**

4   Here we can see that the first transaction has been considered the header by the code. Hence, we would import the data again, but this time we would specify that headers are equal to `None`:

```
store_dataset = pd.read_csv('store_data.csv', header=None)
```

5 Let's look at the head again (see figure 4.8). This time it looks correct:

```
store_dataset.head()
```

In [10]: `1 store_dataset.head()`

Out[10]:

	0	1	2	3	4	5	6	7	8	9	10	11	12	13	14	15
0	shrimp	almonds	avocado	vegetables mix	green grapes	whole wheat flour	yams	cottage cheese	energy drink	tomato juice	low fat yogurt	green tea	honey	salad	mineral water	salmon
1	burgers	meatballs	eggs	NaN	NaN	NaN	NaN	NaN	NaN	NaN	NaN	NaN	NaN	NaN	NaN	NaN
2	chutney	NaN	NaN	NaN	NaN	NaN	NaN	NaN	NaN	NaN	NaN	NaN	NaN	NaN	NaN	NaN
3	turkey	avocado	NaN	NaN	NaN	NaN	NaN	NaN	NaN	NaN	NaN	NaN	NaN	NaN	NaN	NaN
4	mineral water	milk	energy bar	whole wheat rice	green tea	NaN	NaN	NaN	NaN	NaN	NaN	NaN	NaN	NaN	NaN	NaN

Figure 4.8   Correct results for `.head()`

6 The library we are using for the code accepts the dataset as a list of lists. The entire dataset must be a big list while each transaction is an inner list in the big list. So, to achieve it, we first convert our `store_dataset` dataframe into a list:

```
all_records = []
for i in range(0, 7501):
    all_records.append([str(store_dataset.values[i,j]) for j in
        range(0, 20)])
```

7 Next, we implement the Apriori algorithm.

For the algorithm, we are working on the `all_records` list we created in step 6. The minimum support specified is 0.5 or 50%, the minimum confidence is 25%, the minimum lift is 4, and the minimum length of the rule is 2.

The output of this step is the `apriori_rules` class object. This object is then converted into a list that we can understand. Finally, we print this list:

```
apriori_rules = apriori(all_records, min_support=0.5, min_confidence=0.25,
    min_lift=4, min_length=2)
apriori_rules = list(apriori_rules)
print(len(apriori_rules))
```

The output of the code will be 0. This means that no such rules exist that satisfy the condition we have set for the rules.

We again try to execute the same code, albeit by reducing the minimum support to 25%:

```
apriori_rules = apriori(all_records, min_support=0.25, min_confidence=0.25,
min_lift=4, min_length=2)
apriori_rules = list(apriori_rules)
print(len(apriori_rules))
```

Again, no rules are generated and the output is 0. Even reducing the minimum support to 10% does not lead to any rules:

```
apriori_rules = apriori(all_records, min_support=0.1, min_confidence=0.25,
min_lift=4, min_length=2)
apriori_rules = list(apriori_rules)
print(len(apriori_rules))
```

Now we reduce the minimum lift to 2. This time we get 200 as the output. This means that there are 200 such rules that fulfill the criteria:

```
apriori_rules = apriori(all_records, min_support=0.25, min_confidence=0.25,
min_lift=2, min_length=2)
apriori_rules = list(apriori_rules)
print(len(apriori_rules))
```

8   Let's look at the first rule (see figure 4.9):

```
print(apriori_rules[0])
```

```
print(apriori_rules[0])

RelationRecord(items=frozenset({'almonds', 'burgers'}), support=0.005199306759098787,
ordered_statistics=[OrderedStatistics(items_base=frozenset({'almonds'}),
item_add=frozenset({'burgers'}), confidence=0.25490196078431376, lift=2.923577382023146)])
```

Figure 4.9   Output from `print(apriori_rules[0])`

The rule explains the relationship between almonds and burgers. The support is .005, and the confidence is 0.25. Lift, which is 2.92, indicates that this rule is quite strong.

9   We will now look at all the rules in detail. For that, loop through the rules and extract information from each of the iterations. Each of the rules has the items constituting the rule and respective values for support, confidence, lift, and conviction. We have shown an example in step 8. Now, in step 9, we are just extracting that information for all the rules using a for loop:

```
for rule in apriori_rules:
    item_pair = rule[0]
    items = [x for x in item_pair]
    print("The apriori rule is: " + items[0] + " -> " + items[1])

    print("The support for the rule is: " + str(rule[1]))

    print("The confidence for the rule is: " + str(rule[2][0][2]))
    print("The lift for the rule is: " + str(rule[2][0][3]))
    print("************************")
```

The output for this step is shown in figure 4.10. Here we can observe each rule is listed along with the respective values of support, confidence, lift, and conviction.

```
for rule in apriori_rules:
    item_pair = rule[0]
    items = [x for x in item_pair]
    print("The apriori rule is: " + items[0] + " -> " + items[1])

    print("The support for the rule is: " + str(rule[1]))

    print("The confidence for the rule is: " + str(rule[2][0][2]))
    print("The lift for the rule is: " + str(rule[2][0][3]))
    print("*************************")
```

```
The apriori rule is: almonds -> burgers
The support for the rule is: 0.005199306759098787
The confidence for the rule is: 0.25490196078431376
The lift for the rule is: 2.923577382023146
*************************
The apriori rule is: cereals -> milk
The support for the rule is: 0.007065724570057326
The confidence for the rule is: 0.2746113989637306
The lift for the rule is: 2.119197637476279
*************************
The apriori rule is: chocolate -> tomato sauce
The support for the rule is: 0.005065991201173177
The confidence for the rule is: 0.3584905660377358
The lift for the rule is: 2.1879883936932925
*************************
The apriori rule is: mushroom cream sauce -> escalope
The support for the rule is: 0.005732568990801226
The confidence for the rule is: 0.3006993006993007
The lift for the rule is: 3.790832696715049
```

Figure 4.10   Output for step 9

We can interpret the rules easily. For example, the rule almonds -> burgers has a lift of 2.92 with a confidence of 25.49% and support of 0.51%. This concludes our implementation using Python. This example can be extended to any other real-world business dataset.

> **NOTE**   Not all the rules generated are not worth using. We will examine how to get the best rules from all the rules generated when we deal with the case study in the last section of the chapter.

The Apriori algorithm is a robust and very insightful algorithm. But, like any other solution, it has a few shortcomings.

4.4.2 *Challenges with the Apriori algorithm*

As we have seen, the number of subsets generated in the Apriori algorithm is quite high (see figure 4.5). It is very tedious to generate candidates' item sets, and hence it becomes quite cumbersome to analyze the dataset. Apriori scans the entire dataset multiple times, and hence it requires the database to be loaded in the memory. We can safely deduce that it requires a lot of time to make the computations. This problem is magnified when we are dealing with a very large dataset. In fact, for real-world problems where millions of transactions are generated, quite a huge number of candidate item sets are generated, and it is very time-consuming to use Apriori on the entire dataset.

Due to this very reason, generally, a minimum value of support is set to reduce the number of possible rules. In the previous example, we can calculate the support for level 1 combinations, as shown in table 4.3. Here, if we set the minimum value of support as 0.5, only one rule will be shortlisted. Support is calculated for each of the combination of the items. For example, for milk and bread, the number of transactions is 2, while the total number of transactions is 5. So the support is 2/5, which is 0.4.

Table 4.3   Support for level 1 combinations

Combination	Number of transactions	Total transactions	Support
Milk, Eggs	2	5	0.4
Milk, Bread	2	5	0.4
Milk, Cheese	0	5	0
Eggs, Bread	4	5	0.8
Eggs, Cheese	2	5	0.4
Bread, Cheese	1	5	0.2

Setting up a minimum value of support is hence an intelligent tactic to make the rules much more manageable. It reduces the time and generates rules that are much more significant. After all, the rules generated from the analysis should be generalizable enough so that they can be implemented across the entire database.

Exercise 4.2

Answer these questions to check your understanding:

1. The Apriori algorithm scans the database only once. True or False?
2. If bananas are present in 5 transactions out of a total of 12 transactions, it means the support for bananas is 5/12. True or False?

But the Apriori algorithm is indeed a great solution. It is still highly popular and generally one of the very first algorithms brought up whenever association rules are discussed.

NOTE   Data preparation is one of the key steps and quite a challenge. We will explore this challenge during the case study in section 4.8.

4.5   *Equivalence class clustering and bottom-up lattice traversal*

We will now study the equivalence class clustering and bottom-up lattice traversal algorithm (ECLAT), which sometimes is considered better than Apriori in terms of speed and ease of implementation. ECLAT uses a depth-first search approach. This means that ECLAT performs the search in a vertical fashion throughout the dataset. It starts at the root node and then goes one level deep and continues until it reaches the first terminal note. Let's say the terminal node is at level X. Once the terminal node is reached, the algorithm then takes a step back and reaches level $(X-1)$ and continues until it finds a terminal node again. Let's understand this process by means of a tree diagram, as shown in figure 4.11.

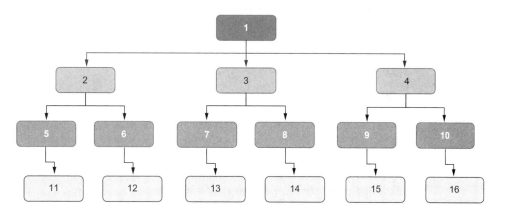

Figure 4.11 Tree diagram to understand the process of the ECLAT algorithm. It starts with 1 and ends at 16.

ECLAT will take the following steps:

1 The algorithm starts at the root node 1.
2 It then goes one level deep to root node 2.
3 It will then continue one more level deep until it reaches terminal node 11.
4 Once it reaches terminal node 11, it then takes a step back and goes to node 5.
5 The algorithm then searches if there is any node available that can be used. At node 5 we can see that there is no such node available.
6 Hence, the algorithm again takes a step back and reaches node 2.
7 At node 2, the algorithm explores again. It finds that it is possible to go to node 6.
8 So, the algorithm goes to node 6 and starts exploring again until it reaches terminal node 12.
9 This process continues until all the combinations have been exhausted.

Obviously, the speed of computation depends on the total number of distinct items present in the dataset. This is because the number of distinct items defines the width of the tree. The items purchased in each of the transactions would define the relationship between each node.

During the execution time of ECLAT, each item (either individually or in a pair) is analyzed. Let us use the same example we have used for Apriori to understand ECLAT better. Refer to table 4.2.

ECLAT will undergo the following steps to analyze the dataset:

1 In the first run, ECLAT will find the invoice numbers for all single items. In other words, it will find the invoice numbers for all the items individually. It is shown in table 4.4, wherein milk is present in invoice numbers 1001 and 1003, while eggs are present in all five invoices.

Table 4.4   **Respective invoices in which each item is present**

Item	Invoice numbers
Milk	1001, 1003
Eggs	1001, 1002, 1003, 1004, 1005
Bread	1001, 1002, 1003, 1005
Cheese	1002, 1004

2 In the next step, all the two-item datasets are explored as shown in table 4.5. For example, milk and eggs are present in invoice numbers 1001 and 1003, while milk and cheese are not present in any invoice.

Table 4.5   **Two-item datasets**

Item	Invoice numbers
Milk, Eggs	1001 ,1003
Milk, Bread	1001, 1003
Milk, Cheese	—
Eggs, Bread	1001, 1002, 1003, 1005
Eggs, Cheese	1002, 1004
Bread, Cheese	1002

3 In the next step, all three-item datasets are explored, as shown in table 4.6. Here we have two combinations only.

Table 4.6   **Three-item datasets**

Item	Invoice numbers
Milk, Eggs, Bread	1001, 1003
Eggs, Bread, Cheese	1002

4 There are no invoices present in our dataset that contain four items.

5 Now, depending on the threshold we set for the value of the support count, we can choose the rules. So, if we want the minimum number of transactions in

which the rule should be true to be three, then only one rule qualifies, which is {eggs, bread}. If we decide the threshold for the minimum number of transactions is two, then rules like {milk, eggs, bread}, {milk, eggs}, {milk, bread}, {eggs, bread}, and {eggs, cheese} qualify as the rules.

We will now create a Python solution for ECLAT.

4.5.1   Python implementation

We will now work on the execution of ECLAT using Python. We use the `pyECLAT` library here. The dataset looks like figure 4.12.

1	shrimp	almonds	avocado	vegetables mix	green grapes	whole wheat flour	yams
2	burgers	meatballs	eggs				
3	chutney						
4	turkey	avocado					
5	mineral water	milk	energy bar	whole wheat rice	green tea		
6	low fat yogurt						
7	whole wheat pasta	french fries					
8	soup	light cream	shallot				
9	frozen vegetables	spaghetti	green tea				
10	french fries						
11	eggs	pet food					
12	cookies						
13	turkey	burgers	mineral water	eggs		cooking oil	
14	spaghetti	champagne	cookies				
15	mineral water	salmon					
16	mineral water						
17	shrimp	chocolate	chicken	honey	oil	cooking oil	low fat yogurt
18	turkey	eggs					
19	turkey	fresh tuna	tomatoes	spaghetti	mineral water	black tea	salmon
20	meatballs	milk	honey	french fries	protein bar		
21	red wine	shrimp	pasta	pepper	eggs	chocolate	shampoo
22	rice	sparkling water					
23	spaghetti	mineral water	ham	body spray	pancakes	green tea	
24	burgers	grated cheese	shrimp	pasta	avocado	honey	white wine
25	eggs						
26	parmesan cheese	spaghetti	soup	avocado	milk	fresh bread	
27	ground beef	spaghetti	mineral water	milk	energy bar	black tea	salmon
28	sparkling water						
29	mineral water	eggs	chicken	chocolate	french fries		

Figure 4.12   ECLAT for the `pyECLAT` library using Python

The steps are as follows:

1   Import the libraries:

```
import numpy as np
import pandas as pd
from pyECLAT import ECLAT
```

2   Import the dataset:

```
data_frame = pd.read_csv('Data_ECLAT.csv', header = None)
```

3   Generate an ECLAT instance:

```
eclat = ECLAT(data=data_frame)
```

There are some properties of ECLAT instance `eclat` generated in the last step like `eclat.df_bin`, which is a binary dataframe, and `eclat.uniq_`, which is a list of all the unique items.

    4   Fit the model. We give a minimum support of 0.02 here. After that, we print the support:

```
get_ECLAT_indexes, get_ECLAT_supports = eclat.fit(min_support=0.02,
                                                   min_combination=1,
                                                   max_combination=3,

separator=' & ')
get_ECLAT_supports
```

The output is shown in figure 4.13.

```
In [11]:   get_ECLAT_supports

Out[11]:  {'pepper': 0.02865711429523492,
           'french fries': 0.15428190603132289,
           'light mayo': 0.02332555814728424,
           'cake': 0.07697434188603798,
           'low fat yogurt': 0.05664778407197601,
           'eggs': 0.17727424191936023,
           'champagne': 0.042652449183605466,
           'ham': 0.027657447517494167,
           'milk': 0.12695768077307565,
           'honey': 0.03865378207264245,
           'cooking oil': 0.04798400533155615,
           'mineral water': 0.23692102632455847,
           'turkey': 0.06597800733088971,
           'cookies': 0.07697434188603798,
           'olive oil': 0.06597800733088971,
           'spaghetti': 0.18293902032655782,
```

```
           'french fries & eggs': 0.03432189270243252,
           'french fries & mineral water': 0.0229233588803732,
           'french fries & spaghetti': 0.02165944685104965,
           'french fries & chocolate': 0.027657447517494167,
           'french fries & green tea': 0.022325891369543487,
           'cake & mineral water': 0.023658780406531157,
           'eggs & milk': 0.027990669776741087,
           'eggs & mineral water': 0.04798400533155615,
           'eggs & spaghetti': 0.03265578140619793,
           'eggs & chocolate': 0.028323892035988004,
           'eggs & green tea': 0.020659780073308896,
           'eggs & burgers': 0.025324891702765744,
           'milk & mineral water': 0.048317227590803064,
           'milk & spaghetti': 0.0386537820726245,
           'milk & chocolate': 0.026991002999000334,
           'milk & ground beef': 0.02165944685104965,
           'mineral water & olive oil': 0.02732422525824725,
           'mineral water & spaghetti': 0.06064645118293902,
           'mineral water & soup': 0.025658113962012664,
           'mineral water & frozen vegetables': 0.03698767077640786,
           'mineral water & shrimp': 0.027990669776741087,
           'mineral water & chocolate': 0.04765078307230923,
           'mineral water & tomatoes': 0.024991669443518827,
           'mineral water & burgers': 0.023992002665778073,
           'mineral water & ground beef': 0.03698767077640786,
```

Figure 4.13   Output for step 4

We can interpret the results provided based on the support. For each of the items and combination of items, we are getting the value of the support. For example, for french fries and eggs, the value of support is 3.43%.

    ECLAT has some advantages over the Apriori algorithm. Since it uses a depth-search approach, it is faster than Apriori and requires less memory to compute. It does not scan the dataset iteratively, and that makes it even faster than Apriori. We will compare these algorithms once more after we have studied the last algorithm.

4.6   *F-P algorithm*

The F-P algorithm is the third algorithm we discuss in this chapter. It is an improvement over the Apriori algorithm. Recall in Apriori we face the challenges of time-consuming and costly computations. F-P resolves these problems by representing the database in the form of a tree called a *frequent pattern tree* or *FP tree*. Because of this frequent pattern, there is no need to generate the candidates as done in the Apriori algorithm. Let's discuss F-P in detail now.

An F-P tree is a tree-shaped structure, and it mines the most frequent items in the datasets. This is visualized in figure 4.14.

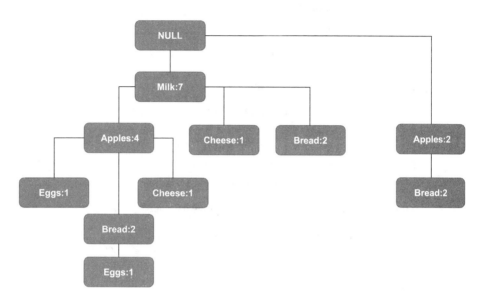

Figure 4.14 An F-P algorithm can be depicted in a tree-diagram structure. Each node represents a unique item. The root node is NULL.

Each node represents a unique item in the dataset. The root node of the tree is generally kept as NULL. The other nodes in the tree are the items in the dataset. The nodes are connected with each other if they are in the same invoice. We will study the entire process in a step-by-step fashion.

Assume we are using the dataset shown in table 4.7. So we have the unique items as Apples, Milk, Eggs, Cheese, and Bread. There are nine transactions, and the respective items in each of the transactions are shown in table 4.7.

Table 4.7 Dataset to understand the F-P algorithm

Transactions	Item sets
T1	Apples, Milk, Eggs
T2	Milk, Cheese
T3	Milk, Bread
T4	Apples, Milk, Cheese

Table 4.7   Dataset to understand the F-P algorithm *(continued)*

Transactions	Item sets
T5	Apples, Bread
T6	Milk, Bread
T7	Apples, Bread
T8	Apples, Milk, Bread, Eggs
T9	Apples, Milk, Bread

Let's apply the F-P algorithm on this dataset now. The steps are as follows:

1 Like Apriori, the entire dataset is scanned first. Occurrences for each of the items is counted, and a frequency is generated. The results are suggested in table 4.8. We have arranged the items in descending order of the frequency or the respective support count in the entire dataset. For example, apples have been purchased in six transactions.

Table 4.8   Respective frequency for each of the item sets

Item	Frequency or support count
Milk	7
Apples	6
Bread	6
Cheese	2
Eggs	2

If two items have exactly same frequency, either can be ordered first. In the example here, Bread and Apples have the same frequency. So we can keep either Bread or Apples as the first one.

2 Start the construction of the F-P tree. We start with creating the root node, which is generally the NULL node, in figure 4.15.

Figure 4.15   The root node for the tree is generally kept NULL.

3 Analyze the first transaction, T1. Here we have Apples, Milk, and Eggs in the first transaction. Out of these three, Milk has the highest support count, which

is 7. So a connection is extended from the root node to Milk, and we denote it as Milk:1 (see figure 4.16).

Figure 4.16 Connection from the root node to Milk. Milk has the highest support; hence we have chosen Milk.

4 Now look at the other items in T1. Apples has a support count of 6 and Eggs have a support count of 2. So we will extend the connection from Milk to Apples and name it Apples:1 and then from Apples to Eggs and call it Eggs:1 (see figure 4.17).

5 Look at T2 now. It has Milk and Cheese. Milk is already connected to the root node. So the count for Milk becomes 2, and it becomes Milk:2. Next, we will create a branch from Milk to Cheese and name it Cheese:1. The addition is shown in figure 4.18.

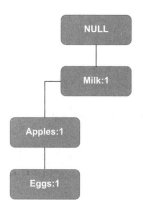

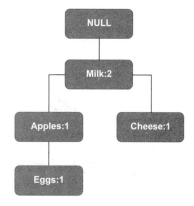

Figure 4.17 Step 4 of the process where we have finished all the items in T1. All the items—Milk, Apples, and Eggs—are now connected.

Figure 4.18 Step 5 of the process where we started to analyze T2. Milk is already connected, so its count increases by 2 while Cheese gets added to the tree.

6 Consider T3. T3 has Milk and Bread. So, similar to step 5, the count for Milk is 3, and it becomes Milk:3. And, similar to step 5, we add another connection

from Milk to Bread and call it Bread:1. The updated tree is shown in figure 4.19.

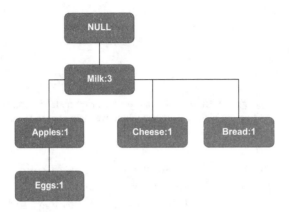

Figure 4.19   In step 6, T3 is analyzed. Milk's count increased by 1 more and becomes 3, while Bread is added as a new connection.

7   In T4, we have Apples, Milk, and Cheese. The count for Milk becomes 4; for Apples it is now 2. Then we create a branch from Apples to Cheese, calling it Cheese:1 (see figure 4.20).

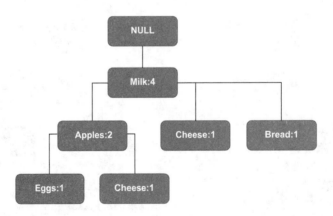

Figure 4.20   In step 7 of the process, T4 is being analyzed. The count of Milk becomes 4, for Apples it increases to 2, and a new branch from Apples to Cheese is added.

8   We find in T5 that we have Apples and Bread. Both are not directly connected to the root node and have an equal frequency of 6. So we can take either to be connected to the root node. The figure gets updated to figure 4.21.

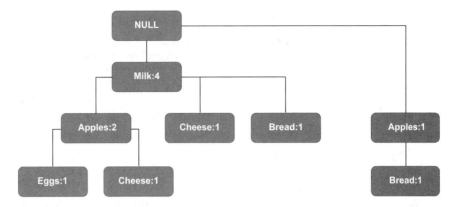

Figure 4.21 After analyzing T5, the diagram changes, as shown here. We have Apples and Bread, which get added to the tree.

9 This process continues until we exhaust all the transactions, resulting in the final figure as shown in figure 4.22.

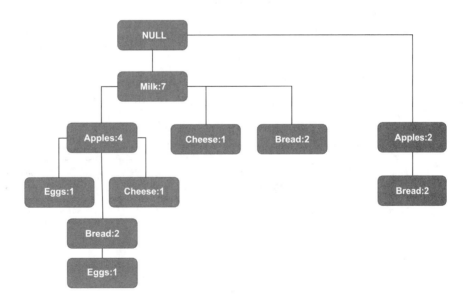

Figure 4.22 The final tree once we have exhausted all the possible combinations

Great job so far! But there are more steps after this. So far, we have created only the tree. Now we need to generate the dataset as shown in table 4.9. This is the output we wish to generate.

Table 4.9　Table for the F-P algorithm

Items	Conditional pattern base	Conditional F-P tree	Frequent pattern generated
Cheese			
Bread			
Eggs			
Apples			

You might be wondering why there are only four items listed. Since Milk has directly originated from the root node and there is no other way to reach it, we need not have a separate row for Milk.

10　Before continuing, we must fix the minimum support count as 2 for any rule to be acceptable. We do this for simplicity's sake as the dataset is quite small.

NOTE　For real-life business problems, you are advised to test with multiple and even much higher values for the support counts; otherwise, the number of rules generated can be very high.

Let's start with Cheese as the first item. We can reach cheese through {NULL-Milk-Cheese} and {NULL-Milk-Apples-Cheese}. For both paths, the count of Cheese is 1. Hence, (if we ignore NULL) our conditional pattern base is {Milk-Cheese} or {Milk:1} and {Milk-Apples:Cheese} or {Milk-Apples:1}. The complete conditional pattern base becomes {{Milk:1}, {Milk-Apples:1}}. This information is added to the second column of table 4.10.

Table 4.10　Step 10 of the process where we have filled the first cell for Cheese

Items	Conditional pattern base	Conditional F-P tree	Frequent pattern generated
Cheese	{{Milk:1}, {Milk-Apples:1}}		
Bread			
Eggs			
Apples			

11　Now if we add the two values in a conditional pattern base, we would get Milk as 2 and Apples as 1. Since we have set up a threshold for the frequency count of 2, we will ignore the count of Apples. The value for the conditional F-P tree, which is the third column in the table, becomes {Milk:2}. Now we simply add the original item to this, which becomes the frequent patten generated or column 4. See table 4.11.

Table 4.11 Step 11 of the process where we have finished the details for the item Cheese

Items	Conditional pattern base	Conditional F-P tree	Frequent pattern generated
Cheese	{{Milk:1}, {Milk-Apples:1}}	{Milk:2}	{Milk-Cheese:2}
Bread			
Eggs			
Apples			

12 In a similar fashion, all the other cells are filled in the table, resulting in the final table (table 4.12).

Table 4.12 Final table after we have analyzed all the combinations for the items

Items	Conditional pattern base	Conditional F-P tree	Frequent pattern generated
Cheese	{{Milk:1}, {Milk-Apples:1}}	{Milk:2}	{Milk-Cheese:2}
Bread	{{Milk-Apples:2}, {Milk:2}, {Apples:2}}	{{Milk:4, Apples:2}, {Apples:2}}	{{Milk-Bread:4}, {Apples-Bread:4}, {Milk-Apples-Bread:2}}
Eggs	{{Milk-Apples:1}, {Milk-Apples-Bread:1}}	{Milk:2, Apples:2}	{{Milk-Eggs:2}, {Milk-Apples:2}, {Milk-Apples:2}}
Apples	{Milk:4}	{Milk:4}	{Milk-Apples:4}

It is a complex process indeed. But once the steps are clear, it is straightforward.

As a result of this exercise, we have received the final set of rules as depicted in the final column Frequent Pattern Generated.

NOTE Notice that none of the rules are similar to each other.

We will use the final column, Frequent Pattern Generated, as the rules for our dataset.

The Python implementation for the F-P growth algorithm is quite simple and is easy to compute using the libraries. In the interest of space, we have uploaded the Jupyter notebook to the GitHub repository of the chapter.

We will now explore another interesting topic: sequence rule mining. It is a very powerful solution that allows a business to tailor its marketing strategies and product recommendations to the customers.

4.7 Sequence rule mining

Consider this: Netflix has a transactional database of all the movies ordered by customers over time. If it analyzes and finds that 65% of customers who viewed a war movie *X* also viewed a romantic comedy *Y* in the following month, then this is very insightful and actionable information. It will allow Netflix to recommend its offerings to customers and customize its marketing strategy.

So far in the chapter, we have covered three algorithms for association rules. But all the data points were limited to the same dataset, and there was no sequencing involved. Sequential pattern mining allows us to analyze a dataset that has a sequence of events happening. By analyzing the dataset, we can find statistically relevant patterns, which allows us to decipher the entire sequence of events. Obviously, the sequence of events is in a particular order, which is a very important property to be considered during sequence rule mining.

> **NOTE**   Sequence rule mining is different from time-series analysis. To learn more about time-series analysis, refer to the appendix.

Sequence rule mining is utilized across multiple domains and functions. It can be used in biology to extract information during DNA sequencing, or it can be used to understand the online search pattern of a user. Sequence rule mining would help us understand what the user is going to search next. During the discussion of association rules, we used the transactions in which milk, bread, and eggs were purchased in the same transaction. Sequence rule mining is an extension to that wherein we analyze consecutive transactions and try to decipher the sequence present, if any.

While studying the Sequential Pattern Discovery Using Equivalence classes (SPADE) algorithm, we cover the mathematical concepts that form the base of the algorithm. These concepts are a little tricky and might require more than one reading to grasp.

4.7.1   *Sequential Pattern Discovery Using Equivalence*

We now explore sequence rule mining using SPADE. It was suggested by Mohammed J. Zaki; the link to the paper is at the end of this chapter.

So we wish to analyze a sequence of events. For example, a customer bought a mobile phone and a charger. After a week, they bought earphones, and after two weeks, they bought a mobile phone cover and screen guard. So, in each of the transactions, there were items purchased. And each transaction can be called an event. Let's understand it in more detail.

Let us assume we have the complete list of items for the discussion. It will contain items like i_1, i_2, i_3, i_4, i_5, and so on. So we can write $I = \{i_1, i_2, i_3, i_4, i_5.........., i_n\}$ where we have n distinct items in total.

Items can be anything. If we consider the same example of a grocery store, items can be milk, eggs, cheese, bread, and so on.

An event will be a collection of items in the same transaction. An event can contain items like (i_1, i_5, i_4, i_8). For example, an event can contain items bought in the same transaction (milk, sugar, cheese, bread). We will denote an event by α.

Next, let's understand a sequence. A sequence is nothing but events in an order. In other words, $\alpha_1 \rightarrow \alpha_2 \rightarrow \alpha_3 \rightarrow \alpha_4$ can be termed a sequence of events. For example, (Milk, Cheese) -> (Bread, Eggs) -> (Cheese, Bread, Sugar) -> (Milk, Bread) is a sequence of transactions. It means that in the first transaction, milk and cheese were bought. In the following transaction, bread and eggs were bought, and so on.

A sequence with k items is a k-item sequence. For example, sequence (Milk, Bread) -> (Eggs) contains three items. Now let's explore the SPADE algorithm step by step.

Let's say we have the following sequences generated. In the first sequence, ID 1001, Milk is bought in the very first transaction. In the second one, Milk, Eggs, and Bread are bought. They are followed by Milk and Bread. In the fourth one, only Sugar is purchased. In the fifth and final transaction of sequence 1001, Bread and Apples are purchased; this is applicable to all the respective sequences. For example, in sequence ID 1001, we have multiple events. In the first purchase, Milk is bought. Then (Milk, Eggs, Bread) are bought and so on. See table 4.13.

Table 4.13   The dataset for sequence mining

Sequence ID	Sequence
1001	<(Milk) (Milk, Eggs, Bread) (Milk, Bread) (Sugar) (Bread, Apples)>
1002	<(Milk, Sugar) (Bread) (Eggs, Bread) (Milk, Cheese)>
1003	<(Cheese, Apples) (Milk, Eggs) (Sugar, Apples) (Bread) (Eggs)>
1004	<(Cheese, Bananas) (Milk, Apples) (Bread) (Eggs) (Bread)>

Table 4.13 can be converted into a vertical data format as shown in table 4.14. In this step, we calculate the frequencies for one-sequence items, which are sequences with only one item. For this, only a single database scan is required. We simply have the sequence ID and element ID for each of the items.

Table 4.14   Vertical format for table 4.13

Sequence ID	Element ID	Items
1001	1	Milk
1001	2	Milk, Eggs, Bread
1001	3	Milk, Bread
1001	4	Sugar
1001	5	Bread, Apples
1002	1	Milk, Sugar
1002	2	Bread
1002	3	Eggs, Bread
1002	4	Milk, Cheese
1003	1	Cheese, Apples
1003	2	Milk, Eggs
1003	3	Sugar, Apples
1003	4	Bread

Table 4.14   Vertical format for table 4.13 *(continued)*

Sequence ID	Element ID	Items
1003	5	Eggs
1004	1	Cheese, Bananas
1004	2	Milk, Apples
1004	3	Bread
1004	4	Eggs
1004	5	Bread

Table 4.14 is nothing but a vertical tabular representation of table 4.13. For example, in sequence ID 1001, at the element ID 1 we have Milk. For sequence ID 1001, at the element ID 2 we have Milk, Eggs, Bread, and so on.

For the purpose of explanation, we are considering only two items—0 Milk and Eggs—and the support threshold of 2.

Then, in the next step, we will break it down for each of the items. For example, Milk appears in sequence ID 1001 and element ID 1, sequence ID 1001 and element ID 2, sequence ID 1001 and element ID 3, sequence ID 1002 and element ID 1, and so on. It results in a table like table 4.15 where we have shown Milk and Eggs. It needs to be applied to all the items in the dataset.

Table 4.15   Respective sequence IDs for Milk and Eggs

Milk		Eggs	
Sequence ID	Element ID	Sequence ID	Element ID
1001	1	1001	2
1001	2	1002	3
1001	3	1003	2
1002	1	1003	5
1002	4	1004	4
1003	2		
1004	2		

Now we wish to count two sequences or those with two-item sequences. We can have two sequences: either Milk -> Eggs or Eggs -> Milk. Let's first take Milk -> Eggs.

For Milk -> Eggs, we need to have Milk in front of Eggs. For the same sequence ID, if the element ID of Milk is less than the element ID of Eggs, then it is an eligible sequence. In the preceding example, for sequence ID 1001, the element ID of Milk is 1, while the element ID of Eggs is 2. So we can add that as the first eligible pair, as shown in the first row of table 4.16. The same is true for sequence ID 1002. In table 4.15, row 4, we have sequence ID 1002. The element ID of Milk is 1, while that of Eggs in row 2 is 3. Again, the element ID of Milk is lesser than the element ID of Eggs, so it becomes the second entry, and the process continues. The key point is to have the same sequence ID while comparing the respective element IDs of Milk and Eggs.

Table 4.16   Sequence for Milk and Eggs

Milk and Eggs		
Sequence ID	Element ID (Milk)	Element ID (Eggs)
1001	1	2
1002	1	3
1003	2	5
1004	2	4

By using the same logic, we can create the table for Eggs -> Milk, which is shown in table 4.17. Again, the key point is to have the same sequence ID while comparing the respective element IDs of Milk and Eggs.

Table 4.17   Sequence for Eggs and Milk

Eggs and Milk		
Sequence ID	Element ID (Eggs)	Element ID (Milk)
1001	2	3
1002	3	4

This can be done for each of the possible combinations. We now move to creating three-item sequences, and we will create Milk, Eggs -> Milk. For this purpose, we have to join the two tables. See table 4.18.

Table 4.18   Combining the sequence Milk -> Eggs and Eggs -> Milk to join the tables

Milk and Eggs			Eggs and Milk		
Sequence ID	Element ID (Milk)	Element ID (Eggs)	Sequence ID	Element ID (Eggs)	Element ID (Milk)
1001	1	2	1001	2	3
1002	1	3	1002	3	4
1003	2	5			
1004	2	4			

The logic of joining is matching the sequence ID and the element ID. We have high-lighted the matching ones in red and green, respectively, although this will not show up in the printed book. For sequence ID 1001, the element ID of Eggs in the left table matches the element ID of Eggs in the right table, and that becomes the first entry of table 4.19, which shows the results. Similarly, for sequence ID 1002, element ID 3 matches.

Table 4.19   Final table after we have analyzed all the combinations for the items

Milk, Eggs -> Milk			
Sequence ID	Element ID (Milk)	Element ID (Eggs)	Element ID (Milk)
1001	1	2	3
1002	1	3	4

This process continues. The algorithm stops when no frequent sequences can be found.

We will now implement SPADE on a dataset using Python. We use the `pyspade` library, and thus we have to load the dataset and call the function. It generates the result for us. The support is kept as 0.6 here, and then we print the results (see figure 4.23):

```
from pycspade.helpers import spade, print_result
spade_result = spade(filename='SPADE_dataset.txt', support=0.6, parse=True)
print_result(spade_result)
```

```
[17]: print_result(spade_result)

         Occurs   Accum  Support   Confid      Lift
Sequence
           88       88 0.7927928      N/A       N/A
(10)
           68       68 0.6126126 0.7727273 0.8168831
(10)->(6)
           67       67 0.6036036 0.7613636 0.7825126
(10)->(9)
           88       88 0.7927928      N/A       N/A
(3)
           71       71 0.6396396 0.8068182 0.8292298
(3)->(9)
          102      560 0.9189189      N/A       N/A
(4)
           79       79 0.7117117 0.7745098 0.8428489
(4)->(4)
           77       77 0.6936937 0.7549020 0.7980392
(4)->(5)
           83       83 0.7477477 0.8137255 0.8602241
(4)->(6)
           80       80 0.7207207 0.7843137 0.8136339
(4)->(7)
           77       77 0.6936937 0.7549020 0.7831226
(4)->(8)
           83       83 0.7477477 0.8137255 0.8363290
(4)->(9)
```

Figure 4.23   SPADE implemented on the pyspade library using Python

4.8   Case study for association rules

Association rule mining is quite a helpful and powerful solution. Next, we are going to solve an actual case study using association rules. Recall that, at the start of the chapter, we suggested you study the pattern of a grocery store. What is the logic of such arrangements in the store?

Consider this: you are working for a grocery retailer like Walmart, Tesco, Spar, Marks & Spencer's, etc., and you are planning the visual layout of a new store. Obviously, it is imperative that retail stores utilize the space in the store wisely and to the maximum capacity. At the same time, it is vital that the movement of the customers is not hindered. Customers should have access to all the items on display and be able to navigate easily. You might have experienced some stores where you feel choked and bombarded with displays while others are neatly stacked.

How do we solve this problem? There can be multiple solutions. Some retailers might wish to group the items based on their categories. For example, they might want to keep all the baking products on one shelf or use some other condition. We are studying the machine learning example here.

Using market basket analysis, we can generate the rules that indicate the respective relationships between various items. We can predict which items are frequently bought together, and they can be kept together in the store. For example, if we know that milk and bread are bought together, then bread can be kept near the milk counter. The customer purchasing milk can locate bread easily and continue with their purchase.

But it is not as easy as it sounds. Let us solve this case step by step:

1   *Business problem definition*—The very first step is defining the business problem, which is clear to us. We wish to discover the relationships between various items so that the arrangement in the store can be made better. Here, *planograms* come into the picture. Planograms help the retailer plan the utilization of the space in the store in a wise manner so that the customer can also navigate and access the products easily. It can be considered a visual layout of the store. An example is shown in figure 4.24.

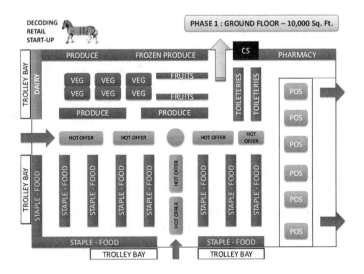

Figure 4.24   An example of a planogram. Planograms are very useful for visual merchandising.

In the figure, we can see that there are specific areas for each item category. Association rules are quite insightful to help generate directions for planograms.

2 *Data discovery*—The next step is data discovery, wherein the historical transactions are scouted and loaded into a database. Typically, a transaction can look like table 4.20. Note it is quite a challenge to convert this data format into one that can be consumed by the association rule algorithms.

Table 4.20   Example of invoices generated in a real-world retail store

Invoice number	Date	Items	Amount
1001	01-Jun-21	Milk, Eggs, Cheese, Bread	$10
1002	01-Jun-21	Bread, Bananas, Apples, Butter	$15
1003	01-Jun-21	Butter, Carrots, Cheese, Eggs, Bread, Milk, Bananas	$19
1004	01-Jun-21	Milk	$1
1005	01-Jun-21	Bread	$0.80

3 *Data preparation*—This step perhaps is the most difficult step. As we have seen, association rules model creation is a very simple task. We have libraries that can do the heavy lifting for us. But the dataset expected by them is in a particular format. This is a tedious task; it is quite time-consuming and requires a lot of data preprocessing skills.

There are a few considerations you should keep in mind while preparing the dataset:

– Sometimes we get NULL or blank values during the data preparation phase. Missing values in the datasets can lead to problems while computing. In other machine learning solutions, we would advise to treat the missing values. In the case of association rules, we suggest ignoring the respective transactions and not considering them in the final dataset.

– Many times, we get junk values in the data. Special characters like !@%^&*()_ are found in the datasets. This can be attributed to incorrect entries in the system. Hence, data cleaning is required. We cover the data preprocessing step in detail in chapter 11, wherein we deal with NULL values and junk values.

– Converting a table into a format that can be understood and consumed by the association rule learning algorithms is an imperative but arduous step. Go through the concept of SQL pivoting to understand the concept better.

4 *Model preparation*—Perhaps the easiest of the steps is modeling. We have already solved Python solutions for different algorithms, so you should be quite comfortable with it.

5 *Model interpretation*—Creating the model might be easy, but interpretation of the rules is not. Sometimes, you have rules like #NA -> (Milk, Cheese). Such a rule is obviously not usable and does not make any sense. It indicates that the data preparation was not correct and some junk values are still present in the dataset. Another example is (Some items) -> (Packaging material); this is perhaps the most obvious rule but, again, not usable. This rule indicates that whenever shopping is done, packaging material is also purchased. That's obvious, right? A final example is (Potatoes, Tomatoes) -> (Onions). This kind of rule might look correct, but it is a common-sense fact that the retailer would already know. Obviously, most of the customers who are buying vegetables will buy potatoes, tomatoes, and onions together. Such rules might not add much value to the business.

The threshold for support, confidence, lift, and conviction allows us to filter out the most important rules. We can sort the rules in the descending order of the lift and then remove the most obvious ones.

It is of vital importance that business stakeholders and subject matter experts are involved at every step. In this case study, the operations team, visual merchandising team, product teams, and marketing teams are the key players, which should be closely aligned at each step.

6 *Improving the planogram*—Once the rules are generated and accepted, then we can use them to improve the planogram for the retail space. The retailer can use them to improve the marketing strategy and improve product promotions. For example, if a rule like (A, B) -> (C) is accepted, the retailer might wish to create a bundle of the products and sell them as a single entity. It will increase the average number of items purchased in the same transaction for the business.

This case study can be extended to any other domain or business function. For example, the same steps can be used if we wish to examine user's movement across web pages. Web developers can analyze the historical clicks and usages of the customers on their websites. By identifying the patterns, they can find out what users tend to click and which features will maximize their engagement. Medical practitioners can use association rules to better diagnose patients. The doctors can compare the probability of the symptoms in relationship with other symptoms and provide a more accurate diagnosis.

4.9 Concluding thoughts

There are some assumptions and limitations in the association rules and sequence rules we have studied:

- The respective significance of an item is ignored while we generate the rules. For example, if a customer purchased five cans of milk and 1 kg of apples in a transaction, it is treated similarly to an invoice in which one can of milk and 5 kg of apples are purchased. Hence, we should bear in mind that the respective *weight* of an item is not being considered.

- The cost of an item indicates the perceived value of a product. Some products that are costly are more important, and hence, if they are purchased by the customer, more revenue can be generated. While analyzing the invoices, we ignore the cost associated with an item.

- While analyzing the sequence, we have not considered the respective time periods between the two transactions. For example, if between T1 and T2 there were 10 days while between T2 and T3 there were 40 days, both are considered as the same.

- In all the analyses, we have considered different categories as the same. Perishable items and nonperishable items are treated in a similar fashion. For example, fresh milk with a shelf life of two to three days is treated similarly to washing powder, which has a much longer shelf life.

- Many times, we receive noninteresting rules after analysis. These results are from common sense (Potatoes, Tomatoes) -> (Onion). Such rules are not of much use. We face such a problem a lot of the time.

- While noninteresting rules are a challenge, a huge number of discovered rules are again one of the problems. We get hundreds of rules, and it becomes difficult to understand and analyze each one of them. Here the thresholding becomes handy.

- The time and memory requirements for computations are huge. The algorithms require scanning the datasets many times, and hence it is quite a time-consuming exercise.

- The rules generated are dependent on the dataset that has been used for analysis. For example, if we analyze the dataset generated during summers only, we cannot use the rules for winters as consumers' preferences change between different weather conditions. Moreover, we should refresh the algorithms over time since with the passage of time, the macro- and micro-economic factors change and hence the algorithms should be refreshed too.

There are some other algorithms that are also of interest. For association rules, we can have multirelation association rules, k-optimal pattern discovery, approximate frequent datasets, generalized association rules, high-order pattern discovery, etc. For sequence mining, we have Generalized Sequence Pattern, FreeSpan, PrefixSpan, mining associated patterns, etc. These algorithms are quite interesting and can be studied for knowledge enhancement.

Association rules and sequence mining are quite interesting topics. Various business domains and functions are increasingly using association rules to understand the pattern of events. These insights allow the teams to make sound and scientific decisions to improve the customer experience and overall engagement. In this chapter, we have explored association rules and sequence mining. These were studied using Apriori, F-P, and ECLAT algorithms, and for sequence mining we used SPADE.

4.10   *Practical next steps and suggested readings*

The following provides suggestions for what to do next and offers some helpful reading:

- Go through these research papers for the association rules algorithm:
  - Fast Discovery of Association Rules: https://mng.bz/eyqv
  - Fast Algorithms for Mining Association Rules: https://mng.bz/64GZ
  - Efficient Analysis of Pattern and Association Rule Mining Approaches: https://arxiv.org/pdf/1402.2892.pdf
  - A Review of Association Rule Mining Techniques with Respect to their Privacy-Preserving Capabilities: https://mng.bz/0Q0N
- For sequence mining, go through these research papers:
  - SPADE: An Efficient Algorithm for Mining Frequent Sequences: https://mng.bz/9YG7
  - Sequential Mining: Patterns and Algorithm Analysis: https://arxiv.org/pdf/1311.0350.pdf
  - Sequential Pattern Mining Algorithm Based on Interestingness: https://ieeexplore.ieee.org/document/8567170
  - A New Approach for Problem of Sequential Pattern Mining: https://mng.bz/jpxr

Summary

- Association rule learning identifies relationships between variables in datasets, like the beer and diaper example.
- Through data analysis, such associations can inform marketing strategies, product placement, and pricing in supermarkets.
- Market basket analysis in retail uses association rules to find buying patterns and is applicable in other industries like bioinformatics.
- Association rules consist of antecedents leading to consequents, denoted as P -> Q, with no common elements between them.
- Rule significance depends on support (frequency), confidence (accuracy), lift (dependence measurement), and conviction.
- High support, confidence, lift, and conviction indicate stronger, more useful rules.
- The Apriori algorithm generates item sets for association rules using a "bottom-up" approach but faces challenges with large datasets.
- The ECLAT algorithm uses a depth-first search for faster, memory-efficient computation of frequent item sets.
- The F-P growth algorithm improves on Apriori by using a frequent pattern tree to eliminate candidate generation.

- Sequence rule mining helps explain user behavior over time, distinct from time-series analysis.
- The SPADE algorithm analyzes sequences of events and dependencies over time for sequence rule mining.
- Python implementations of the Apriori, ECLAT, F-P growth, and SPADE algorithms are achievable with appropriate libraries.
- Evaluation metrics and threshold settings for support, confidence, and lift are crucial for efficient rule generation.
- Sequence rule mining has applications in marketing, bioinformatics, and user interaction analysis, allowing for actionable insights.

Clustering

5

This chapter covers

- Spectral clustering
- Fuzzy clustering
- Gaussian mixture models clustering

Out of complexity, find simplicity.

—Einstein

Sometimes life is very simple, and sometimes we experience quite complex situations. We sail through both situations and change our approach as needed.

In part 1, we covered the fundamentals to prepare you for the journey ahead. We are now in part 2, which is slightly more complex than part 1. Part 3 will be more advanced than the first two parts. So please give careful attention to the coming chapters, as the skills and knowledge gained here will prepare you for the later chapters in the book.

Before starting this chapter, we should refresh our memory on what we covered in chapter 2. We studied clustering algorithms in part 1 of the book. In chapter 2, we learned that clustering is an unsupervised learning technique where we wish to group the data points by discovering interesting patterns in the datasets. We went through the meaning of clustering solutions and different categories of clustering algorithms and looked at a case study. In that chapter, we explored k-means clustering, hierarchical clustering, and DBSCAN clustering in depth. We went through the mathematical background, process, and Python implementation and the pros and cons of each algorithm.

You may often encounter datasets that do not conform to a simple shape and form. Moreover, we have to find the best fit before making a choice of the final algorithm we wish to implement. Here we might need help with more complex clustering algorithms—the topic of this chapter. In this chapter, we are going to again study three such complex clustering algorithms: spectral clustering, fuzzy clustering, and Gaussian mixture models (GMM) clustering. As always, Python implementation will follow the mathematical and theoretical concepts. This chapter is slightly heavy on mathematical concepts. There is no need to be an advanced student of mathematics, but it is sometimes important to understand how the algorithms work in the background. At the same time, you will be surprised to find that Python implementation of such algorithms is not tedious. This chapter does not have a case study.

Welcome to the fifth chapter, and all the very best!

5.1 Technical toolkit

We will continue to use the same version of Python and Jupyter Notebook as we have used so far. The codes and datasets used in this chapter have been checked in at GitHub (https://mng.bz/6epo).

We are going to use the regular Python libraries we have used so far: `numpy`, `pandas`, `sklearn`, `seaborn`, `matplotlib`, etc. You need to install two other Python libraries in this chapter: `skfuzzy` and `network`. Using libraries, we can implement the algorithms very quickly. Otherwise, coding these algorithms is quite a time-consuming and painstaking task.

Let's get started with a refresh of clustering!

5.2 Clustering: A brief recap

Recall from chapter 2, clustering is used to group similar objects or data points. It is an unsupervised learning technique where we intend to find natural grouping in the data, as shown in figure 5.1.

Here, we can observe that on the left side, we have ungrouped data, and on the right side, the data points have been grouped into logical groups. We can also observe that there can be two methodologies to do the grouping or clustering, and both result in different clusters. Clustering as a technique is quite heavily used in business solutions like customer segmentation, market segmentation, etc.

We learned about k-means and hierarchical and DBSCAN clustering in chapter 2. We also covered various distance measurement techniques and indicators to measure the performance of clustering algorithms. You are advised to revisit the concepts.

In this chapter, we focus on advanced clustering methods. We start with spectral clustering in the next section.

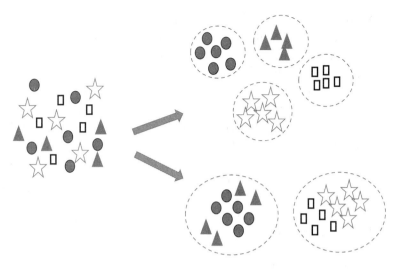

Figure 5.1 Clustering of objected results into natural grouping

5.3 *Spectral clustering*

Spectral clustering is one of the unique clustering algorithms, and a lot of research has been done in this field. Revered researchers include Prof. Andrew Yang, Prof. Michael Jordan, Prof. Yair Weiss, Prof. Jianbo Shi, and Prof. Jitendra Malik, to name a few. We provide links to some of their papers at the end of the chapter.

Spectral clustering works on the affinity and not the absolute location of the data points for clustering. When we consider the absolute location of the points, the similarity is simply based on the distances between the points, whereas affinity considers the similarity between the points. If the affinity is 0 between the points, they are dissimilar, whereas if the affinity is 1, they are very similar. Hence, wherever the data is in complicated shapes (i.e., some kind of special relationship exists between the data points), spectral clustering is the answer. We show a few examples in figure 5.2 where spectral clustering can provide a logical solution.

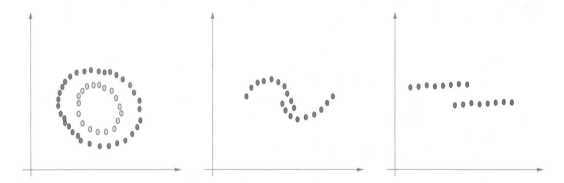

Figure 5.2 Examples of various complex data shapes that can be clustered using spectral clustering

For figure 5.2, we could have used other algorithms like k-means clustering too. But they might not be able to do justice to such complicated shapes of data. You can see from figure 5.2 that the various data points are in a certain pattern. Algorithms like k-means clustering utilize the compactness of the data points and are driven by centroids of the respective clusters. In other words, the closeness of the points to each other and compactness toward the cluster center drive the clustering in k-means. On the other hand, in spectral clustering, *connectivity* is the driving logic. In connectivity, either the data points are immediately close to one another or they are connected in some way. Some examples of such connectivity-based clustering are depicted in figure 5.2. The points in the inner circle belong to one cluster while those in the outer circle belong to another cluster.

Now look at the first diagram in figure 5.3, where the data points are in a doughnut pattern. There can be data points that follow this doughnut pattern. We need to cluster this data, and it is indeed a complex pattern. Imagine that by using a clustering method, the circles inside a square are made a part of the same cluster, which is shown in the middle diagram in figure 5.3. After all, they are close to each other. But if we look closely, the points are in a circle and in a pattern, and hence, the actual cluster should be as shown in the far right diagram in figure 5.3.

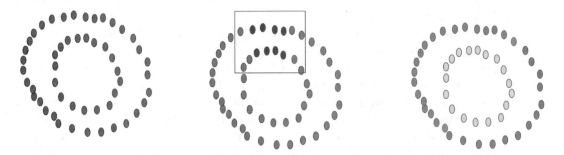

Figure 5.3   We can have a complex representation of data points that need to be clustered. Observe the doughnut shape (left). An explanation can be that the dots in a square are a part of the same cluster as what would be based on the distance only, but clearly, they are not part of the same cluster (middle). We have two circles here. The points in the inner circle belong to one cluster, whereas the outer points belong to another cluster (right).

The example shown in figure 5.3 depicts the advantages of spectral clustering as opposed to k-means clustering. In the second figure, the dots in red (those in the square in the print book) will be incorrectly clustered into a different cluster, and in the third figure, the correct clustering is shown. Spectral clustering may group the data from the inner circle in a separate cluster.

As we said earlier, spectral clustering utilizes the connectivity approach. In spectral clustering, data points that are immediately next to each other are identified in a graph. These data points are sometimes referred to as *nodes*. These data points or nodes are then mapped to a low-dimensional space. A low-dimensional space is one that has a fewer number of input features. During this process, spectral clustering uses eigenvalues, affinity matrix, Laplacian matrix, and degree matrix derived from the dataset. The low-dimensional space can then be segregated into clusters.

> **NOTE**   Spectral clustering utilizes the connectivity approach for clustering. It relies on graph theory, wherein we identify clusters of nodes based on the edges connecting them.

We will study the process in detail. But first, there are a few important mathematical concepts that form the foundation of spectral clustering, which we will cover now.

5.3.1   *Building blocks of spectral clustering*

We know that the goal of clustering is to group data points that are similar into one cluster and the data points that are not similar into another. One important mathematical concept is similarity graphs, which are a representation of data points.

SIMILARITY GRAPHS

A graph is one of the intuitive methods to represent data points. The first diagram in figure 5.4 shows an example of a graph that is simply a connection between data points represented by the edge. Two data points are connected if the similarity between them is positive or it is above a certain threshold, which is shown in the second diagram. Instead of absolute values for the similarity, we can use weights. So in the second diagram in figure 5.4, as point 1 and 2 are similar compared to points 1 and 3, the connection between points 1 and 2 has a higher weight than points 1 and 3.

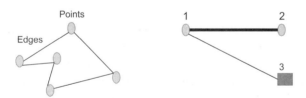

Figure 5.4   A graph is a simple representation of data points. The points or nodes are connected by edges if they are very similar (left). The weight is higher if the similarity between data points is high; for dissimilar data points, the weight is less (right).

So, we can say that, using similarity graphs, we wish to cluster the data points such that the edges of the data points have

- Higher weight values and hence are similar to each other and so are in the same cluster
- Lower values of weight and hence are not similar to each other and so are in different clusters

Apart from similarity graphs, we should also know the concept of eigenvalues and eigenvectors, which we covered in detail in the previous chapter. You are advised to refresh your memory on it should you need to.

ADJACENCY MATRIX

Have a close look at figure 5.5. We can see those various points from 1 to 5 are connected. We represent the connection in a matrix. That matrix is called an *adjacency matrix*. In an adjacency matrix, the rows and columns are the respective nodes. The values inside the matrix represent the connection: if the value is 0, that means there is no connection, and if the value is 1, it means there is a connection.

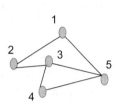

	1	2	3	4	5
1	0	1	0	0	1
2	1	0	1	0	0
3	0	1	0	1	1
4	0	0	1	0	1
5	1	0	1	1	0

Figure 5.5   An adjacency matrix represents the connection between various nodes. There is a connection between node 1 and node 5; hence the value is 1. There is no connection between node 1 and node 4; hence the corresponding value is 0.

So, for an adjacency matrix, we are only concerned if there is a connection between two data points. With the way that we are defining the edges (as nonoriented), the matrix is always symmetric. This is because if there is a connection from 1 to 2, there must also be a connection from 2 to 1, and if there is no connection between 3 and 1, there is no connection between 1 and 3 either. If we extend the concept of the adjacency matrix, we get a degree matrix, which is our next topic.

DEGREE MATRIX

A degree matrix is a diagonal matrix, where the degree of a node along the diagonal is the number of edges connected to it. If we use the same example as previously, we get the degree matrix shown in figure 5.6. Nodes 3 and 5 have three connections each, so they have values of 3 along the diagonal; the other nodes have only two connections each, so they have 2 as the value along the diagonal.

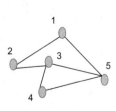

	1	2	3	4	5
1	2	0	0	0	0
2	0	2	0	0	0
3	0	0	3	0	0
4	0	0	0	2	0
5	0	0	0	0	3

Figure 5.6   While an adjacency matrix represents the connection between various nodes, a degree matrix is for the number of connections each node has. It is shown on the diagonal of the matrix. For example, node 5 has three connections and hence has a value of 3 in the adjacency matrix, while node 1 has only two connections and so has a value of 2.

You might be wondering: Why do we use these matrices? Matrices provide an elegant representation of the data and can clearly depict the relationships between two points. Also, computers can more easily deal with matrix representation than alternative ways for manipulating the graph.

Now that we have covered both the adjacency matrix and degree matrix, we can move to the Laplacian matrix.

LAPLACIAN MATRIX

There are quite a few variants of the Laplacian matrix, but if we take the simplest form, it is nothing but a subtraction of the adjacency matrix from the degree matrix—in other words, $L = D - A$. We can demonstrate it as shown in figure 5.7.

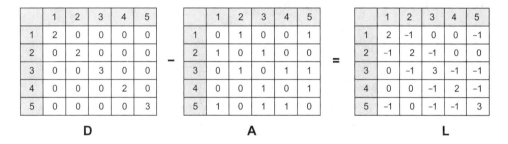

Figure 5.7   The Laplacian matrix is quite simple to understand. To get a Laplacian matrix, we can simply subtract an adjacency matrix from the degree matrix as shown in the example here. Here, D represents the degree matrix, A is the adjacency matrix, and L is the Laplacian matrix.

The Laplacian matrix is an important concept, and we use the eigenvalues of L to develop spectral clustering. Once we get the eigenvalues and eigenvectors, we can define two other values: spectral gap and Fielder value. The very first nonzero eigenvalue is the *spectral gap*, which defines the density of the graph. The *Fielder value* is the second eigenvalue; it provides an approximation of the minimum cut required to separate the graph into two components. The corresponding vector for the Fielder value is called the *Fielder vector*.

> **NOTE** The Fielder vector has both negative and positive components, and their resultant sum is zero.

We will use this concept once we study the process of spectral clustering in detail in the next section. We cover one more concept—the affinity matrix—before moving on to the process of spectral clustering.

AFFINITY MATRIX

In the adjacency matrix, if we replace the number of connections with the similarity of the weights, we will get the affinity matrix. If the points are completely dissimilar, the affinity will be 0; if they are completely similar, the affinity will be 1. The values in the matrix represent different levels of similarity between data points.

> ### Exercise 5.1
> Answer these questions to check your understanding:
>   1 The degree matrix is created by counting the number of connections. True or False?
>   2 Laplacian is a transpose of the division of degree and adjacency matrix. True or False?
>   3 Draw a graph on paper and then derive its adjacency and degree matrix.

5.3.2   *The process of spectral clustering*

Now we have covered all the building blocks for spectral clustering. At a high level, the various steps can be noted as follows:

1 We get the dataset and calculate its degree matrix and adjacency matrix.
2 Using them, we calculate the Laplacian matrix.
3 Then we calculate the first k eigenvectors of the Laplacian matrix. The k eigenvectors are the ones that correspond to the k smallest eigenvalues.
4 The resultant matrix formed is used to cluster the data points in k-dimensional space.

NOTE For more clarity on eigenvalues, the affinity matrix, and the Laplacian matrix, refer to the appendix.

We cover the process of spectral clustering using an example, as shown in figure 5.8. These steps are generally not done in real-world implementation, as we have packages and libraries to achieve them, but they are covered here to give you an idea of how the algorithm can be developed from scratch and how it works so that you have a better understanding on how to effectively utilize it. For the Python solution, we will use the libraries and packages only. Though it is possible to develop an implementation from scratch, it is not time-efficient to reinvent the wheel.

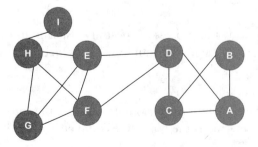

Figure 5.8 Consider the example shown where we have some data points and they are connected. We will perform spectral clustering on this data.

When we wish to perform the spectral clustering on this data, we follow these steps:

1 Create the adjacency matrix and degree matrix. We will leave this step up to you.
2 Create the Laplacian matrix (see figure 5.9).

	A	B	C	D	E	F	G	H	I
A	3	-1	-1	-1	0	0	0	0	0
B	-1	2	-1	0	0	0	0	0	0
C	-1	-1	3	-1	0	0	0	0	0
D	-1	0	-1	4	-1	-1	0	0	0
E	0	0	0	-1	4	-1	-1	-1	0
F	0	0	0	-1	-1	4	-1	-1	0
G	0	0	0	0	-1	-1	4	-1	-1
H	0	0	0	0	-1	-1	-1	3	0
I	0	0	0	0	0	0	-1	0	-1

Figure 5.9   The Laplacian matrix of the data. You are advised to create the degree and adjacency matrix and check the output.

3 Create the Fielder vector, as shown in figure 5.10, for the preceding Laplacian matrix. We create the Fielder vector as described in the Laplacian Matrix section. Observe how the sum of the matrix is zero.

0.33	-0.38
0.33	-0.48
0.33	-0.38
0.33	-0.12
0.33	0.16
0.33	0.30
0.33	0.24
0.33	0.51
0.33	0.16

Figure 5.10   The Fielder vector is the output for the Laplacian matrix.

4 We can see that there are a few positive values and a few negative values. Based on the positive or negative values, we can create two distinct clusters. Figure 5.11 illustrates the process of spectral clustering.

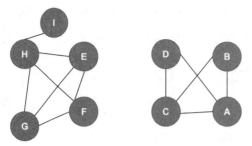

Figure 5.11   The two clusters are identified. This is a very simple example to illustrate the process of spectral clustering.

Spectral clustering is useful for image segmentation, speech analysis, text analytics, entity resolution, etc. The method does not make any assumptions about the shape of the data. Methods like k-means assume that the points are in a spherical form around the center of the cluster, whereas there is no such strong assumption in spectral clustering.

Another significant difference is that in spectral clustering the data points need not have convex boundaries as compared to other methods where compactness drives clustering. Spectral clustering is sometimes slow since various matrices and their eigenvalues, Laplacians, etc., have to be calculated. With a large dataset, the complexity increases, and hence, spectral clustering can become slow, but it is a fast method when we have a sparse dataset.

Spectral clustering requires building a matrix that nominally has the size of the number of items in a dataset squared because there is one column and one row for each element. For example, a modest dataset of a few million elements will require a matrix of several trillion elements! Storing that matrix verbatim requires terabytes of RAM and is something that is at the edge of what a very powerful and expensive server could do. There are techniques to mitigate the memory needs (such as not storing every single element separately), but they make working with the matrix more complicated. Moreover, finding the eigenvalues and even one eigenvector of such a large matrix is very time-intense. As such, spectral clustering is a viable approach generally for small datasets.

We will now proceed to the Python solution of the spectral clustering algorithm.

5.4   *Python implementation of spectral clustering*

We have covered the details of spectral clustering—it is time to get into the code. For this, we will create an artificial dataset and run a k-means algorithm and then spectral clustering to compare the results. The steps are as follows:

1 Import all the necessary libraries. These libraries are standard, except for a few that we will cover. `sklearn` is one of the most famous and sought-after libraries, and from `sklearn` we import `SpectralClustering`, `make_blobs`, and `make_circles`:

```
from sklearn.cluster import SpectralClustering
from sklearn.datasets import make_blobs
import matplotlib.pyplot as plt
```

```
from sklearn.datasets import make_circles
from numpy import random
import numpy as np
from sklearn.cluster import SpectralClustering, KMeans
from sklearn.metrics import pairwise_distances
from matplotlib import pyplot as plt
import networkx as nx
import seaborn as sns
```

2 Curate a dataset. We will use the `make_circles` method. Here, we take 2,000 samples and represent them in a circle. The output is as follows (see figure 5.12):

```
data, clusters = make_circles(n_samples=2000, noise=.01, factor=.3,
    random_state=5)
plt.scatter(data[:,0], data[:,1])
```

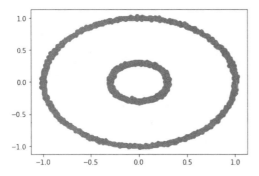

Figure 5.12   Curating a dataset using the `make_circles` method

3 Test this dataset with k-means clustering. The two colors show two different clusters, which overlap each other. The print version of the book will not show the colors, but the output of the Python code will. The same output is available in the GitHub repository (see figure 5.13):

```
kmeans = KMeans(init='k-means++', n_clusters=2)
km_clustering = kmeans.fit(data)
plt.scatter(data[:,0], data[:,1], c=km_clustering.labels_, cmap='prism',
alpha=0.5, edgecolors='g')
```

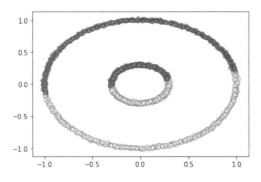

Figure 5.13   Testing the dataset with k-means clustering

4 Run the same data with spectral clustering. We find that the two clusters are being handled separately here (see figure 5.14):

```
spectral = SpectralClustering(n_clusters=2,
    affinity='nearest_neighbors', random_state=5)
sc_clustering = spectral.fit(data)
plt.scatter(data[:,0], data[:,1], c=sc_clustering.labels_,
    cmap='prism', alpha=0.5, edgecolors='g')
```

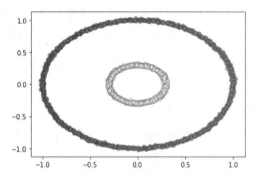

Figure 5.14   **The two clusters are being handled separately when using spectral clustering.**

We can observe here that the same dataset is handled differently by the two algorithms. Spectral clustering handles the dataset arguably better, as the circles that are separate are depicted separately.

5 Simulate various cases by changing the values in the dataset and running the algorithms. Observe the different outputs for comparison.

5.5   *Fuzzy clustering*

So far we have covered quite a few clustering algorithms. Did you wonder why a data point should belong to only one cluster? Why can't a data point belong to more than one cluster? Have a look at figure 5.15: the red points in the right image (shown with an x in the print version) can belong to more than one cluster.

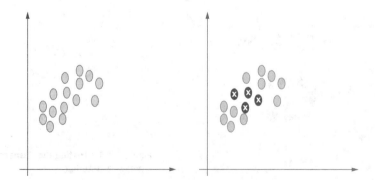

Figure 5.15   **The figure on the left represents all the data points. The red points (those with an x in the print version) can belong to more than one cluster. In fact, we can allocate more than one cluster to each point. A probability score can be given for a point to belong to a particular cluster.**

We know that clustering is used to group items in cohesive groups based on their similarities. The items that are similar are in one cluster, whereas the items that are dissimilar are in different clusters. The idea of clustering is to ensure the items in the same cluster are similar. When the items can be only in one cluster, it is called *hard clustering*. K-means clustering is a classic example of hard clustering. But if we reflect on figure 5.15, we can observe that an item can belong to more than one cluster. This is called *soft clustering*.

> **NOTE**   It is computationally cheaper to create fuzzy boundaries than to create hard clusters.

In fuzzy clustering, an item can be assigned to more than one cluster. The items that are closer to the center of a cluster will have a stronger belongingness to that cluster as compared to the points that are at the edge of the cluster. This is referred to as *membership*. It employs the least-square algorithm to find the most optimal location of an item. The optimal location that we derive from the least-square algorithm will be the probability space between two or more clusters. We will examine this concept in detail later.

5.5.1   *Types of fuzzy clustering*

Fuzzy clustering can be further divided into classical fuzzy algorithms and shape-based fuzzy algorithms. See figure 5.16.

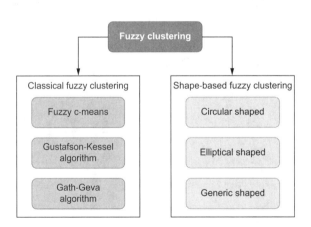

Figure 5.16   Fuzzy algorithms can be divided into the classical fuzzy algorithm and the shape-based fuzzy algorithm.

We will cover the fuzzy c-means (FCM) algorithm in detail next, but first we will review the rest of the algorithms briefly:

- The Gustafson-Kessel algorithm, sometimes called the GK algorithm, works by associating an item with a cluster and a matrix. GK results in elliptical clusters, and to modify as per varied structures in the datasets, GK uses the covariance matrix. It allows the algorithm to capture the elliptical properties of the cluster.

GK can result in narrower clusters, and wherever the number of items is higher, those areas can be thinner.

- The Gath-Geva algorithm is not based on an objective function. The clusters can result in any shape, because it is a fuzzification of statistical estimators.

- The shape-based clustering algorithms are self-explanatory as per their names. A circular fuzzy clustering algorithm will result in circular-shaped clusters and so on.

The FCM algorithm is the most popular fuzzy clustering algorithm. It was initially developed in 1973 by J.C. Dunn, and it has been improved multiple times. It is quite similar to k-means clustering.

Refer to figure 5.17. In the first part of the figure (left), we have some items or data points. These data points can be a part of a clustering dataset like customer transactions, etc. In the second part of the figure (middle), we create a cluster for these data points. While this cluster is created, membership grades are allocated to each of the data points. These membership grades suggest the degree or the level to which a data point belongs to a cluster. We will shortly examine the mathematical function to calculate these values.

TIP Do not get confused by the degree and the probabilities. If we sum these degrees, we may not get 1, as these values are normalized between 0 and 1 for all the items.

In the third part of the figure (right), we can see that point 1 is closer to the cluster center and thus belongs to the cluster to a higher degree than point 2, which is closer to the boundary or the edge of the cluster.

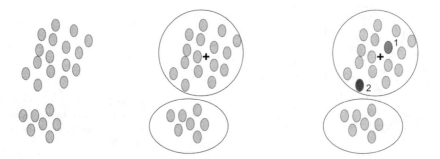

Figure 5.17 Data points that can be clustered (left). The data points can be grouped into two clusters. For the first cluster, the cluster centroid is represented using a + sign (middle). Point 1 is much closer to the cluster center as compared to point 2. So we can conclude that point 1 belongs to this cluster to a higher degree than cluster 2.

We will now venture into the technical details of the algorithm. This can get a little mathematically heavy.

Consider we have a set of n items (equation 5.1):

$$x = \{x_1, x_2, x_3, x_4, x_5, \ldots, x_n\} \tag{5.1}$$

We apply the FCM algorithm to these items. These n items are clustered into c fuzzy clusters based on some criteria. Let's say that we will get from the algorithm a list of c cluster centers (equation 5.2):

$$c = \{c_1, c_2, c_3, c_4, c_5, \ldots, c_c\} \tag{5.2}$$

The algorithm also returns a partition matrix, which can be defined as equation 5.3:

$$W = w_{i,j} \in [0, 1], i = 1, \ldots, n, j = 1, \ldots, c \tag{5.3}$$

Here, each of the elements in $w_{i,j}$ is the degree to which each of the elements in X belong to cluster c_j. This is the purpose of the partition matrix.

Mathematically, we can get $w_{i,j}$ as shown in equation 5.4. The proof of the equation is beyond the scope of this book.

$$w_{i,j} = \frac{1}{\sum_{k=1}^{c} \left(\frac{\|x_i - c_j\|}{\|x_i - c_k\|} \right)^{\frac{2}{m-1}}} \tag{5.4}$$

The algorithm generates centroids for the clusters too. The centroid of a cluster is the mean of all the points in that cluster, and the mean is weighted by their respective degrees of belonging to that cluster. If we represent it mathematically, we can write it like in equation 5.5:

$$c_k = \frac{\sum_x w_k(x)^m x}{\sum_x w_k(x)^m} \tag{5.5}$$

In equations 5.4 and 5.5, we have a very important term: m. m is the hyperparameter used to control the fuzziness of the clusters. The values of $m \geq 1$ and can be kept as 2 (a typically used value).

NOTE The higher the value of m, the fuzzier the clusters.

We now examine the step-by-step process in the FCM algorithm:

1 Start as we start in k-means clustering by choosing the number of clusters we wish to have in the output.
2 Allocate the weights randomly to each of the data points.
3 The algorithm iterates until it has converged. Recall how the k-means algorithm converges, wherein we initiate the process by randomly allocating the centroids of clusters. And then iteratively we refine the centroids for each of the clusters until we get convergence. This is how k-means works. For FCM, we will utilize a similar process albeit with slight differences. We have added a membership value $w_{i,j}$ and m.

4 For FCM, for the algorithm to converge we calculate the centroid for each of the clusters as per equation 5.6:

$$c_k = \frac{\sum_x w_k(x)^m x}{\sum_x w_k(x)^m}$$

(5.6)

5 For each of the data points, we also calculate its respective coefficient for being in that particular cluster. We will use equation 5.4.

6 Now we should iterate until the FCM algorithm has converged. The cost function that we wish to minimize is given by equation 5.7:

$$\text{Objective function} = \arg\min_c \sum_{i=1}^{n} \sum_{j=1}^{c} w_{i,j}^m \|\mathbf{x}_i - \mathbf{c}_j\|^2$$

(5.7)

Once this function has been minimized, we can conclude that the FCM algorithm has converged. In other words, we can stop the process as the algorithm has finished processing.

This is a good time to compare this with the k-means algorithm. In k-means, we have a strict objective function that will allow only one cluster membership, while for FCM clustering, we can get different clustering membership based on the probability scores.

FCM is very useful for business cases where the boundary between clusters is not clear and stringent. Consider the field of bioinformatics, wherein a gene can belong to more than one cluster of genes. Another example is when we have overlapping datasets like in the fields of the marketing analytics or image segmentation where we might have a lot of complex, overlapping, and confusing datasets. FCM can give comparatively more robust results than k-means.

We will now proceed to the Python solution of FCM clustering using the libraries.

Exercise 5.2

Answer these questions to check your understanding:

1 Fuzzy clustering allows us to create overlapping clusters. True or False?
2 A data point can belong to one and only one cluster. True or False?
3 If the value of *m* is lower, we get clusters with more precise boundaries. True or False?

5.5.2 *Python implementation of FCM*

We have covered the process of FCM. We will now work on the Python implementation of FCM by following these steps:

1 Import the necessary libraries:

```
import skfuzzy as fuzz
import pandas as pd
import numpy as np
import matplotlib.pyplot as plt
```

```
import seaborn as sns
%matplotlib inline
```

2 Declare a color palette, which will be used later for color coding the clusters:

```
color_pallete = ['r','m','y','c', 'brown', 'orange','m','k',
'gray','purple','seagreen']
```

3 Define the cluster centers:

```
cluster_centers = [[1, 1],
            [2, 4],
            [5, 8]]
```

4 Assign the weights:

```
sigmas = [[0.5, 0.6],
          [0.4, 0.5],
          [0.1, 0.6]]
```

5 Set the seed and then loop through the cluster centers:

```
np.random.seed(5)

xpts = np.zeros(1)
ypts = np.zeros(1)
labels = np.zeros(1)
for i, ((xmu, ymu), (xsigma, ysigma)) in enumerate(zip(cluster_centers,
sigmas)):
    xpts = np.hstack((xpts, np.random.standard_normal(500) * xsigma + xmu))
    ypts = np.hstack((ypts, np.random.standard_normal(500) * ysigma + ymu))
    labels = np.hstack((labels, np.ones(500) * i))
```

6 We will represent the data points first. See figure 5.18:

```
fig0, ax0 = plt.subplots()
for label in range(5):
    ax0.plot(xpts[labels == label], ypts[labels == label], '.')
ax0.set_title('Data set having 500 points.')
plt.show()
```

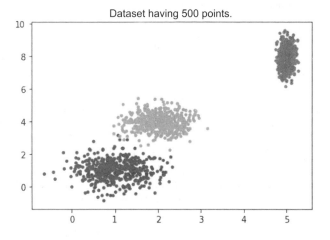

**Figure 5.18
Representation of
the data points**

7 Iterate different outputs with different values of cluster values and FPC (see figure 5.19):

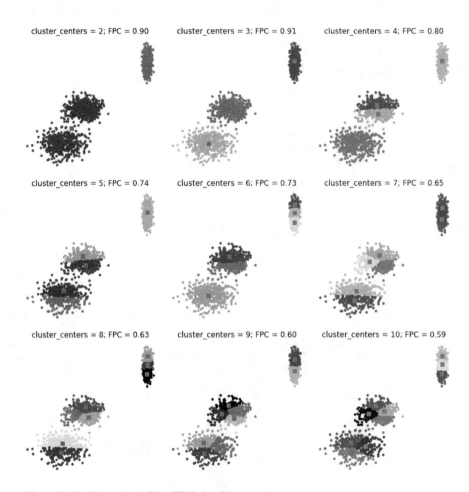

Figure 5.19   The output of the FCM algorithm

```
fig1, axes1 = plt.subplots(3, 3, figsize=(10, 10))
alldata = np.vstack((xpts, ypts))
fpcs = []

for ncenters, ax in enumerate(axes1.reshape(-1), 2):
    cntr, u, u0, d, jm, p, fpc = fuzz.cluster.cmeans(
        alldata, ncenters, 2, error=0.005, maxiter=1000, init=None)

    # Store fpc values for later
    fpcs.append(fpc)

    # Plot assigned clusters, for each data point in training set
    cluster_membership = np.argmax(u, axis=0)
    for j in range(ncenters):
```

```
        ax.plot(xpts[cluster_membership == j],
                ypts[cluster_membership == j], '.', color=colors[j])

    # Mark the center of each fuzzy cluster
    for pt in cntr:
        ax.plot(pt[0], pt[1], 'rs')

    ax.set_title('cluster_centers = {0}; FPC =
    {1:.2f}'.format(ncenters,
fpc), size=12)
    ax.axis('off')

fig1.tight_layout()
```

Observe the output of the code, where for the same datasets you can see the different clusters with different positions of the centers. To appreciate the colors, you will have to run the code.

5.6 Gaussian mixture model

Next, we continue our discussion of soft clustering. Recall we introduced the GMM at the start of the chapter. Now we will study the concept and see the Python implementation of it.

First, let's get an understanding of the *Gaussian distribution* or what is sometimes called *normal distribution*. You might recognize it as a bell curve; it usually refers to the same thing.

In figure 5.20, observe that the distribution where the μ (mean) is 0 and σ^2 (standard deviation) is 1. It is a perfect normal distribution curve. Compare the distribution in different curves here.

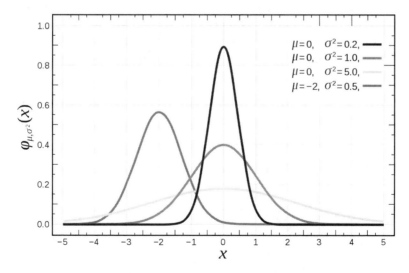

Figure 5.20 A Gaussian distribution is one of the most famous distributions. Observe how the values of mean and standard deviation are changed and their effect on the corresponding curve.

168

CHAPTER 5 *Clustering*

The mathematical expression for Gaussian distribution is

$$f(x) = \frac{1}{\sigma\sqrt{2\pi}}e^{-\frac{1}{2}\left(\frac{x-\mu}{\sigma}\right)^2}$$

$f(x)$ = probability density function **(5.8)**

σ = standard deviation

μ = mean

The equation is also called the probability density function. In figure 5.20, observe the shape of the probability distribution where the μ is 0 and σ^2 is 1. It is a perfect normal distribution curve. Compare the distribution in different curves in figure 5.20 where, by changing the values of the mean and standard distribution, we get different graphs.

You might be wondering why we are using Gaussian distribution here. There is a very famous statistical theorem called the *central limit theorem*. The theorem states that if the variability of the data is due to a large number of unrelated causes, then the distribution can be approximated by a Gaussian curve. Also, the approximation becomes more and more accurate the more data is collected; that is, the more data we collect, the more Gaussian the distribution. This normal distribution can be observed across all walks of life and in chemistry, physics, mathematics, biology, or any other branch of science. That is the beauty of Gaussian distribution.

The plot shown in figure 5.20 is 2D. We can have multidimensional Gaussian distribution too. In the case of a multidimensional Gaussian distribution, we will get a 3D figure as shown in figure 5.21. Our input was a scalar in 1D. Now, instead of scalar, our input is a vector; the mean is also a vector and represents the center of the data. Hence, the mean has the same dimensionality as the input data. The variance is now the covariance matrix Σ. This matrix not only tells us the variance in the inputs but also comments on the relationship between different variables—for example, how the values of y are affected if the value of x is changed. Have a look at figure 5.21. We can understand the relationship between the x and y variables here.

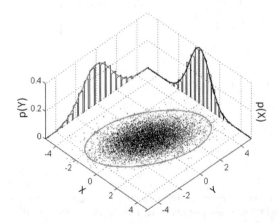

Figure 5.21 3D representation of a Gaussian distribution

NOTE Covariance plays a significant role here. K-means does not consider the covariance of a dataset, which is used in the GMM model.

Let's examine the process of GMM clustering. Imagine we have a dataset with n items. When we use GMM clustering, we do not find the clusters using the centroid method; instead, we fit a set of k Gaussian distributions to the dataset at hand. In other words, we have k clusters. We should determine the parameters for each of these Gaussian distributions, which are mean, variance, and weight of a cluster. Once the parameters for each of the distributions are determined, then we can find the respective probability for each of the n items to belong to k clusters.

Mathematically, we can calculate the probability as shown in equation 5.9. The equation is used so we know that a particular point x is a linear combination of k Gaussians. The term ϕ_j is used to represent the strength of the Gaussian, and it can be seen in the second equation that the sum of such strength is equal to 1.

$$p(x) = \sum_{j=1}^{k} \phi_j \mathcal{N}(x; \mu_j, \Sigma_j)$$

$$\sum_{j=1}^{k} \phi_j = 1$$

(5.9)

For spectral clustering, we must identify the values of ϕ, Σ, and μ. As you can imagine, getting the values of these parameters can be tricky. It is indeed a slightly complex process called the expectation-maximization (EM) technique, which we will cover next. This section is quite heavy on mathematical concepts and is optional. It is recommended for readers interested in understanding the deeper workings of the techniques.

5.6.1 EM technique

EM is a statistical method to determine the correct parameters for a model. There are quite a few techniques that are popular; maximum likelihood estimation might be the most famous. But at the same time, there could be a few challenges with maximum likelihood. The dataset might have missing values or, in other words, be incomplete. Or it is possible that a point in the dataset is generated by two different Gaussian distributions. Hence, it will be very difficult to determine which distribution generated that data point. Here, EM can be helpful.

NOTE K-means uses only mean while GMM utilizes both mean and variance of the data.

The variables that are generated in the process are called *latent variables*. Since we do not know the exact values of these latent variables, EM first estimates their optimum values using the current data. Once this is done, then the model parameters are estimated. Using these model parameters, the latent variables are again determined. And, using these new latent variables, new model parameters are derived. The process continues until a good enough set of latent values and model parameters are achieved that fit the data well. Let's study that in more detail now. We will use the same example as in the last section.

Imagine we have a dataset with n items. As mentioned, when we use GMM clustering, we do not find the clusters using the centroid method; instead, we fit a set of k Gaussian distributions to the dataset at hand. In other words, we have k clusters. We determine the parameters for each of these Gaussian distributions (mean, variance, and weight). Let's say that mean is $\mu_1, \mu_2, \mu_3, \mu_4\ldots. \mu_k$ and covariance is $\Sigma_1, \Sigma_2, \Sigma_3, \Sigma_4\ldots.\Sigma_k$. We can also have one more parameter to represent the density or strength of the distribution, and it can be represented by ϕ.

We start with the expectation, or the E step. In this step, each data point is assigned to a cluster probabilistically. So, for each point, we calculate its probability of belonging to a cluster; if this value is high, the point is in the correct cluster; otherwise, the point is in the wrong cluster. In other words, we calculate the probability that each data point is generated by each of the k Gaussians.

NOTE Since we are calculating probabilities, these are called soft assignments.

The probability is calculated using the formula in equation 5.10. If we look closely, the numerator is the probability, and then we normalize by the denominator.

$$W_j^{(i)} = \frac{\phi_j \mathcal{N}(x^{(i)}; \mu_j, \Sigma_j)}{\sum_{q=1}^{k} \phi_q \mathcal{N}(x^{(i)}; \mu_q, \Sigma_q)} \tag{5.10}$$

In the expectation step, for a data point $x_{i,j}$, where i is the row and j is the column, we are getting a matrix where rows are represented by the data points and columns are their respective Gaussian values.

When the expectation step is finished, we will perform the maximization or the M step. In this step, we will update the values of μ, Σ, and ϕ using the formula in equation 5.7. Recall, in k-means clustering, we simply take the mean of the data points and move ahead. We do something similar here albeit use the probability or the expectation we calculated in the last step.

The three values can be calculated using the equations below. Equation 5.7 is the calculation of the covariances Σ_j, of all the points, which is then weighted by the probability of that point being generated by Gaussian j as shown in equation 5.11. The mathematical proofs are beyond the scope of this book.

$$\Sigma_j = \frac{\sum_{i=1}^{N} W_j^{(i)} \left(x^{(i)} - \mu_j\right) \left(x^{(i)} - \mu_j\right)^T}{\sum_{i=1}^{N} W_j^{(i)}} \tag{5.11}$$

The mean μ_j, is determined by equation 5.12. Here, we determine the mean for all the points, weighted by the probability of that point being generated by Gaussian j.

$$\mu_j = \frac{\sum_{i=1}^{N} W_j^{(i)} x^{(i)}}{\sum_{i=1}^{N} W_j^{(i)}} \tag{5.12}$$

Similarly, the density or the strength is calculated by equation 5.13, where we add all the probabilities for each point to be generated by Gaussian j and then divide by the total number of points N.

$$\phi_j = \frac{1}{N} \sum_{i=1}^{N} W_j^{(i)} \tag{5.13}$$

Based on these values, new values for Σ, μ, and ϕ are derived, and the process continues until the model converges. We stop when we can maximize the log-likelihood function.

It is a complex mathematical process. We have covered it to give you an in-depth understanding of what happens in the background of the statistical algorithm. The Python implementation is much more straightforward than the mathematical concept.

Exercise 5.3

Answer these questions to check your understanding:

1 Gaussian distribution has a mean equal to 1 and a standard deviation equal to 0. True or False?
2 GMM models do not consider the covariance of the data. True or False?

5.6.2 *Python implementation of GMM*

We will first import the data, and then we will compare the results using k-means and GMM. We follow these steps:

1 Import all the libraries and the dataset:

```
import pandas as pd
data = pd.read_csv('vehicle.csv')
import matplotlib.pyplot as plt
```

2 Drop any NA from the dataset:

```
data = data.dropna()
```

3 Fit a `kmeans` algorithm. We are keeping the number of clusters as 5. Please note that we are not saying that this is an ideal number of clusters. The number of

clusters is only for illustrative purposes. We declare a variable k-means and then use five clusters. The dataset is fit next:

```
from sklearn.cluster import KMeans
kmeans = KMeans(n_clusters=5)
kmeans.fit(data)
```

4 Plot the clusters. First, a prediction is made on the dataset, and then the values are added to the data frame as a new column. The data is then plotted with different colors representing different clusters. The print version of the book will not show the different colors, but the output of the Python code will. The same output is available in the GitHub repository.

  The output is as follows (see figure 5.22):

```
pred = kmeans.predict(data)
frame = pd.DataFrame(data)
frame['cluster'] = pred

color=['red','blue','orange', 'brown', 'green']
for k in range(0,5):
    data = frame[frame["cluster"]==k]
    plt.scatter(data["compactness"],data["circularity"],c=color[k])
plt.show()
```

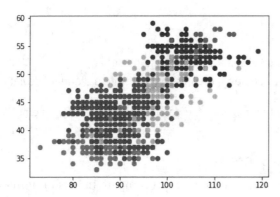

Figure 5.22   Outcome of plotting the clusters after fitting the kmeans algorithm

5 Fit a GMM model. Note that the code is the same as the k-means algorithm, only the algorithm's name has changed from k-means to `GaussianMixture`:

```
from sklearn.mixture import GaussianMixture
gmm = GaussianMixture(n_components=5)
gmm.fit(data)

#predictions from gmm
labels = gmm.predict(data)
frame = pd.DataFrame(data)
frame['cluster'] = labels
```

6 Plot the results. The output is as follows (figure 5.23):

```
color=['red','blue','orange', 'brown', 'green']
for k in range(0,5):
    data = frame[frame["cluster"]==k]
    plt.scatter(data["compactness"],data["circularity"],c=color[k])
plt.show()
```

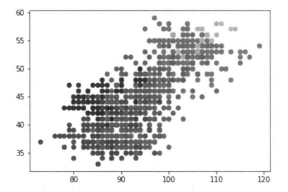

Figure 5.23 Outcome of plotting the clusters after fitting a GMM algorithm

7 Run the code with different values of clusters to observe the difference. In the following plots, the left one is k-means with two clusters, while the right is GMM with two clusters. There are a few points that are classified differently in the two clustering approaches. The print version of the book will not show the different colors, but the output of the Python code will. The same output is available in the GitHub repository, too (see figure 5.24).

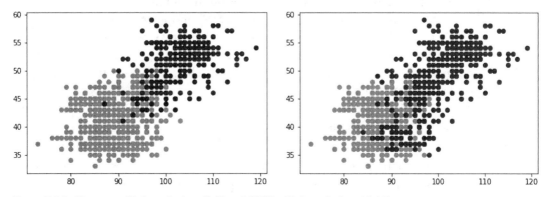

Figure 5.24 K-means with two clusters (left) and GMM with two clusters (right)

Gaussian distribution is one of the most widely used data distributions used. If we compare k-means and the GMM model, we see that k-means does not consider the normal distribution of the data. The relationship of various data points is also not considered in k-means.

> **NOTE** K-means is a distance-based algorithm; GMM is a distribution-based algorithm.

In short, it is advantageous to use GMM models for creating clusters, particularly when we have overlapping datasets. It is a useful technique for financial and price modeling, natural language processing-based solutions, etc.

5.7   *Concluding thoughts*

In this chapter, we have explored three complex clustering algorithms. You might have felt the mathematical concepts were a bit heavy. They are indeed, but they provide a deeper understanding of the process. These algorithms are not necessarily the best ones for every problem. Ideally, in a real-world business problem, we start with classical clustering algorithms (k-means, hierarchical, and DBSCAN). If we do not get acceptable results, we can try the more complex algorithms.

Many times, a data science problem is equated to the choice of algorithm, which it is not. The algorithm is certainly an important ingredient of the entire solution, but it is not the only one. In real-world datasets, there are a lot of variables, and the amount of data is also quite high. The data has a lot of noise. We should account for all of these factors when we shortlist an algorithm. Algorithm maintenance and refreshing are also considerations. All of these aspects are covered in detail in the last chapter of the book.

5.8   *Practical next steps and suggested readings*

The following provides suggestions for what to do next and offers some helpful reading:

- In chapter 2, we did clustering using various techniques. Use the datasets from there and perform spectral clustering, GMM, and FCM clustering to compare the results. Datasets provided at the end of chapter 2 can be used for clustering.
- Get the credit card dataset for clustering from Kaggle (https://mng.bz/oKwd) and data from the famous Iris dataset, which we used earlier (https://www.kaggle.com/uciml/iris).
- Refer to the book *Computational Network Science* by Henry Hexmoor to study the mathematical concepts.
- Get spectral clustering papers from the following links and study them:
  - On spectral clustering: analysis and an algorithm: https://mng.bz/nRwa
  - Spectral clustering with eigenvalue selection: https://mng.bz/vKw7
  - The mathematics behind spectral clustering and the equivalence to principal component analysis: https://arxiv.org/pdf/2103.00733v1.pdf
- Get GMM papers from the following links and explore them:
  - "GMM Estimation for High Dimensional Panel Data Models": https://mng.bz/4agw

- "Application of Compound Gaussian Mixture Model in the Data Stream": https://ieeexplore.ieee.org/document/5620507
- Get FCM papers from the following links and study them:
  - "FCM: The Fuzzy c-Means *Clustering* Algorithm": https://mng.bz/QDXG
  - A Survey on Fuzzy c-Means Clustering Techniques: https://www.ijedr.org/papers/IJEDR1704186.pdf
  - "Implementation of Fuzzy C-Means and Possibilistic C-Means Clustering Algorithms, Cluster Tendency Analysis and Cluster Validation": https://arxiv.org/pdf/1809.08417.pdf

Summary

- Spectral clustering focuses on data point affinity rather than location for clustering. It works well with complex data shapes where traditional algorithms like k-means may not suffice.
- Spectral clustering utilizes graph theory and connectivity, relying on eigenvalues, the Laplacian matrix, and the affinity matrix.
- The process includes calculating degree, adjacency, Laplacian matrices, and the Fielder vector for clustering.
- K-means clustering uses centroids, whereas spectral clustering's focus is on connectivity and data point similarities.
- Spectral clustering can require substantial computational resources due to matrix operations and is suitable for smaller datasets.
- Fuzzy clustering allows data points to belong to multiple clusters, introducing "membership" for data items.
- FCM is a key algorithm in fuzzy clustering, utilizing membership degrees and controlling fuzziness through hyperparameter m.
- GMM employs Gaussian distributions for soft clustering, factoring in dataset covariance.
- GMM is suitable for overlapping datasets and considers the relationship between data points, unlike k-means.
- The EM technique is used in GMM to estimate parameters iteratively.
- GMM models are advantageous for financial modeling, natural language processing, and cases with overlapping data.
- Fuzzy and GMM are soft clustering methods, allowing detailed membership and probability assignment to data points.
- Spectral clustering supports applications in image segmentation, speech analysis, and text analytics without assuming data shape constraints.

Dimensionality reduction

6

This chapter covers
- t-distributed stochastic neighbor embedding
- Multidimensional scaling
- Uniform manifold approximation and projection
- Python implementations of the algorithms

Life is really simple, but we insist on making it complicated.

—Confucius

Simplicity is a virtue—both in life and in data science. We have discussed a lot of algorithms so far. A few of them are simple enough, and some of them are a bit complicated. In part 1 of the book, we studied simpler clustering algorithms, and in the last chapter, we examined advanced clustering algorithms. Similarly, we studied a few dimensionality algorithms like principal component analysis (PCA) in chapter 3. Continuing on the same note, we will study three advanced dimensionality reduction techniques in this chapter.

The advanced topics we cover in this and the next part of the book are meant to prepare you for complex problems. While you can apply these advanced solutions, it is always advisable to start with the classical solutions like PCA for dimensionality reduction. And if that solution doesn't appropriately address the problem, then you can try the advanced solutions.

Dimensionality reduction is one of the most sought-after solutions, particularly when we have a large number of variables. Recall the "curse of dimensionality" we discussed in chapter 3. You are advised to refresh your memory on chapter 3 before moving forward if needed. We will cover t-distributed stochastic neighbor embedding (t-SNE), multidimensional scaling (MDS), and uniform manifold approximation and projection (UMAP) in this chapter. This chapter will cover some mathematical concepts that create the foundation of the advanced techniques we are going to discuss. As always, the concept discussion will be followed by a Python solution. This chapter also has a short case study. We will also develop a solution using an images dataset.

There may be a dilemma in your mind: What is the level of mathematics required, and is an in-depth statistical knowledge a prerequisite? The answer is both yes and no. While having a mathematical understanding will allow you to understand the algorithms and appreciate the process in greater depth; at the same time, for real-world business implementation, sometimes one might want to skip the mathematics and directly move to the examples in Python. We suggest having at least more than a basic understanding of the mathematics to fully grasp the concept. In this book, we provide that level of mathematical support without going into too much depth, presenting instead an optimal mix of practical world and mathematical concepts.

Welcome to the sixth chapter, and all the very best!

6.1 Technical toolkit

We will continue to use the same version of Python and Jupyter Notebook as we have used so far. The codes and datasets used in this chapter have been checked in at https://mng.bz/XxOv.

You will need to install `Keras` as an additional Python library in this chapter. Along with this, you will need the regular modules: `numpy`, `pandas`, `matplotlib`, `seaborn`, and `sklearn`.

6.2 Multidimensional scaling

As you know, maps prove to be quite handy while traveling. Now imagine you are given a task. You receive distances between some cities around the world—for example, between London and New York, London and Paris, Paris and New Delhi, and so forth. Then you are asked to re-create the map from which these distances have been derived. If we have to re-create that 2D map, that will be through trial and error; we will make some assumptions and move ahead with the process. It will surely be a tiring exercise prone to error and quite time-consuming indeed. MDS can do this task easily for us.

NOTE While thinking of the preceding example, ignore the fact that the earth is not flat, and assume that the distance measurement metric is constant—for example, there is no confusion in miles or kilometers.

As an illustration, consider figure 6.1. Formally put, if we have x data points, MDS can help us convert the information of the pairwise distance between these x points to a configuration of points in a Cartesian space. Or, simply put, MDS transforms a large dimensional dataset into a lower dimensional one and, in the process, keeps the distance or the similarity between the points the same.

	Atlanta	Boston	Chicago	Dallas	Denver	Houston	Las Vegas	Los Angeles	Miami	New Orleans	New York	Phoenix	San Francisco	Seattle	Washington, DC
Atlanta		1095	715	805	1437	844	1920	2230	675	499	884	1832	2537	2730	657
Boston	1095		983	1815	1991	1886	2500	3036	1539	1541	213	2664	3179	3043	44
Chicago	715	983		931	1050	1092	1500	2112	1390	947	840	1729	2212	2052	695
Dallas	805	1815	931		801	242	1150	1425	1332	504	1604	1027	1765	2122	1372
Denver	1437	1991	1050	801		1032	885	1174	2094	1305	1780	836	1266	1373	1635
Houston	844	1886	1092	242	1032		1525	1556	1237	365	1675	118	1958	2348	1443
Las Vegas	1920	2500	1500	1150	885	1525		289	2640	1805	2486	294	573	1188	2568
Los Angeles	2230	3036	2112	1425	1174	1556	289		2757	1921	2825	398	403	1150	2680
Miami	675	1539	1390	1332	2094	1237	2640	2757		892	1328	2359	3097	3389	1101
New Orleans	499	1541	947	504	1305	365	1805	1921	892		1330	1523	2269	2626	1098
New York	884	213	840	1604	1780	1675	2486	2825	1328	1330		2442	3036	2900	229
Phoenix	1832	2664	1729	1027	836	1158	294	398	2359	1523	2442		800	1482	2278
San Francisco	2537	3179	2212	1765	1266	1958	573	403	3097	2269	3036	800		817	2864
Seattle	2730	3043	2052	2122	1373	2348	1188	1150	3389	2626	2900	1482	817		2755
Washington, DC	657	440	695	1372	1635	1443	2568	2680	1101	1098	229	2278	2864	2755	

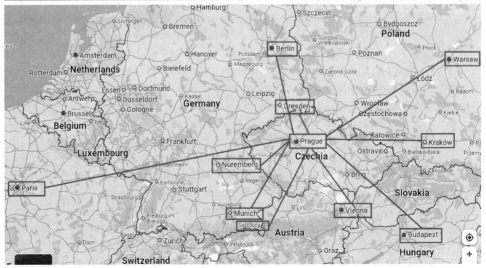

Figure 6.1 Illustration of distance between the cities and if they are represented on a map. The figure is only to help develop an understanding and does not represent the actual results.

To simplify, consider figure 6.2. Here we have three points: A, B, and C. We are representing these points in a 3D space. Then we represent the three points in a 2D space, and finally they are represented in a 1D space. The distance between the points is not up to scale in the diagrams in the figure. The example represents the meaning of lowering the number of dimensions.

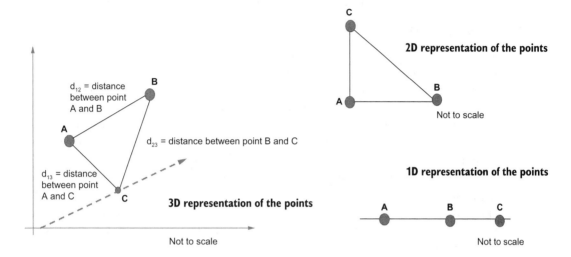

Figure 6.2   Representation of three points

Hence, in MDS, multidimensional data is reduced to a lower number of dimensions. There are three types of MDS algorithms:

- Classical MDS
- Metric multidimensional scaling
- Nonmetric multidimensional scaling

6.2.1   *Classic MDS*

We will examine the metric MDS process in detail in the book, while we will cover the classical and nonmetric briefly. Imagine we have two points: i and j. Let us assume that the original distance between two points is d_{ij} and the corresponding distance in the lower dimensional space is δ_{ij}.

In classical MDS, the distances between the points are treated as Euclidean distances, and the original and fitted distances are represented in the same metric. It means that if the original distances in a higher dimensional space are calculated using the Euclidean method, the fitted distances in the lower dimensional space are also calculated using Euclidean distance. We already know how to calculate Euclidean distances. For example, we have to find the distance between points i and j, and let's say the distance is d_{ij}. The distance can be given by the Euclidean distance formula given by equation 6.1 in a 2D space:

$$d_{ij} = \sqrt{(x_i - x_j)^2 + (y_i - y_j)^2} \qquad (6.1)$$

Recall in chapter 2, we discussed other distance functions like Manhattan distance, Euclidean distance, etc. You are advised to refresh your memory on chapter 2.

6.2.2   *Nonmetric MDS*

We just now noted that Euclidean distance can be used to calculate the distance between two points. Sometimes it is not possible to take the actual values of the distances, like when d_{ij} is the result of an experiment where subjective assessments were made or, in other words, where a rank was allocated to the various data parameters. For example, if the distance between points 2 and 5 was at rank 4 in the original data, in such a scenario, it will not be wise to use absolute values of d_{ij}, and hence relative values or *rank values* have to be used. Here, distance can mean a kind of ranking—for example, who came first in a race. This is the process in nonmetric MDS. For example, imagine we have four points: A, B, C, and D. We wish to rank the respective distances between these four points. The respective combinations of points can be A and B, A and C, A and D, B and C, B and D, and C and D. Their distances can be ranked as shown in table 6.1.

Table 6.1   **The respective distance between four points and the ranks of the distances**

Pair of points	Distance	Ranks of the respective distances
A and B	100	3
A and C	105	4
A and D	95	2
B and C	205	6
B and D	150	5
C and D	55	1

So, in the nonmetric MDS method, instead of using the actual distances, we use the respective ranks of the distance. We next move on to the metric MDS method.

We know that in classical MDS, the original and fitted distances are represented in the same metric. In metric MDS, it is assumed that the values of d_{ij} can be transformed into Euclidean distances by employing some parametric transformation on the datasets. In some articles, you might find classical and metric MDS used interchangeably.

In MDS, as a first step, the respective distances between the points are calculated. Once the respective distances have been calculated, then MDS will try to represent the higher dimensional data point in a lower dimensional space. To perform this, an optimization process has to be carried out so that the optimum number of resultant dimensions can be chosen. Hence, a loss function or cost function has to be optimized.

COST FUNCTION

We use algorithms to predict the values of a variable. For example, we might use some algorithm to predict the expected demand of a product next year. We would want the algorithm to predict as accurately as possible. Cost functions are a simple method to check the performance of the algorithms.

Cost function is a simple technique to measure the effectiveness of our algorithms. It is the most common method used to gauge the performance of a predictive model. It compares the original values and the predicted values by the algorithm and calculates how wrong the model is in its prediction.

As you would imagine, in an ideal solution, we would want the predicted values to be the same as the actual values, which is very difficult to achieve. If the predicted values differ a lot from the actual values, the output of a cost function is higher. If the predicted values are closer to the actual values, then the value of a cost function is lower. A robust solution is one that has the lowest value of the cost function. Hence, the objective to optimize any algorithm will be to minimize the value of the cost function. Cost function is also referred to as loss function; these two terms can be used interchangeably.

In metric MDS, we can also call the cost function *stress*. It is just another name for cost function. The formula for stress is given in equation 6.2:

$$\text{Stress}_D(x_1, x_2, \ldots, x_N) = \left(\sum_{i \neq j = 1, \ldots, N} (d_{ij} - \|x_i - x_j\|)^2 \right)^{\frac{1}{2}} \tag{6.2}$$

In the equation,

- Term Stress_D is the value the MDS function has to minimize.
- The data points with the new set of coordinates in a lower dimensional space are represented by $x_1, x_2, x_3 \ldots x_N$.
- The term $\|x_i - x_j\|$ is the distance between two points in their lower dimensional space.
- The term d_{ij} is the original distance between the two points in the original multidimensional space.

By looking at the equation, we can see that if the values of $\|x_i - x_j\|$ and d_{ij} are close to each other, the value of the resultant stress will be small.

NOTE Minimizing the value of stress is the objective of the loss function.

To optimize this loss function, we can use multiple approaches. One of the most famous methods is using a gradient descent that was originally proposed by Kruskal and Wish in 1978. The gradient descent method is very simple to understand and can be explained using a simple analogy.

Imagine you are standing on top of a mountain and you want to get down. You want to choose the fastest path because you want to get down as fast as possible (no, you cannot jump!). So, to take the first step, you look around and, whichever is the steepest path, you take a step in that direction and reach a new point. Then again, you take a step in the steepest direction. This process is shown in the first diagram in figure 6.3.

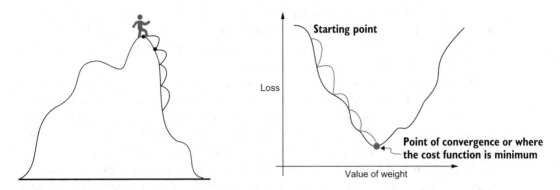

Figure 6.3   A person standing on top of a mountain and trying to get down. The process of gradient descent follows this method (left). The actual process of optimization of a cost function in gradient descent process. Note that at the point of convergence, the value of the cost function is minimal (right).

Now say an algorithm has to achieve a similar feat; the process is represented in the right diagram in figure 6.3, wherein a loss function starts at a point and finally reaches the point of convergence. At this point of convergence, the cost function is minimal.

MDS differs from the other dimensionality reduction techniques. As compared to techniques like PCA, MDS does not make any assumptions about the dataset and hence can be used for a larger number of datasets. Moreover, MDS allows the use of any distance measurement metric. Unlike PCA, MDS is not an eigenvalue-eigenvector technique. Recall in PCA, the first axis captures the maximum amount of variance, the second axis has the next best variance, and so on. In MDS, there is no such condition. The axes in MDS can be inverted or rotated as needed. Also, in most of the other dimensional reduction methods used, the algorithms do calculate a lot of axes, but they cannot be viewed. In MDS, a smaller number of dimensions are explicitly chosen at the start. Hence there is less ambiguity in the solution. Further, in other algorithms, generally, there is only one unique solution, whereas MDS tries to iteratively find the most acceptable solution. It means that in MDS there can be multiple solutions for the same dataset.

But at the same time, the computation time required for MDS is greater for bigger datasets—and there is a catch in the gradient descent method used for optimization (see figure 6.4). Let's refer to the mountain example we covered earlier. Imagine that while you are coming down from the top of the mountain, the starting point is A, and the bottom of the mountain is point C. While you are coming down, you reach point B. As you can see in the left diagram in the figure, there is a slight elevation around point B. At this point B, you might incorrectly conclude that you have reached the bottom of the mountain. In other words, you will think that you have finished your task. This is the problem of the local minima.

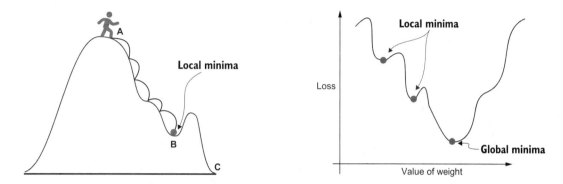

Figure 6.4   **While the first figure is the point of convergence and represents the gradient descent method, note that in the second figure the global minima is somewhere else, while the algorithm can be stuck at a local minima. The algorithm might check that it has optimized the cost function and reached the point of global minima, whereas it has only reached the local minima. In a local minima, there is no direction that is ascending; all the directions descend. The algorithm, if purely local, has no information about other deeper minima existing beyond a potentially small hill.**

It is a possibility that instead of a global minimum, the loss function might be stuck in a local minima. The algorithm might think that it has reached the point of convergence, while the complete convergence might not have been achieved, and we are at a local minimum.

There is still a question to be answered about the efficacy of the MDS solution. How can we measure the effectiveness of the solution? In the original paper, Kruskal recommended the stress values to measure the goodness-of-fit of the solution, which are shown in table 6.2. The recommendations are mostly based on the empirical experience of Kruskal. These stress values are based on Kruskal's experience.

Table 6.2   Stress values and their goodness of fit

Stress values	Goodness of fit
0.200	Poor
0.100	Fair
0.050	Good
0.025	Excellent
0.000	Perfect

The next logical question is: How many final dimensions should we choose? A scree plot provides the answer, as shown in figure 6.5. Recall in chapter 2 we used a similar elbow method to choose the optimal number of clusters in k-means clustering. For MDS too, we can use the elbow method to determine the optimal number of components to represent the data.

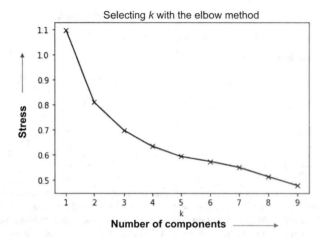

Figure 6.5   Scree plot to find the optimal number of components. It is similar to the k-means solution; we have to look for the elbow in the plot.

Exercise 6.1

Answer these questions to check your understanding:

1 What is the difference between metric and nonmetric MDS algorithms?
2 Gradient descent is used to maximize the cost. True or False?
3 Explain the gradient descent method using a simple example.

6.3   *Python implementation of MDS*

For the Python implementation of the MDS method we will use the famous Iris dataset, which we have used previously. Using the algorithm is quite simple, thanks to the libraries available in the scikit learn package.

NOTE   The implementation is generally simple as the heavy lifting is done by the libraries.

The steps are as follows:

1 Load the libraries. The usual suspects are sklearn, matplotlib, and numpy, and we also load MDS from sklearn:

```
import numpy as np
from sklearn.datasets import load_iris
```

```
import matplotlib.pyplot as plt
from sklearn.manifold import MDS
from sklearn.preprocessing import MinMaxScaler
import pandas as pd
import warnings
warnings.filterwarnings("ignore")
```

2 Load the dataset. The Iris dataset is available in the `sklearn` library, so we need not import Excel or .csv files here:

```
raw_data = load_iris()
dataset = raw_data.data
```

3 A requirement for MDS is that the dataset should be scaled before the actual visualization is done. We use the `MixMaxScalar()` function to achieve this. Min-Max scaling simply scales the data using the formula in equation 6.3:

$$x_{scaled} = \frac{x - x_{min}}{x_{max} - x_{min}} \tag{6.3}$$

```
d_scaler = MinMaxScaler()
dataset_scaled = d_scaler.fit_transform(dataset)
```

As an output of this step, the data is scaled and ready for the next step of modeling.

4 Invoke the MDS method from the `sklearn` library. The `random_state` value allows us to reproduce the results. We have chosen the number of components as 3 for the example:

```
mds_output = MDS(3,random_state=5)
```

5 Fit the scaled data created earlier using the MDS model:

```
data_3d = mds_output.fit_transform(dataset_scaled)
```

6 Declare the colors we wish to use for visualization. Next, the data points are visualized in a scatter plot:

```
mds_colors = ['purple','blue', 'yellow']
for i in np.unique(raw_data.target):
  d_subset = data_3d[raw_data.target == i]

  x = [row[0] for row in d_subset]
  y = [row[1] for row in d_subset]
  plt.scatter(x,y,c=mds_colors[i],label=raw_data.target_names[i])
plt.legend()
plt.show()
```

The output of the preceding code is shown in figure 6.6.

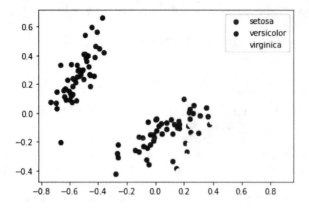

Figure 6.6   Output for the Iris data

This example of Python implementation is a visualization of the Iris data. It is quite a simple example, as it does not involve stress and optimization for the number of components. In other words, we need a more complex dataset to really optimize MDS. We will now work on a curated dataset to implement MDS (see figure 6.7).

Distance	A	B	C	D	E
A	0	40	50	30	40
B	40	0	40	50	20
C	50	40	0	20	50
D	30	50	20	0	20
E	40	20	50	20	0

Figure 6.7   Various cities and their respective distances between each other

Let us assume we have five cities and the respective distance between them is given in figure 6.7. The steps are as follows:

1 We have already imported the libraries in the last code:

```
import numpy as np
from sklearn.datasets import load_iris
import matplotlib.pyplot as plt
from sklearn.manifold import MDS
from sklearn.preprocessing import MinMaxScaler
import pandas as pd
import warnings
warnings.filterwarnings("ignore")
```

2   Create the dataset. Although we create a dataset here, in real business scenarios, it will be in the form of distances only (see figure 6.8):

```
data_dummy_cities = {'A':[0,40,50,30,40],
            'B':[40,0,40,50,20],
            'C':[50,40,0,20,50],
            'D':[30,50,20,0,20],
            'E':[40,20,50,20,0],
            }
cities_dataframe = pd.DataFrame(data_dummy_cities, index
=['A','B','C','D','E'])
cities_dataframe
```

```
1  cities_dataframe
```

	A	B	C	D	E
A	0	40	50	30	40
B	40	0	40	50	20
C	50	40	0	20	50
D	30	50	20	0	20
E	40	20	50	20	0

Figure 6.8   Creating the dataset

3   Use the `MinMaxScalar()` function to scale the dataset as we did in the last coding exercise:

```
scaler = MinMaxScaler()
df_scaled = scaler.fit_transform(cities_dataframe)
```

Now we work toward finding the most optimal number of components. We will iterate for different values of the number of components. For each of the values of the number of components, we will get the value of stress. The point at which a kink is observed is the optimal number of components.

As a first step, we will declare an empty dataframe, which can be used to store the values of the number of components and corresponding stress values. Then we iterate from 1 to 10 in a `for` loop. Finally, for each of the values of components (1 to 10), we get the respective values of stress:

```
MDS_stress = []
for i in range(1, 10):
    mds = MDS(n_components=i)
    pts = mds.fit_transform(df_scaled)
    MDS_stress.append(mds.stress_)
```

4   Now that we have the values of stress, we will plot these values in a graph. The respective labels for each of the axes are also given. Look at the kink at values 2 and 3 in figure 6.9. These can be the optimal values of the number of components:

```
plt.plot(range(1, 10), MDS_stress)
plt.xticks(range(1, 5, 2))
plt.title('Plot of stress')
plt.xlabel('Number of components')
plt.ylabel('Stress values')
plt.show()
```

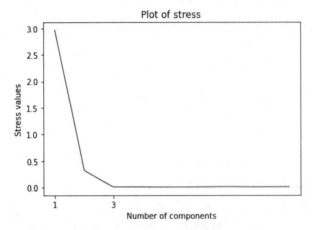

Figure 6.9   Scree plot to select the optimized number of components

5   Run the solution for the number of components = 3. If we look at the values of stress, number of components = 3, it generates the minimum value of stress as 0.00665 (see figure 6:10):

```
mds = MDS(n_components=3)
x = mds.fit_transform(df_scaled)
cities = ['A','B','C','D','E']

plt.figure(figsize=(5,5))
plt.scatter(x[:,0],x[:,1])
plt.title('MDS with Sklearn')
for label, x, y in zip(cities, x[:, 0], x[:, 1]):
    plt.annotate(
        label,
        xy = (x, y),
        xytext = (-10, 10),
        textcoords = 'offset points'
    )
plt.show()
print(mds.stress_)
```

This concludes our discussion on the MDS algorithm. We discussed the foundation and concepts, pros and cons, algorithm assessment, and Python implementation of MDS. As one of the nonlinear dimensionality reduction methods, it is a great solution for visualization and dimensionality reductions.

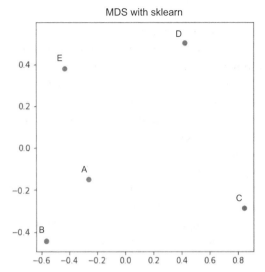

MDS with sklearn

Figure 6.10 Output for the MDS dataset: representation of the five cities in a plot

6.4 *t-distributed stochastic neighbor embedding*

If a dataset is really high dimensional, the analysis becomes cumbersome. The visualization is even more confusing. We have covered that in great detail in the curse of dimensionality section in chapter 3. You are advised to revisit the concept before proceeding if you need a refresher.

One such really high-dimensional dataset can be image data. We find it difficult to comprehend such data due to anything beyond 3 dimensions being increasingly difficult for us to intuit.

You may have used facial recognition software on your smartphone. For such solutions, facial images have to be analyzed, and machine learning models have to be trained. Look at the pictures in figure 6.11: we have a human face, a bike, a vacuum cleaner, and a screen capture of a phone.

Image is a complex data type. Each image is made up of pixels, and each pixel can be made up of RGB (red, green, blue) values. Values for each of the RGB can range from 0 to 255. The resulting dataset will be a very high-dimensional dataset.

Figure 6.11 Images are quite complex to decipher by an algorithm. Images can be of any form and can be of a person, a piece of equipment, or even a phone screen.

Now recall PCA, which we studied in chapter 3. PCA is a linear algorithm. Thus, its capability to resolve nonlinear and complex polynomial functions is limited. More-over, when a high-dimensional dataset has to be represented in a low-dimensional space, the algorithm should keep similar data points close to each other, which can be a challenge in linear algorithms. PCA, as a linear dimension reduction technique, tries to separate the different data points as far away from each other as possible, and tries to maximize the variance captured in the data. The resulting analysis is not robust and might not be best suited for further use and visualization. Hence, we have nonlinear algorithms like t-SNE to help.

t-SNE is a nonlinear dimensionality reduction technique that is quite handy for high-dimensional data. It is based on stochastic neighbor embedding, which was devel-oped by Sam Roweis and Geoffrey Hinton. The t-distributed variant was proposed by Lauren van der Maaten. Thus, t-SNE is an improvement of the SNE algorithm.

At a high level, SNE measures the similarity between instance pairs in a high-dimen-sional space and in a low-dimensional space. A good solution is where the difference between these similarity measures is the least, and SNE then optimizes these similarity measures using a cost function similar to what we have discussed for MDS.

We examine the step-by-step process of t-SNE next. The process described is a little heavy on mathematics:

1 Consider a high-dimensional space and some points in it.
2 Measure the similarities between the various points in the high-dimensional space mentioned in the last point. For a point x_i, we will then create a Gaussian distribution centered at that point. We have already studied Gaussian or normal distribution in chapter 2. The Gaussian distribution is shown in figure 6.12.

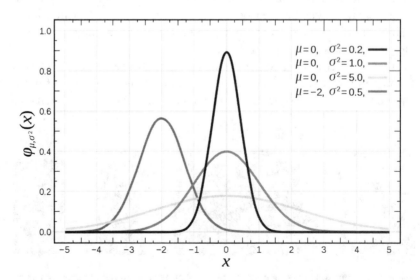

Figure 6.12   Gaussian or normal distribution.

3 Measure the density of points (let's say x_j) that fall under that Gaussian distribution and then renormalize them to get the respective conditional probabilities ($p_{j|i}$). For the points that are nearby and hence similar, this conditional probability will be high, and for the points that are far and dissimilar, the value of conditional probabilities ($p_{j|i}$) will be very small. These values of probabilities are those in the high-dimensional space. For curious readers, the mathematical formula for this conditional probability is presented as equation 6.4

$$p_{j|i} = \frac{\exp\left(-\frac{\|x_i - x_j\|^2}{2\sigma_i^2}\right)}{\sum_{k \neq i} \exp\left(-\frac{\|x_i - x_k\|^2}{2\sigma_i^2}\right)} \tag{6.4}$$

where σ is the variance of the Gaussian distribution centered at x_i. The mathematical proof is beyond the scope of this book.

4 Measure one more set of probabilities in the low-dimensional space. For this set of measurements, we use the Cauchy distribution, described next. We use Kullback-Liebler (KL) divergence for measuring the difference between two probability distributions.

6.4.1   Cauchy distribution

The Cauchy distribution belongs to the family of continuous probability distributions. Though there is a resemblance with the normal distribution, as we have represented in figure 6.13, the Cauchy distribution has a narrower peak and spreads out more

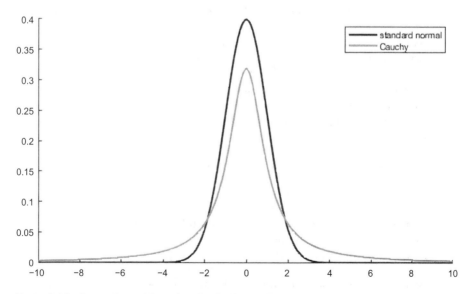

Figure 6.13   Comparison of Gaussian distribution vs. Cauchy distribution. (Image source: Quora)

slowly. It means that, compared to a normal distribution, the probability of obtaining values far from the peaks is higher. Sometimes, the Cauchy distribution is known as the *Lorentz distribution*. It is interesting to note that Cauchy does not have a well-defined mean, but the median is the center of symmetry.

1 Consider we get y_i and y_j as the low-dimensional counterparts for the high-dimensional data points x_i and x_j. So we can calculate the probability score like we did in the last step. Using the Cauchy distribution, we can get a second set of probabilities $q_{j|i}$ too. The mathematical formula is shown in equation 6.5:

$$q_{j|i} = \frac{\exp\left(-\|y_i - y_j\|^2\right)}{\sum_{k \neq i} \exp\left(-\|y_i - y_k\|^2\right)} \tag{6.5}$$

2 So far, we have calculated two set of probabilities $(p_{j|i})$ and $(q_{j|i})$. In this step, we compare the two distributions and measure the difference between the two. In other words, while calculating $(p_{j|i})$ we measured the probability of similarity in a high-dimensional space whereas for $(q_{j|i})$ we did the same in a low-dimensional space. Ideally, the mapping of the two spaces is similar, and for that, there should not be any difference between $(p_{j|i})$ and $(q_{j|i})$. So the SNE algorithm tries to minimize the difference in the conditional probabilities $(p_{j|i})$ and $(q_{j|i})$, similar to what we have done with MDS for the distance in high- and low-dimensional spaces.

3 The difference between the two probability distributions is done using KL divergence.

DEFINITION KL divergence or relative entropy is used to measure the difference between two probability distributions. Usually, one probability distribution is the data or the measured scores, and the second probability distribution is an approximation or the prediction of the original probability distribution—for example, if the original probability distribution is X and the approximated one is Y. KL divergence can be used to measure the difference between X and Y probability distributions. In absolute terms, if the value is 0, then it means that the two distributions are identical. The KL divergence is applicable for neurosciences, statistics, and fluid mechanics, among others.

4 To minimize the KL cost function, we use the gradient descent approach. We have already discussed the gradient descent approach in section 6.2 where we discussed the MDS algorithm.

There is one more important factor we should be aware of while we work on t-SNE, and that is *perplexity*. Perplexity is a hyperparameter that allows us to control and optimize the number of close neighbors each of the data points has.

NOTE As per the official paper, a typical value for perplexity lies between 5 and 50.

There can be one additional nuance: the output of a t-SNE algorithm might never be the same on successive runs. We have to optimize the values of the hyperparameters to receive the best output.

> **Exercise 6.2**
>
> Answer these questions to check your understanding:
> 1 Explain Cauchy distribution in your own words.
> 2 PCA is a nonlinear algorithm. True or False?
> 3 KL divergence is used to measure the difference between two probability distributions. True or False?

6.4.2 Python implementation of t-SNE

We will use two datasets in this example. The first one is the Iris dataset, which we have already used more than once in this book. The second dataset is quite an interesting one: the MNIST dataset is a database of handwritten digits. It is one of the most famous datasets used to train image processing solutions and generally is considered the "Hello World" program for image detection solutions. An image representation is shown figure 6.14.

Figure 6.14 MNIST dataset

The steps for the Iris dataset are as follows:

1 Import the necessary libraries. Note that we have imported the MNIST dataset from the `keras` library.

```
rom sklearn.manifold import TSNE
from keras.datasets import mnist
from sklearn.datasets import load_iris
from numpy import reshape
import seaborn as sns
import pandas as pd
```

TIP If you are not able to install modules in your Python code, refer to the appendix where we provide a solution.

2 Load the Iris dataset. The dataset comprises two parts: one is the "data" and the second is the respective label or "target" for it. It means that "data" is the description of the data and "target" is the type of iris. We print the features and the labels using code:

```
iris = load_iris()
iris_data = iris.data
iris_target = iris.target
iris.feature_names
iris.target_names
```

3 Invoke the t-SNE algorithm. We are using the n_components=2, verbose=1, and random_state=5 to reproduce the results. Then the algorithm is used to fit the data (see figure 6.15):

```
tsne = TSNE(n_components=2, verbose=1, random_state=5)
fitted_data = tsne.fit_transform(iris_data)
```

```
In [31]:    1  tsne = TSNE(n_components=2, verbose=1, random_state=5)
            2  fitted_data = tsne.fit_transform(iris_data)
            3

[t-SNE] Computing 91 nearest neighbors...
[t-SNE] Indexed 150 samples in 0.000s...
[t-SNE] Computed neighbors for 150 samples in 0.003s...
[t-SNE] Computed conditional probabilities for sample 150 / 150
[t-SNE] Mean sigma: 0.509910
[t-SNE] KL divergence after 250 iterations with early exaggeration: 52.932037
[t-SNE] KL divergence after 1000 iterations: 0.123070
```

Figure 6.15   Output of the code when we are fitting the algorithm

4 Plot the data. This step allows us to visualize the data fitted by the algorithm in the last step.

First, we will initiate an empty dataframe. We will add three columns, one at a time. We start with iris_target, followed by tSNE_first_component and tSNE_second_component. tSNE_first_component is the first column of the fitted_data dataframe, and therefore the index is 0. tSNE_second_component is the second column of the fitted_data dataframe and hence the index is 1. Finally, we represent the data in a scatterplot in figure 6.16:

```
iris_df = pd.DataFrame()
iris_df["iris_target"] = iris_target
iris_df["tSNE_first_component"] = fitted_data[:,0]
iris_df["tSNE_second_component"] = fitted_data[:,1]
```

```
sns.scatterplot(x="tSNE_first_component", y="tSNE_second_component",
hue=iris_df.iris_target.tolist(),
                palette=sns.color_palette("hls", 3),
                data=iris_df).set(title="Iris data tSNE projection")
```

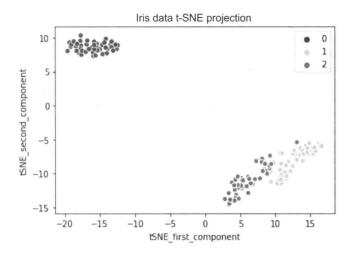

Figure 6.16 **t-SNE projection of the Iris dataset. Note how we are getting
three separate clusters for the three classes we have in the dataset.**

To implement the algorithm for the MNIST dataset, load the libraries and dataset.
The libraries were already loaded in the last code example. Now load the dataset. The
dataset requires `reshape`, which is done here (see figure 6.17):

```
(digit, digit_label), (_ , _) = mnist.load_data()
digit = reshape(digit, [digit.shape[0], digit.shape[1]*digit.shape[2]])
Step 2: the subsequent steps are exactly same to the last example we used.
tsne_MNIST = TSNE(n_components=2, verbose=1, random_state=5)
fitted_data = tsne_MNIST.fit_transform(digit)

mnist_df = pd.DataFrame()
mnist_df["digit_label"] = digit_label
mnist_df["tSNE_first_component"] = fitted_data[:,0]
mnist_df["tSNE_second_component"] = fitted_data[:,1]

sns.scatterplot(x="tSNE_first_component", y="tSNE_second_component",
    hue=mnist_df.digit_label.tolist(),
                palette=sns.color_palette("hls", 10),
                data=mnist_df).set(title="MNIST data T-SNE projection")
```

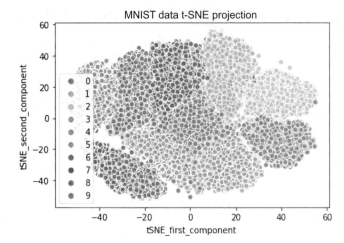

Figure 6.17   Output of t-SNE for the 10 classes of digits represented in different shades of gray

There are a few important points to keep in mind while running t-SNE:

- Run the algorithm with different values of hyperparameters before finalizing a solution.
- Ideally, perplexity should be between 5 and 50, and for an optimized solution, the value of perplexity should be less than the number of points.
- T-SNE guesses the number of close neighbors for each of the points. For this reason, a dataset that is denser will require a much higher perplexity value.
- Note that perplexity is the hyperparameter that balances the attention given to both the local and the global aspects of the data.

t-SNE is a widely popular algorithm. It can be used for studying the topology of an area, but a single t-SNE cannot be used for making a final assessment. Instead, multiple t-SNE plots should be created to make any final recommendation. Sometimes there are complaints that t-SNE is a black-box algorithm. This might be true to a certain extent. What makes the adoption of t-SNE harder is that it does not generate the same results in successive iterations. Hence, you might find t-SNE recommended only for exploratory analysis.

6.5   *Uniform manifold approximation projection*

UMAP is a powerful and popular dimensionality reduction technique. It is designed to preserve both the local and global structures of the dataset while reducing the complexity and dimensions of the high-dimensional dataset to a low-dimensional dataset.

UMAP was introduced in 2018 by Lealand McInnes, John Healy, and James Melville. UMAP makes the data more suitable for visualizations and data analysis. This relates to the concepts of topology and manifold theory. UMAP assumes that the high-dimensional dataset often lies on a manifold, which means a low-dimensional structure is embedded in a higher-dimensional space. Hence, it attempts to project this manifold into a lower dimensional space, preserving both the nearest neighbor relationships, which is nothing but the local structure, and the larger relationships, which is the global structure.

6.5.1 *Working with UMAP*

UMAP methodology uses the concept of fuzzy simplicity sets. These sets represent the probability distribution of distances between various data points and capture the underlying manifold structures.

The first step in UMAP is to construct a weighted graph where each of the data points is connected to its nearest neighbor based on a distance metric. Generally, the Euclidean distance is used as the distance metric. This graph construction is an abstract representation of the data structure in high dimensions.

The next step is to optimize the graph. The graph is optimized in a lower dimension space by minimizing cross-entropy loss between the original high-dimensional relationships and the newly created low-dimensional relationships. This uses the stochastic gradient descent, producing the UMAP embeddings. We will study stochastic gradient descent in chapter 9.

There are two key parameters for UMAP:

- `n_neighbours`—The number of nearest neighbors to consider for each point. Using this parameter, we balance the preservation of the local data structure as compared to the global data structure.
- `min_dist`—This is used to control how tightly the points are clustered together. Smaller values of minimum distance keep the points much closer and hence create deeper clusters. The larger value for minimum distance will create lighter clusters, which are spread out.

6.5.2 *Using UMAP*

The various uses of UMAP are as follows:

- One of the most popular uses of UMAP is the visualization of high-dimensional datasets in the bioinformatics field. Gene datasets are quite complex and multi-dimensional, where each data point might be represented by hundreds or thousands of attributes. Using UMAP, researchers can virtually inspect the clusters and the underlying relationships in the dataset. The solution helps them identify cell types, developmental stages, and gene expression patterns.
- UMAP is also applied to the natural language processing field by reducing the dimensionality of embeddings. It helps in the visualization of relationships between words or sentences or documents, making it easier to understand the similarities.
- UMAP can also be applied to images. It helps in the visualization of the plastering of images based on various similarities, hence it is quite useful for competitive vision tasks to understand how similar images can be clustered together.
- UMAP can be used with other clustering algorithms like k-means or DBSCAN. It can uncover the hidden patterns in large datasets and since it preserves both

local and global structures, the clusters found in lower dimensional representations often provide more important groupings as compared to the original high-dimensional dataset.

In addition to helping with visualizations, UMAP can also be used as a preprocessing step to reduce the dimensions of data. It can be used as an alternative to PCA or other solutions. By reducing the number of dimensions in a dataset, the model's performance might be improved and the computation time is reduced.

The use of UMAP in Python is straightforward. The library `umap-learn` allows us to use the power of UMAP.

6.5.3   *Key points of UMAP*

Let's now cover the key points of UMAP and compare it to other algorithms:

- Since UMAP is a nonlinear solution, it can capture more complex datasets and patterns as compared to PCA. Recall that PCA is a linear dimensionality tradition technique, so when the data is not on a simple linear manifold, UMAP proves to be more accurate.
- The goal of PCA is to explain the maximum variance in the entire dataset. On the other hand, UMAP balances both local and global structures and hence is more versatile for tasks like anomaly detection.
- As compared to PCA, UMAP can be used for larger datasets.
- UMAP is faster than the other nonlinear solution, t-SNE. t-SNE can preserve the local structure of the data, but it struggles with preserving the global structure, and it can lead to a misleading interpretation of the clusters. UMAP does a better job as it preserves both local and global structures.
- UMAP results are much more stable and consistent across multiple iterations. For other algorithms, the results can be unstable and might change with different values of random seeds.

UMAP has gained a lot of popularity recently and has become a go-to tool for machine learning and AI solutions. It is fast and can preserve both local and global data structures. Hence it is a strong option compared to other dimensionality reduction solutions like PCA, t-SNE, and autoencoders.

6.6   *Case study*

In chapter 3, we explored a case study for the telecom industry reducing dimensionality. In this chapter, we will examine a small case study wherein t-SNE or MDS can be utilized for dimensionality reduction.

Have you heard about hyperspectral images? As you know, we humans see the colors of visible light in mostly three bands: long, medium, and short wavelengths. The long wavelengths are perceived as red, medium as green, and short as blue. All the other colors human beings perceive are simply mixtures of these three, and that is what allows screens and printers to work with only three colors. Spectral imaging, on the other hand, divides the spectrum into many more bands, and this technique can be extended beyond the visible and hence is used across biology, physics, geoscience, astronomy, agriculture, and many more avenues. Hyperspectral imaging collects and processes information from across the electromagnetic spectrum. It obtains the spectrum for each of the pixels in the image. See figure 6.18.

One such dataset is the Pavia University dataset. The dataset is curated by the ROSIS sensor in Pavia, northern Italy. The details of the dataset are given next, and the dataset can be downloaded from https://mng.bz/nRVa.

There are 103 spectral bands in this dataset. The HIS size is 610 * 340 pixels, and it contains nine classes. Such a type of data can be used for

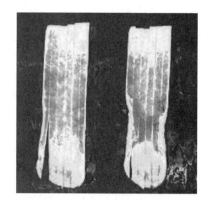

Figure 6.18 Hyperspectral image of "sugar end" potato strips shows invisible defects (Source: SortingExpert, CC BY-SA 3.0)

crop analysis, mineral examination and exploration, etc. Since this data also contains information about geological patterns, it is quite useful for scientific purposes. Before developing any image recognition solution, we have to reduce the number of dimensions for this dataset. The computation cost will be much higher if we have a large number of dimensions. Hence, we want a lower representative number of dimensions. Figure 6.19 shows a few example bands. You are advised to download the dataset (which is also pushed at the GitHub repository) and use the various dimensionality reduction techniques on the dataset to reduce the number of dimensions. There can be many other image datasets and complex business problems where t-SNE and MDS can be of pragmatic use.

Band - 25

Band - 9

Band - 53

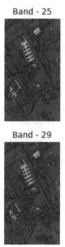

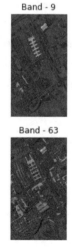

Band - 29

Band - 63

Band - 14

Figure 6.19 Example of bands in the dataset. These are only random examples.

6.7   Concluding thoughts

Dimensionality reduction is quite an interesting and useful field. It makes machine learning less expensive and less time-consuming. Imagine that you have a dataset with thousands of attributes or features. You do not know the data very well, the business understanding is limited, and, at the same time, you have to find the patterns in the dataset. You are not even sure if the variables are all relevant or just random noise. At such a moment, when we want to make the dataset less complex to crack and reduce the computational time, dimensionality reduction is the solution.

We covered dimensionality reduction techniques earlier in the book. This chapter covers three advanced techniques: t-SNE, MDS, and UMAP. All three techniques should not be considered a substitute for the other, easier techniques we discussed. Rather, they can be useful if we are not getting meaningful results with basic algorithms. It is always advised to use PCA first and then try the advanced techniques.

The complexity of the book is increasing. This chapter started with images—but we have only wet our toes. In the next chapter, we deal with text data. Perhaps you will find it very interesting and useful.

6.8   Practical next steps and suggested readings

The following provides suggestions for what to do next and offers some helpful reading:

- Use the vehicles dataset used in chapter 2 for clustering and implement MDS on it. Compare the performance on clustering before and after implementing MDS.
- Get the datasets used in chapter 2 for Python examples and use them for implementing MDS.
- For MDS, refer to the following research papers:
    - "Dimensionality Reduction: A Comparative Review," by Lauren van der Maaten, Eric Postma, and H. Japp Van Den Herik: https://mng.bz/eyxQ
    - "Multidimensional Scaling-Based Data Dimension Reduction Method for Application in Short-Term Traffic Flow Prediction for Urban Road Network," by Satish V. Ukkusuri and Jian Lu: https://mng.bz/pKmz
- Get t-SNE research papers from the following links and study them:
    - "Visualizing Data Using t-SNE," by Laurens van der Maaten and Geoffrey Hinton: https://mng.bz/OBaE
    - "The Art of Using t-SNE for Single Cell Transcriptomics": https://mng.bz/YD9A
- See the paper "Performance Evaluation of t-SNE and MDS Dimensionality Reduction Techniques with KNN, SNN, and SVM Classifiers": https://arxiv.org/pdf/2007.13487.pdf

Summary

- MDS is a dimensionality reduction technique that transforms high-dimensional data into a lower-dimensional space while preserving distances.
- There are three types of MDS: classical, metric, and nonmetric.
- Classical MDS uses Euclidean distances, aligning original and fitted distances.
- Nonmetric MDS ranks distances rather than using absolute values.
- Metric MDS transforms distances to fit a lower dimensional space.
- MDS involves calculating distances and optimizing a stress cost function with gradient descent, though it can be computationally intensive and is prone to local minima problems.
- MDS works iteratively and does not make assumptions about data distribution, making it versatile for choosing distance metrics compared to PCA.
- t-SNE is a nonlinear dimensionality reduction technique and is particularly effective for high-dimensional and complex datasets like images.
- t-SNE optimizes similarity between data points in both high- and low-dimensional spaces using the Cauchy distribution and KL divergence.
- t-SNE has an edge over PCA due to its nonlinear nature, though it involves hyperparameters like perplexity.
- UMAP is another dimensionality reduction method that efficiently preserves both local and global data structures and is faster and more stable than t-SNE.
- Python implementations are available for both MDS and t-SNE.
- MDS is one of the advanced dimensionality reduction techniques, requiring optimization of a loss function or cost function.

Unsupervised learning for text data

7

This chapter covers

- Text data analysis: use cases and challenges
- Preprocessing and cleaning text data
- Vector representation methods for text data
- Sentiment analysis and text clustering using Python
- Generative AI applications for text data

Everybody smiles in the same language.

—George Carlin

Our world has so many languages. These languages are the most common medium of communication to express our thoughts and emotions. These words can be written into text. In this chapter, we explore the sorts of analysis we can do on text data. Text data falls under unstructured data and carries a lot of useful information and hence is a useful source of insights for businesses. We use natural language processing (NLP) to analyze the text data.

At the same time, to analyze text data, we have to make the data analysis-ready. Or, in very simple terms, since our algorithms and processors can only understand numbers, we have to represent the text data in numbers or *vectors*. We will explore all these steps in this chapter. Text data holds the key to quite a few important use cases, such as sentiment analysis, document categorization, and language translation, to name a few. We will cover the use cases using a case study and develop a Python solution on the same.

The chapter starts with defining text data, sources of text data, and various use cases of text data. We will then move on to the steps and processes to clean and handle the text data. We cover the concepts of NLP, mathematical foundations, and methods to represent text data into vectors. We will create Python codes for the use cases. Toward the end, we share a case study on text data. Finally, we will also look into the generative AI-based (GenAI) solutions. We have not covered GenAI concepts yet in the book, as they are in part 3. But here we introduce the concepts in the light of text data.

Welcome to the seventh chapter, and all the very best!

7.1 Technical toolkit

We will continue to use the same version of Python and Jupyter Notebook as we have used so far. The codes and datasets used in this chapter have been checked in at the same GitHub location.

You need to install the following Python libraries for this chapter: `re`, `string`, `nltk`, `lxml`, `requests`, `pandas`, `textblob`, `matplotlib`, `sys`, `sklearn`, `scikitlearn`, and `warnings`. Along with these, you will need `numpy` and `pandas`. With libraries, we can use the algorithms very quickly.

7.2 Text data is everywhere

Recall in the very first chapter of the book we explored structured and unstructured datasets. Unstructured data can be text, audio, image, or video. Examples of unstructured data and their respective sources are given in figure 7.1, where we explain the primary types of unstructured data—text, images, audio, and video—along with examples. The focus of this chapter is on text data.

Figure 7.1 Unstructured data can be text, images, audio, or video. We deal with text data in this chapter. This list is not exhaustive.

Language is perhaps our greatest tool for communication. When in written form, this becomes text data. Today, thanks to widely accessible computers and smartphones, text is everywhere. It is generated by writing blogs and social media posts, tweets, comments, stories, reviews, chats, and comments, to name a few. Text data is generally much more direct than images and can be emotionally expressive. It is useful for businesses to unlock the potential of text data and derive insights from it. They can understand customers better, explore the business processes, and gauge the quality of services offered.

Have you ever reviewed a product or a service on Amazon? You award stars to a product; at the same time, you can also input free text. Go to Amazon and look at some of the reviews. You might find some reviews have a good amount of text as the feedback. This text is useful for the product/service providers to enhance their offerings. Also, you might have participated in a few surveys that ask you to share your feedback. Moreover, with the advent of Alexa, Siri, Cortona, etc., the voice command acts as an interface between humans and machines—which is again a rich source of data. Even the customer calls we make to a call center can be transcribed so that they become a source of text data. These calls can be recorded, and using speech-to-text conversion, we can generate a huge amount of text data.

7.3 Use cases of text data

Not all the use cases discussed in this section can implement unsupervised learning. Some require supervised learning too. Nevertheless, for your knowledge, we share both types of use cases, based on supervised learning and unsupervised learning:

- *Sentiment analysis*—You might have participated in surveys or given your feedback on products/surveys. These surveys generate tons of text data. That text data can be analyzed, and we can determine whether the sentiment in the review is positive or negative. In simple words, sentiment analysis gauges the positivity or negativity of the text data. Hence, we can see the sentiment about a product or service in the minds of the customers. We can use both supervised and unsupervised learning for sentiment analysis.

- *News categorization or document categorization*—Look at the Google News web page and you will find that each news item has been categorized to sports, politics, science, business, or another category. Incoming news is classified based on the content of the news, which is the actual text. Imagine the thousands of documents that are sorted in this manner. In this use case, it is clear that machine learning is ideal, given the unfeasible amount of time and effort that would be required to sort such items manually. Supervised learning solutions work well for such problems.

- *Language translation*—Translation of text from one language to another is a very interesting use case. Using NLP, we can translate between languages. Language translation is very tricky, as different languages have different grammatical rules. Generally, deep learning–based solutions are the best fit for language translation.

- *Spam filtering*—Email spam filters can be set up using NLP and supervised machine learning. A supervised learning algorithm can analyze incoming mail parameters and give a prediction if that email belongs to a spam folder or not. The prediction can be based on various parameters like sender email ID, subject line, body of the mail, attachments, time of mail, etc. Generally, supervised learning algorithms are used here.

- *Part-of-speech tagging*—This is one of the popular use cases. It means that we can distinguish the nouns, adjectives, verbs, adverbs, etc., in a sentence. Named-entity recognition is also one of the famous applications of NLP. It involves identifying a person, place, organization, time, or number in a sentence. For example, John lives in London and works for Google. Named-entity recognition can generate understanding like [John]$_{Person}$ lives in [London]$_{Location}$ and works for [Google]$_{organization}$.

- *Sentence generation, captioning the images, speech-to-text or text-to-speech tasks, and handwriting recognition*—These are a few other significant and popular use cases.

The use cases listed here are not exhaustive. There are tons of other use cases that can be implemented using NLP. NLP is a very popular research field too. We share some significant papers at the end of the chapter.

You might have also heard about large language models (LLMs) like ChatGPT, Bard, and Claude. They are algorithms that process natural language inputs and predict the next word based on what they have already seen. With GenAI in the picture, a lot of the use cases can be solved by simply calling the API. ChatGPT can communicate like a human with memory and serves as customer support for many services. LLMs can summarize hundreds of pdf documents. You can even create applications that can be used for getting answers from multiple documents and websites. Certainly, GenAI has enhanced the power here.

While text data is very important, at the same time it is quite difficult to analyze. Remember, our computers and processors understand only numbers. So the text needs to be represented as numbers so we can perform mathematical and statistical calculations on it. Before diving into the preparation of text data, we cover some of the challenges we face while working on text datasets.

7.4 Challenges with text data

Text is a difficult data type to work with. There are a large number of permutations to express the same thought. For example, I might ask, "Hey buddy, what is your age?" or "Hello there, may I know how old are you?"—they mean the same, right? The answer to both the questions is the same, and it is quite easy for humans to decipher, but it can be a daunting task for a machine.

Some of the most common challenges we face in this area are as follows:

- Text data can be complex to handle. There can be a lot of junk characters like $^%*& present in the text.
- With the advent of modern communications, we have started to use short forms of words; for example, "u" can be used for "you," "brb" for "be right back," and so on. Additionally, the challenge is where the same word might mean something different to different people, or misspelling a single letter can change the complete meaning of the word.
- Language is changing, unbounded, and ever-evolving. It changes every day and new words are added to the language. If you do a simple Google search, you will find that quite a few words are added to the dictionary each year.
- The world has close to 6,500 languages, and each one carries its own unique characteristics. Each and every one completes our world. Each language follows its own rules and grammar, which are unique in usage and pattern. Even the writing can be different: some are written left to right, some right to left, and some even vertically. The same emotion might take fewer or more words in different languages.
- The meaning of a word is dependent on the context. A word can be both an adjective and a noun, depending on the context. Consider these examples:
  - "This book is a must-read" and "Please book a room for me."
  - "Tommy" can be a name, but when used as "Tommy Hilfiger" its usage is completely changed.
  - "Apple" is both a fruit and a company.
  - "April" is a month and can be a name too.
- Look at one more example: "Mark traveled from the UK to France and is working with John over there. He misses his friends." Humans can easily understand that "he" in the second sentence is Mark and not John, which might not be that simple for a machine.
- There can be many synonyms for the same word, like "good" can be replaced by "positive," "wonderful," "superb," or "exceptional" in different scenarios. Words like "studying," "studious," and "studies" are related to the same root word "study."
- The size of text data can be daunting too. Managing a text dataset, storing it, cleaning it, and refreshing it is a herculean task.

Like any other machine learning project, text analytics follows the principles of machine learning, albeit the precise process is slightly different. Recall in chapter 1 we examined the process of a machine learning project, as shown in figure 7.2. You are advised to refresh your memory on the process from chapter 1 if needed.

Data science project steps

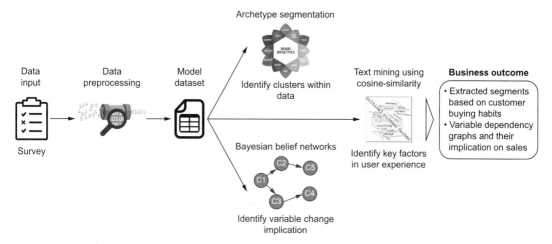

Figure 7.2   The overall steps in a data science project are the same for text data. The preprocessing of text data is very different from the structured dataset.

Defining the business problem, data collection and monitoring, etc., remain the same. The major difference is in the processing of the text, which involves data cleaning, creation of features, representation of text data, etc. We will cover this in the next section.

Exercise 7.1
Answer these questions to check your understanding:

1 Note the three most effective use cases for the text data.
2 Why is working on text data so tedious?

7.5   *Preprocessing the text data*

Text data, like any other data source, can be messy and noisy. We clean some of it in the data discovery phase and a lot of it in the preprocessing phase. At the same time, we should extract the features from our dataset. Some of the steps in the cleaning process are common and can be implemented on most text datasets. Some text datasets might require a customized approach. We start with cleaning the raw text data.

7.6   *Data cleaning*

As with any form of data analysis, ensuring good data quality is vital. The cleaner the text data, the better the analysis. At the same time, preprocessing is not a straightforward task but rather is complex and time-consuming.

Text data must be cleaned as it contains a lot of junk characters, irrelevant words, noise and punctuation, URLs, etc. The primary ways of cleaning the text data are

- *Stopping word removal*—Out of all the words that are used in any language, there are some words that are most common. Stop words are the most common words in a vocabulary that carry less importance than key words. Examples are "is," "an," "the," "a," "be," "has," "had," "it," etc. Once we remove the stop words from the text, the dimensions of the data are reduced and hence the complexity of the solution is reduced.

  We can define a customized list of stop words and remove them that way, or there are standard libraries to remove the stop words.

  At the same time, it is imperative that we understand the context very well while removing the stop words. For example, if we ask a question "is it raining?" then the answer "it is" is a complete answer in itself. When we are working with solutions where contextual information is important, we do not remove stop words.

- *Frequency-based removal of words*—Sometimes you might wish to remove the words that are most common in your text or that are very unique. The process is to get the frequency of the words in the text and then set a threshold of frequency. We can remove the most common ones. Or maybe you wish to remove the ones that have occurred only once/twice in the entire dataset. Based on the requirements, you will decide. At the same time, we should be cautious and observe due diligence while removing the words.

- *Library-based cleaning*—This is done when we wish to clean the data using a predefined and customized library. We can create a repository of words that we do not want in our text and iteratively remove them from the text data. This approach allows us flexibility to implement the cleaning of our own choice.

- *Junk or unwanted characters*—Text data, particularly tweets, comments, etc., might contain a lot of URLs, hashtags, numbers, punctuations, social media mentions, special characters, etc. We might need to clean them from the text. At the same time, we should be careful as some words that are not important for one domain might be required for a different domain. If data has been scraped from websites or HTML/XML sources, we need to get rid of all the HTML entities, punctuations, nonalphabet characters, and so on.

TIP Always keep business context in mind while cleaning the text data.

As we know, a lot of new types of expressions have entered the language—for example, lol, hahahaha, brb, rofl, etc. These expressions are to be converted to their original meanings. Even emojis like :-), ;-), etc., should be converted to their original meanings.

- *Data encoding*—There are a few data encodings available like ISO/IEC, UTF-8, etc. Generally, UTF-8 is the most popular one. But it is not a hard and fast rule to always use UTF-8 only.

- *Lexicon normalization*—Depending on the context and usage, the same word might get represented in different ways. During lexicon normalization, we clean such ambiguities. The basic idea is to reduce the word to its root form. Hence, words that are derived from each other can be mapped to the central word, provided they have the same core meaning.

Figure 7.3 shows that the same word, "eat," has been used in various forms. The root word is "eat," but these different forms demonstrate the many different representations for "eat."

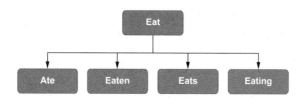

Figure 7.3 "Ate," "eaten," "eats," and "eating" all have the same root word: "eat." Stemming and lemmatization can be used to get the root word.

Here, we wish to map all these words like "eating," "eaten," etc., to their central word, "eat," as they have the same core meaning. There are two primary methods to work on this:

- Stemming is a basic rule-based approach for mapping a word to its core word. It removes "es," "ing," "ly," "ed," etc., from the end of the word. For example, studies will become "studi" and "studying" will become "study." Being a rule-based approach, the output spellings might not always be accurate.
- Lemmatization is an organized approach that reduces words to their dictionary form. The *lemma* of a word is its dictionary or canonical form. For example, "eats," "eating," "eaten," etc., all have the same root word "eat." Lemmatization provides better results than stemming, but it takes more time.

These are only some of the methods to clean text data. These techniques will help, but business acumen is required to further make sense of the dataset. We will clean the text data using these approaches by developing a Python solution.

Once the data is cleaned, we start with the representation of data so that it can be processed by machine learning algorithms, which is our next topic.

7.7 Extracting features from the text dataset

We have explored the concepts and techniques to clean up messy text data. Now we have cleaned the data, and it is ready to be used. The next step is to represent this data in a format that can be understood by our algorithms. As we know, our algorithms can only understand numbers.

A very simple technique to encode text data in a way that it can be useful for machine learning can be to simply perform one-hot encoding on our words and represent them in a matrix—but certainly not a scalable one if you have a complete document.

NOTE One-hot encoding is covered in the appendix.

The words can be first converted to lowercase and then sorted in alphabetical order. Then a numeric label can be assigned to them. Finally, words are converted to binary vectors. Let us understand using an example.

If the text is "It is raining heavily," we will use these steps:

1 Lowercase the words so the output will be "it is raining heavily."
2 Arrange them in alphabetical order. The result is heavily, is, it, raining.
3 Assign place values to each word as heavily:0, is:1, it:2, raining:3.
4 Transform them into binary vectors as shown here:

> [0. 0. 1. 0.] #it
> [0. 1. 0. 0.] #is
> [0. 0. 0. 1.] #raining
> [1. 0. 0. 0.]] #heavily

As we can see, we are able to represent each of the words in binary vectors, where 0 or 1 is the representation for each of the words. Though this approach is quite intuitive and simple to comprehend, it is pragmatically not possible when we have a massive corpus and vocabulary.

NOTE Corpus refers to a collection of texts. It is Latin for "body." It can be a body of written words or spoken words, which can be used to perform a linguistic analysis.

Moreover, handling massive data sizes with so many dimensions will be computationally very expensive. The resulting matrix thus created will be very sparse too. Hence, we should consider other means and ways to represent our text data.

There are better alternatives than one-hot encoding. These techniques focus on the frequency of the word or the context in which the word is being used. This scientific method of text representation is much more accurate, robust, and explanatory. There are multiple such techniques like term frequency-inverse document frequency (TF-IDF), the bag of words approach, etc. We discuss a few of these techniques later in the chapter. First, we need to examine the important concept of tokenization.

7.8   *Tokenization*

Tokenization is simply breaking a text or a set of text into individual tokens. It is the building block of NLP. Look at the example in figure 7.4, where we have created individual tokens for each word of the sentence. Tokenization is an important step as it allows us to assign unique identifiers or tokens to each of the words. Once we have allocated each word a specific token, the analysis becomes less complex.

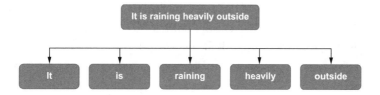

Figure 7.4   Tokenization can be used to break a sentence into different tokens of words.

Tokens are usually used on individual words, but this is not always necessary. We are allowed to tokenize a word or the subwords or characters in a word. In the case of subwords, the same sentence can have subword tokens as rain-ing (i.e., rain and ing as separate subtokens).

If we wish to perform tokenization at a character level, it can be r-a-i-n-i-n-g. In fact, in the first step of the one-hot encoding approach discussed in the last section, tokenization was done on the words. Tokenization at a character level might not always be used.

> **NOTE**   Tokenization is the building block for NPL solutions.

Once we have obtained the tokens, the tokens can be used to prepare a vocabulary. A vocabulary is the set of unique tokens in the corpus.

There are multiple libraries for tokenization. *Regexp* tokenization uses the given pattern arguments to match the tokens or separators between the tokens. *Whitespace* tokenization treats any sequence of whitespace characters as a separator. Then we have *blankline,* which uses a sequence of blank lines as a separator. Finally, *wordpunct* tokenizes by matching a sequence of alphabetic characters and a sequence of nonalphabetic and nonwhitespace characters. We will perform tokenization when we create Python solutions for our text data.

Next, we will explore more methods to represent text data. The first such method is the bag of words (BOW) approach.

7.9   BOW approach

As the name suggests, all the words in the corpus are used. In the BOW approach, the text data is tokenized for each word in the corpus, and then the respective frequency of each token is calculated. During this process, we disregard the grammar, the order, and the context of the word. We simply focus on the simplicity. Hence, we will represent each text (sentence or document) as a *bag of its own words.*

In the BOW approach for the entire document, we define the vocabulary of the corpus as all the unique words present in the corpus. Please note we use all the unique words in the corpus. If we want, we can also set a threshold (i.e., the upper and lower limit for the frequency of the words to be selected). Once we have the unique words, each of the sentences can be represented by a vector of the same dimension as the base vocabulary vector. This vector representation contains the frequency of each word of the sentence in the vocabulary. It might sound complicated, but it is actually a straightforward approach.

Let us understand this approach with an example. Let's say that we have two sentences: "It is raining heavily" and "We should eat fruits." To represent these two sentences, we calculate the frequency of each of the words in these sentences, as shown in figure 7.5.

Words	Freq
It	1
is	1
raining	1
heavily	1

It is raining heavily

Words	Freq
We	1
should	1
eat	1
fruits	1

We should eat fruits

Figure 7.5 The frequency of each word has been calculated. In this example, we have two sentences.

Now if we assume that the words in these two sentences represent the entire vocabulary, we can represent the first sentence as shown in figure 7.6. Note that the table contains all the words, but the words that are not present in the sentence have received a value of 0.

Words	Freq
eat	0
fruits	0
heavily	1
is	1
it	1
raining	1
should	0
we	0

It is raining heavily

Figure 7.6 We are assuming that in the vocabulary only two sentences are present and the first sentence will be represented as shown.

In this example, we examined how the BOW approach has been used to represent a sentence as a vector. But the BOW approach has not considered the order of the words or the context. It focuses only on the frequency of the word. Hence, it is a very fast approach to represent the data and is computationally less expensive compared to its peers. Since it is frequency based, it is commonly used for document classifications.

But, due to its pure frequency-based calculation and representation, solution accuracy using the BOW approach can take a hit. In language, the context of the word plays a significant role. As we have seen earlier, apple is both a fruit as well as a well-known brand and organization. That is why we have other advanced methods that consider more parameters than frequency alone. One such method is TF-IDF, which we will study next.

Exercise 7.2

Answer these questions to check your understanding:

1. Explain tokenization in simple language as if you are explaining it to a person who does not know NLP.
2. The bag of words approach uses the context of the words and not frequency alone. True or False?
3. Lemmatization is a less rigorous approach than stemming. True or False?

7.10   Term frequency and inverse document frequency

In the BOW approach, we give importance to the frequency of a word only. But the words that have a higher frequency might not always offer meaningful information as compared to words that are rare but carry more importance. For example, say we have a collection of medical documents, and we wish to compare two words: "disease" and "diabetes." Since the corpus consists of medical documents, the word "disease" is bound to be more frequent, while the word "diabetes" will be less frequent but more important to identify the documents that deal with diabetes. The term frequency and inverse document frequency (TF-IDF) approach allows us to resolve this problem and extract information on the more important words.

In TF-IDF, we consider the relative importance of the word. TF means term frequency, and IDF means inverse document frequency. We can define TF-IDF in this way:

- TF is the count of a term in the entire document (for example, the count of the word "a" in document "D").
- IDF is the log of the ratio of total documents (N) in the entire corpus and the number of documents (df) that contain the word "a."

So the TF-IDF formula will give us the relative importance of a word in the entire corpus. The mathematical formula is the multiplication of TF and IDF and is given by equation 7.1:

$$w_{i,j} = tf_{i,j} \times \log\left(\frac{N}{df_i}\right) \tag{7.1}$$

where N is the total number of documents in the corpus, $tf_{i,j}$ is the frequency of the word in the document, and df_i is the number of documents in the corpus that contain that word.

The concept might sound complex. Let's understand this with an example. Say we have a collection of 1 million sports journals. These sports journals contain many articles of various lengths. We also assume that all the articles are in the English language only. So, let's say, in these documents, we want to calculate the TF-IDF value for the words "ground" and "backhand."

Let's assume we have a document of 100 words with the word "ground" appearing five times and "backhand" only twice. So the TF for ground is $5/100 = 0.05$, and for backhand, it is $2/100 = 0.02$.

We understand that the word "ground" is quite a common word in sports, while the word "backhand" will be used less often. Now we assume that "ground" appears in 100,000 documents out of 1 million documents while "backhand" appears only in 10. So the IDF for "ground" is $\log (1,000,000/100,000) = \log (10) = 1$. For "backhand" it will be $\log (1,000,000/10) = \log (100,000) = 5$.

To get the final values for "ground," we multiply TF and IDF $= 0.05 \times 1 = 0.05$. To get the final values for "backhand," we multiply TF and IDF $= 0.02 \times 5 = 0.1$.

We can observe in this case that the relative importance of the word "backhand" is more than the relative importance of the word "ground." This is the advantage of TF-IDF over the frequency-based BOW approach. But TF-IDF takes more time to compute as compared to BOW, since all the TF and IDF have to be calculated. Nevertheless, TF-IDF offers a better and more mature solution as compared to the BOW approach in such cases. So, in scenarios where the relative importance of a word is in discussion, we can use TF-IDF. For example, if the task is to shortlist medical documents on cardiology, the importance of the word "angiogram" will be higher as it is much more related to cardiology.

We have so far covered BOW and the TF-IDF approach. But in neither of these approaches did we take the sequence of the words into consideration, which is covered in language models. We cover language models next.

7.11   *Language models*

Language models assign probabilities to the sequence of words. N-grams are the simplest in language models. We know that to analyze the text data, they must be converted to feature vectors. N-gram models create the feature vectors so that text can be represented in a format that can be analyzed further.

N-gram is a probabilistic language model. In an n-gram model, we calculate the probability of the Nth word given the sequence of $(N - 1)$ words. To be more specific, an n-gram model will predict the next word x_i based on the words $x_{i-(n-1)}$, $x_{i-(n-2)}...x_{i-1}$. If we wish to use the probability terms, we can represent them as the conditional probability of x_i given the previous words, which can be represented as $P(x_i \mid x_{i-(n-1)}, x_{i-(n-2)}...x_{i-1})$. The probability is calculated by using the relative frequency of the sequence occurring in the text corpus.

NOTE   If the items are words, n-grams may be referred to as *shingles.*

Let's study this using an example. We will take a sentence and then break down the meaning by using words in the sentence. Consider we have the sentence "It is raining heavily." We show the respective representations of this sentence by using different values of *n* in figure 7.6. You should note how the sequence of words and their respective combinations are getting changed for different values of *n*. If we wish to use *n* = 1 or a single word to make a prediction, the representation will be as shown in figure 7.7. Note that each word is used separately here. They are referred to as *unigrams.*

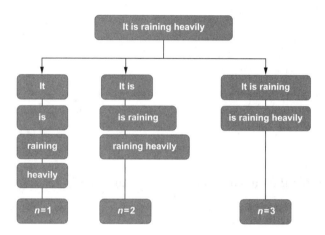

Figure 7.7 Unigrams, bigrams, and trigrams can be used to represent the same sentence. The concept can be extended to n-grams too.

If we wish to use *n* = 2, the number of words used will become two. They are referred to as *bigrams.* If we use *n* = 3, the number of words becomes three, and they are referred to as *trigrams,* and so on.

Hence, if we have a unigram, it is a sequence of one word; for two words, it is a bigram; for three words, it is a trigram; and so on. So, a trigram model will approximate the probability of a word given all the previous words by using the conditional probability of only the preceding two words, whereas a bigram will do the same by considering only the preceding word. This is a valid assumption, indeed, that the probability of a word will depend only on the preceding word and is referred to as the *Markov* assumption. Generally, *n* > 1 is considered to be much more informative than unigrams. But obviously, the computation time will increase too.

The n-gram approach is very sensitive to the choice of *n*. It also depends significantly on the training corpus that has been used, which makes the probabilities heavily dependent on the training corpus. So, if an unknown word is encountered, it will be difficult for the model to work on that new word.

Next we create a Python example. We will show a few examples of text cleaning using Python.

7.12   Text cleaning using Python

There are a few libraries you may need to install. We will show a few small code snippets. You are advised to use them as per the examples. We are also including the respective screenshots of the code snippets and their results:

Code 1: Remove the blank spaces in the text. Import the library re; it is called the Regular Expression (Regex) expression. The text is "It is raining outside" with a lot of blank spaces in between (see figure 7.8):

```
import re
doc = "It is      raining          outside"
new_doc = re.sub("\s+"," ", doc)
print(new_doc)
```

```
1  import re
2  doc = "It is      raining          outside"
3  new_doc = re.sub("\s+"," ", doc)
4  print(new_doc)
```

Figure 7.8   Removing the blank spaces

```
It is raining outside
```

Code 2: Now we will remove the punctuation in the text data (see figure 7.9):

```
text_d = "Hey!!! How are you doing? And how is your health! Bye, take care."
re.sub("[^-9A-Za-z ]", "" , text_d)
```

```
1  text_d = "Hey!!! How are you doing? And how is your health! Bye, take care."
2  re.sub("[^-9A-Za-z ]", "" , text_d)
```

```
'Hey How are you doing And how is your health Bye take care'
```

Figure 7.9   Removing the punctuation

Code 3: Here is one more method to remove the punctuation (see figure 7.10):

```
import string
text_d = "Hey!!! How are you doing? And how is your health! Bye, take care."
cleaned_text = "".join([i for i in text_d if i not in string.punctuation])
cleaned_text
```

```
1  import string
2  text_d = "Hey!!! How are you doing? And how is your health! Bye, take care."
3  cleaned_text = "".join([i for i in text_d if i not in string.punctuation])
4  cleaned_text
```

```
'Hey How are you doing And how is your health Bye take care'
```

Figure 7.10   An alternative way to remove punctuation

Code 4: We will now remove the punctuation as well as convert the text to lowercase (see figure 7.11):

```
text_d = "Hey!!! How are you doing? And how is your health! Bye, take care."
cleaned_text = "".join([i.lower() for i in text_d if i not in
string.punctuation])
cleaned_text
```

```
1
2  text_d = "Hey!!! How are you doing? And how is your health! Bye, take care."
3  cleaned_text = "".join([i.lower() for i in text_d if i not in string.punctuation])
4  cleaned_text
```

```
'hey how are you doing and how is your health bye take care'
```

Figure 7.11   Converting the text to lowercase

Code 5: Tokenization is done here using the standard `nltk` library (see figure 7.12):

```
import nltk
text_d = "Hey!!! How are you doing? And how is your health! Bye, take care."
nltk.tokenize.word_tokenize(text_d)
```

```
1  import nltk
2  text_d = "Hey!!! How are you doing? And how is your health! Bye, take care."
3  nltk.tokenize.word_tokenize(text_d)
```

```
['Hey',
 '!',
 '!',
 '!',
 'How',
 'are',
 'you',
 'doing',
 '?',
 'And',
 'how',
 'is',
 'your',
 'health',
 '!',
 'Bye',
 ',',
 'take',
 'care',
 '.']
```

Figure 7.12   Tokenization

Note that in the output of the code, we have all the words, including the punctuation marks, as different tokens. If you wish to exclude the punctuation, you can clean the punctuation marks using the code snippets shared earlier.

Code 6: Next comes the stop words. We will remove the stop words using the `nltk` library. After that, we tokenize the words (see figure 7.13):

```
stopwords = nltk.corpus.stopwords.words('english')
text_d = "Hey!!! How are you doing? And how is your health! Bye, take care."
text_new = "".join([i for i in text_d if i not in string.punctuation])
print(text_new)
words = nltk.tokenize.word_tokenize(text_new)
print(words)
words_new = [i for i in words if i not in stopwords]
print(words_new)
```

```
1  stopwords = nltk.corpus.stopwords.words('english')
2  text_d = "Hey!!! How are you doing? And how is your health! Bye, take care."
3  text_new = "".join([i for i in text_d if i not in string.punctuation])
4  print(text_new)
5  words = nltk.tokenize.word_tokenize(text_new)|
6  print(words)
7  words_new = [i for i in words if i not in stopwords]
8  print(words_new)

Hey How are you doing And how is your health Bye take care
['Hey', 'How', 'are', 'you', 'doing', 'And', 'how', 'is', 'your', 'health', 'Bye', 'take', 'care']
['Hey', 'How', 'And', 'health', 'Bye', 'take', 'care']
```

Figure 7.13   Removing stop words and tokenizing words

Code 7: We will now perform stemming on a text example. We use `nltk` library for it. The words are first tokenized, and then we apply stemming (see figure 7.14):

```
import nltk
from nltk.stem import PorterStemmer
stem = PorterStemmer()
text = "eats eating studies study"
tokenization = nltk.word_tokenize(text)
for word in tokenization:
    print("Stem for {} is {}".format(word, stem.stem(word)))
```

```
1  import nltk
2  from nltk.stem import PorterStemmer
3  stem = PorterStemmer()
4  text = "eats eating studies study"
5  tokenization = nltk.word_tokenize(text)
6  for word in tokenization:
7      print("Stem for {} is {}".format(word, stem.stem(w)))

Stem for eats is eat
Stem for eating is eat
Stem for studies is studi
Stem for study is study
```

Figure 7.14   Tokenizing and then stemming the words

Code 8: We now perform lemmatization on a text example. We use the `nltk` library for it. The words are first tokenized, and then we apply lemmatization (see figure 7.15):

```
import nltk
from nltk.stem import WordNetLemmatizer
wordnet_lemmatizer = WordNetLemmatizer()
text = "eats eating studies study"
tokenization = nltk.word_tokenize(text)
for word in tokenization:
    print("Lemma for {} is {}".format(word,
     wordnet_lemmatizer.lemmatize(word)))
```

```
1  import nltk
2  from nltk.stem import WordNetLemmatizer
3  wordnet_lemmatizer = WordNetLemmatizer()
4  text = "eats eating studies study"
5  tokenization = nltk.word_tokenize(text)
6  for word in tokenization:
7      print("Lemma for {} is {}".format(word, wordnet_lemmatizer.lemmatize(w)))
```

```
Lemma for eats is eat
Lemma for eating is eat
Lemma for studies is study
Lemma for study is study
```

Figure 7.15   Tokenizing and then lemmatizing the words

Observe and compare the difference between the two outputs of stemming and lemmatization. For "studies" and "studying," stemming generated the output as "studi" while lemmatization generated the correct output as "study."

We have covered BOW, TF-IDF, and n-gram approaches so far. But in all these techniques, the relationship between words has been neglected. This relationship is used in word embeddings, our next topic.

7.13   Word embeddings

> *A word is characterized by the company it keeps.*
>
> —John Rupert Firth

So far we have studied several approaches, but all the techniques ignore the contextual relationship between words. Let's take a closer look using an example.

Imagine we have 100,000 words in our vocabulary, starting from "aa" (the basaltic lava) to "zoom." Now, if we perform one-hot encoding, all these words can be represented in a vector form. Each word will have a unique vector. For example, if the position of the word "king" is 21000, the vector will have a shape like the following vector, which has 1 at the 21,000th position and the rest of the values as 0:

`[0,0,0,0,0,0,0,0,0,0,0,0,0,0,0,0.................1, 0,0,0,0,0,0,0,0,0,0,0,0,0,0,0,0]`

There are a few glaring problems with this approach:

- The number of dimensions is very high, and it is complex to compute.
- The data is very sparse in nature.
- If n new words have to be entered, the vocabulary increases by n, and hence each vector dimensionality increases by n.
- This approach ignores the relationship between words. We know that "ruler," "king," and "monarch" are sometimes used interchangeably. In the one-hot-encoding approach, any such relationships are ignored.

If we wish to perform language translation, or generate a chat-bot, we need to pass such knowledge to the machine learning solution. Word embeddings provide a solution to the problem. They convert the high-dimensional word features into lower dimensions while maintaining the contextual relationship. Word embeddings allow us to create much more generalized models. We can understand the meaning by looking at an example.

> **NOTE** In an LLM-enabled solution, you might not need to do a lot of these steps.

In the example shown in figure 7.16, the relation of "man" to "woman" is similar to "king" to "queen"; "good" to "nice" is similar to "bad" to "awful"; or the relationship of "UK" to "London" is similar to "Japan" to "Tokyo."

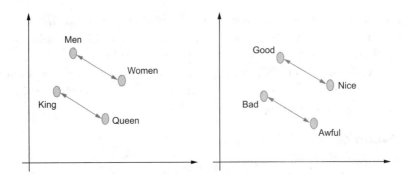

Figure 7.16 Word embeddings can be used to represent the relationships between words. For example, there is a relation from "men" to "women" that is similar to "king" to "queen" as both "men-women" and "king-queen" represent the male-female gender relationship.

In simple terms, using word embeddings, we can represent the words that have similar meanings. Word embeddings can be thought of as a class of techniques where we represent each of the individual words in a predefined vector space. Each of the words in the corpus is mapped to one vector. The distributed representation is understood based on the word's usage. Hence, words that can be used similarly have similar representations. This allows the solution to capture the underlying meaning of the words and their relationships. Hence, the meaning of the word plays a significant role. This representation is more intelligent as compared to the BOW approach where each word is treated differently, irrespective of its usage. Also, the number of dimensions is fewer as compared to one-hot encoding. Each word is represented by 10s or 100s of dimensions, which is significantly less than the one-hot encoding approach where 1000s of dimensions are used for representation.

We cover the two most popular techniques—Word2Vec and global vectors for word representation (GloVe)—in the next section. The mathematical foundation for Word2Vec and GloVe are beyond the scope of this book. We provide an understanding of the working mechanism of the solutions and then develop Python code using Word2Vec and GloVe. This section is more technically involved, so if you are interested only in the application of the solutions, you can skip the next section.

7.14 Word2Vec and GloVe

Word2Vec was first published in 2013. It was developed by Tomas Mikolov and others at Google. We share the link to the paper at the end of the chapter. You are advised to study the paper thoroughly if you wish to learn about the more technical elements in detail.

Word2Vec is a group of models used to produce word embeddings. The input is a large corpus of text. The output is a vector space with a very large number of dimensions. In this output, each of the words in the corpus is assigned a unique and corresponding vector. The most important point is that the words that have a similar or common context in the corpus are located nearby in the vector space produced.

In Word2Vec, the researchers introduced two different learning models—the continuous bag of words (CBOW) and the continuous skip-gram model:

- In CBOW, the model makes a prediction of the current word from a window of surrounding context words. So the CBOW model predicts a target word based on the context of the surrounding words in the text. Recall that in the BOW approach, the order of the words does not play any part. In contrast, in CBOW, the order of the words is significant.

- The continuous skip-gram model uses the current word to predict the surrounding window of context words. While doing so, it allocates more weight to the neighboring words as compared to the distant words.

GloVe is an unsupervised learning algorithm for generating vector representation for words. It was developed by Pennington and others at Stanford and launched in 2014. It is a combination of two techniques: matrix factorization techniques and local context-based learning used in Word2Vec. GloVe can be used to find relationships like zip codes and cities, synonyms, etc. It generates a single set of vectors for words with the same morphological structure.

Both Word2Vec and GloVe learn and understand vector representation of their words from the co-occurrence information. Co-occurrence means how frequently the words appear together in a large corpus. The prime difference is that Word2Vec is a prediction-based model, while GloVe is a frequency-based model. Word2Vec predicts the context given a word while GloVe learns the context by creating a co-occurrence matrix on how frequently a word appears in a given context.

> **Exercise 7.3**
>
> Answer these questions to check your understanding:
>
>   1 BOW is more rigorous than the TF-IDF approach. True or False?
>   2 Differentiate between Word2Vec and GloVe.

We will now move to the case study and Python implementation.

7.15 *Sentiment analysis case study with Python implementation*

So far, we have discussed a lot of concepts on NLP and text data. In this section, we first explore a business case and then develop a Python solution based on it. Here we are working on sentiment analysis.

Product reviews are a rich source of information—both for customers and organizations. Whenever we wish to buy any new product or service, we tend to look at the reviews by fellow customers. You might have reviewed products and services yourself. These reviews are available at Amazon and on blogs, surveys, etc.

Let's consider a case. A telecom operator receives complaints from its customers, reviews about the service, and comments about the overall experience. The streams can be product quality, pricing, onboarding experience, ease of registration, payment process, general reviews, customer service, etc. We want to determine the general context of the review—whether it is positive, negative, or neutral. The reviews include the number of stars allocated, actual text reviews, pros and cons about the product/service, attributes, etc. However, there are a few business problems—for instance,

- Sometimes the number of stars received by a product/service is very high, while the actual reviews are quite negative.
- The organizations and the product owners need to know which features are appreciated by the customers and which features are disliked by the customers. The team can then work on improving the features that are disliked.
- There is a need to gauge and keep an eye on the competition! The organizations need to know the attributes of the popular products of their competitors.
- The product owners want to better plan for the upcoming features they wish to release in the future.

So the business teams will be able to answer these important questions:

- What are our customers' satisfaction levels for the products and services?
- What are the major pain points and dissatisfactions of the customers?

- What drives the customers' engagement?
- Which services are complex and time-consuming, and which are the most liked services/products?

This business use case will drive the following business benefits:

- The products and services that are most satisfactory and are the most liked should be continued.
- The ones that are not liked and are receiving a negative score should be improved and challenges mitigated.
- The respective teams, like finance, operations, complaints, CRM, etc., can be notified, and they can work individually to improve the customer experience.
- The precise reasons for liking or disliking the services will be useful for the respective teams to work in the right direction.
- Overall, it will provide a benchmark to measure the Net Promoter Score for the customer base. The business can strive to enhance the overall customer experience.

We might want to represent these findings by means of a dashboard. This dashboard will be refreshed on a regular cycle, like monthly or quarterly.

To solve this business problem, the teams can collect relevant data from websites, surveys, Amazon, blogs, etc. Then an analysis can be done on that dataset. It is relatively easy to analyze the structured data. In this example, we work on text data.

The Python Jupyter notebook is pushed to the GitHub location. You are advised to use the Jupyter notebook from the GitHub location as it contains more steps. The steps are as follows:

1 Import all the libraries:

```
#### Loading all the required libraries here
from lxml import html
import requests
import pandas as pd
from nltk.corpus import stopwords
from textblob import TextBlob
import matplotlib.pyplot as plt
import sys
import numpy as np
import pandas as pd
import matplotlib
import matplotlib.pyplot as plt
import sklearn
import scikitplot as skplt
import nltk
#to ignore warnings
import warnings
warnings.filterwarnings("ignore")
nltk.download('stopwords')
nltk.download('punkt')
nltk.download('wordnet')
```

2 Define the tags. These tags are used to get the attributes of the product from the reviews:

```
xpath_reviews = '//div[@data-hook="review"]'
reviews = parser.xpath(xpath_reviews)
xpath_rating  = './/i[@data-hook="review-star-rating"]//text()'
xpath_title   = './/a[@data-hook="review-title"]//text()'
xpath_author  = './/a[@data-hook="review-author"]//text()'
xpath_date    = './/span[@data-hook="review-date"]//text()'
xpath_body    = './/span[@data-hook="review-body"]//text()'
xpath_helpful = './/span[@data-hook="helpful-vote-statement"]//text()'
```

3 Make everything ready to extract the data. We create a dataframe to store the customer reviews. Then we iterate through all the reviews and extract the information:

```
# Create a dataframe here.

reviews_df = pd.DataFrame()
for review in reviews:
    rating  = review.xpath(xpath_rating)
    title   = review.xpath(xpath_title)
    author  = review.xpath(xpath_author)
    date    = review.xpath(xpath_date)
    body    = review.xpath(xpath_body)
    helpful = review.xpath(xpath_helpful)

    review_dict = {'rating': rating,
                   'title': title,
                   'author': author,
                   'date': date,
                   'body': body,
                   'helpful': helpful}
    reviews_df = reviews_df.append(review_dict, ignore_index=True)
all_reviews = pd.DataFrame()
```

4 Iterate through the reviews and then fill in the details:

```
# Fill the values of the reviews here.

for i in range(1,90):
    amazon_url = 'https://www.amazon.co.uk/Hive-Heating-Thermostat-
    Professional-Installation/product-reviews/B011B3J6KY/
    ref=cm_cr_othr_d_show_all?ie=UTF8&reviewerType=all_revie
ws&pageNumber='+str(i)
    headers = {'User-Agent': user_agent}
    page = requests.get(amazon_url, headers = headers)
    parser = html.fromstring(page.content)
    xpath_reviews = '//div[@data-hook="review"]'
    reviews = parser.xpath(xpath_reviews)
    reviews_df = pd.DataFrame()
    xpath_rating  = './/i[@data-hook="review-star-rating"]//text()'
    xpath_title   = './/a[@data-hook="review-title"]//text()'
    xpath_author  = './/a[@data-hook="review-author"]//text()'
```

```
xpath_date    = './/span[@data-hook="review-date"]//text()'
xpath_body    = './/span[@data-hook="review-body"]//text()'
xpath_helpful = './/span[@data-hook="helpful-vote-statement"]//text()'
#print(i)
for review in reviews:
    rating  = review.xpath(xpath_rating)
    title   = review.xpath(xpath_title)
    author  = review.xpath(xpath_author)
    date    = review.xpath(xpath_date)
    body    = review.xpath(xpath_body)
    helpful = review.xpath(xpath_helpful)

    review_dict = {'rating': rating,
                   'title': title,
                   'author': author,
                   'date': date,
                   'body': body,
                   'helpful': helpful}
    reviews_df = reviews_df.append(review_dict, ignore_index=True)
#print(reviews_df)
all_reviews = all_reviews.append(reviews_df)
```

5 Have a look at the output we generated:

```
all_reviews.head()
```

6 Save the output to a path. You can give your own path:

```
out_folder = '/Users/Data/'
all_reviews.to_csv(out_folder + 'Reviews.csv')
```

7 Load the data and analyze it:

```
#Load the data now and analyse it
data_path = '/Users/vaibhavverdhan/Book/UnsupervisedLearningBookFinal/'
reviewDataCSV = 'Reviews.csv'
reviewData = (pd.read_csv(data_path+reviewDataCSV,index_col=0,))
```

8 Look at the basic information about the dataset:

```
reviewData.shape
reviewData.rating.unique()
reviewData.rating.value_counts()
```

9 Look at the distribution of the stars given in the reviews. This will allow us to
   understand the reviews given by the customers:

```
labels = '5 Stars', '1 Star', '4 Stars', '3 Stars', '2 Stars'
sizes = [reviewData.rating.value_counts()[0],
    reviewData.rating.value_counts()[1],reviewData.rating.value_counts(
    )[2],rev
iewData.rating.value_counts()[3],reviewData.rating.value_counts()[4]]
colors = ['green', 'yellowgreen', 'coral', 'lightblue', 'grey']
explode = (0, 0, 0, 0, 0)  # explode 1st slice
```

```
# Plot
plt.pie(sizes, explode=explode, labels=labels, colors=colors,
        autopct='%1.1f%%', shadow=True, startangle=140)

plt.axis('equal')
plt.show()
```

10 Make the text lowercase, and then remove the stop words and the words that have the highest frequency:

```
reviewData.body = reviewData.body.str.lower()
reviewData.body = reviewData.body.str.replace('[^\w\s]','')
stop = stopwords.words('english')
reviewData.body = reviewData.body.apply(lambda x: " ".join(x for x in
x.split() if x not in stop))
freq = list(freq.index)
reviewData.body = reviewData.body.apply(lambda x: " ".join(x for x in
    x.split() if x not in freq))
freq = pd.Series(' '.join(reviewData.body).split()).value_counts()[-10:]
freq = list(freq.index)
reviewData.body = reviewData.body.apply(lambda x: " ".join(x for x in
x.split() if x not in freq))
```

11 Tokenize the data:

```
from nltk.tokenize import word_tokenize
tokens = word_tokenize(reviewData.iloc[1,1])
print(tokens)
```

12 Perform lemmatization:

```
from textblob import Word
reviewData.body = reviewData.body.apply(lambda x: "
    ".join([Word(word).lemmatize() for word in x.split()]))
reviewData.body.head()
```

13 Append all the reviews to the string:

```
sentimentString = reviewData.iloc[1,1]
# append to this string
for i in range(2,len(reviewData)):
    sentimentString = sentimentString + reviewData.iloc[i,1]
```

14 Do the sentiment analysis. From `textblob`, we take the sentiment method. It generates polarity and subjectivity for a sentiment. Sentiment polarity for an element is the orientation of the sentiment in the expression; that is, it tells us if the text expresses a negative, positive, or neutral sentiment in the text. It subjectively measures and quantifies the amount of opinion and factual information in the text. If the subjectivity is high, it means that the text contains more opinion than facts:

```
# the functions generates polarity and subjectivity here, subsetting the
polarity only here
```

```
allReviewsSentiment = reviewData.body[:900].apply(lambda x:
TextBlob(x).sentiment[0])
# this contains boths subjectivity and polarity
allReviewsSentimentComplete = reviewData.body[:900].apply(lambda x:
TextBlob(x).sentiment)
allReviewsSentimentComplete.head()
```

15 Save the sentiment to a .csv file:

```
allReviewsSentiment.to_csv(out_folder + 'ReviewsSentiment.csv')
```

16 Allocate a meaning or a tag to the sentiment. We classify each of the scores from extremely satisfied to extremely dissatisfied:

```
allReviewsSentimentDF = allReviewsSentiment.to_frame()
# Create a list to store the data
grades = []

# For each row in the column,
for row in allReviewsSentimentDF['body']:
    # if more than a value,
    if row >= 0.75:
        grades.append('Extremely Satisfied')
    elif (row >= 0.5) & (row < 0.75):
        grades.append('Satisfied')
    elif (row >= 0.2) & (row < 0.5):
        grades.append('Nice')
    elif (row >= -0.2) & (row < 0.2):
        grades.append('Neutral')
    elif (row > -0.5) & (row <= -0.2):
        grades.append('Bad')
    elif (row >= -0.75) & (row < -0.5):
        grades.append('Dis-satisfied')
    elif  row < -0.75:
        grades.append('Extremely Dis-satisfied')
    else:
        # Append a failing grade
        grades.append('No Sentiment')

# Create a column from the list
allReviewsSentimentDF['SentimentScore'] = grades
allReviewsSentimentDF.head()
```

17   Look at the sentiment scores and plot them too. Finally, we merge them with the main dataset:

```
allReviewsSentimentDF.SentimentScore.value_counts()
allReviewsSentimentDF['SentimentScore'].value_counts().plot(kind='bar')
#### Merge the review data with Sentiment generated

reviewData['polarityScore'] = allReviewsSentimentDF['body']        ◁
```

**Adds column
polarityScore**

In this case study, you not only scraped the reviews from the website but you also analyzed the dataset. If we compare the sentiments, we can see that the stars given to a product do not represent a true picture.

Figure 7.17 compares the actual stars and the output from sentiment analysis. We can observe that 73% of customers have given five stars and 7% have given four stars, while in the sentiment analysis most of the reviews have been classified as neutral. This is the real power of sentiment analysis!

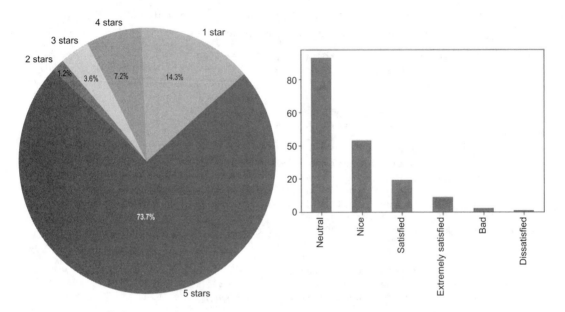

Figure 7.17   Compare the original distribution of number of stars on the left side and the real results from the sentiment analysis on the right.

Sentiment analysis is quite an important use case. It is very useful for business and product teams. The preceding code can be scaled to any such business problem at hand.

We now move to the second case study on document classification using Python.

7.16 *Text clustering using Python*

Consider this: we have a bunch of text datasets or documents, but they all are mixed up. We do not know which text belongs to which class. In this case, we will assume that we have two types of text datasets: one that has all the data related to football and one that is related to travel. We will develop a model that can segregate these two classes. To do that, we follow these steps:

1 Import all the libraries:

```
from sklearn.feature_extraction.text import TfidfVectorizer
from sklearn.cluster import KMeans
```

```
import numpy as np
import pandas as pd
```

2   Create a dummy dataset. This text data has a few sentences we have written our-
    selves. There are two categories:

```
text = ["It is a good place to travel",
        "Football is a nice game", "Lets go for holidays and travel to
Egypt",
        "It is a goal, a great game.", "Enjoy your journey and forget
the rest", "The teams are ready for the same" ]
```

3   Use TF-IDF to vectorize the data:

```
tfidf_vectorizer = TfidfVectorizer(stop_words='english')
X = tfidf_vectorizer.fit_transform(text)
```

4   Do the clustering:

```
k = 2
model = KMeans(n_clusters=k, init='k-means++', max_iter=10, n_init=2)
model.fit(X)
```

5   Represent the centroids and print the outputs (see figure 7.18):

```
centroids = model.cluster_centers_.argsort()[:, ::-1]
features = vectorizer.get_feature_names()

for i in range(k):
    print("Cluster %d:" % i),
    for ind in centroids[i, :10]:
        print("%s" % terms[ind])
```

```
1   for i in range(k):
2       print("Cluster %d:" % i),
3       for ind in centroids[i, :10]:
4           print("%s" % terms[ind])
```

```
Cluster 0:
travel
ready
teams
good
place
lets
holidays
egypt
journey
rest
Cluster 1:
game
great
football
nice
goal
travel
enjoy
fortget
good
holidays
```

Figure 7.18
Printed output

You can extend this example to other datasets too. Get the datasets from the internet and replicate the code in the preceding example.

We have pushed the code to the GitHub location of the book. You are advised to use it. It is really an important source to represent text data.

7.17 GenAI for text data

GenAI solutions are a new kind of unsupervised solution. You surely have heard about ChatGPT and LLMs. They have revolutionized the world. GenAI for text data uses machine learning models to create human-like text. It is trained on large-scale data patterns and hence can generate a variety of content pieces—for example, essays, technical reports, and summaries of a book—and can act like a human chat interface. Even the complex translation of languages is made easy with GenAI.

GenAI for text data involves the use of advanced algorithms, like transformers, to generate coherent, contextually appropriate text. These algorithms are trained on mammoth datasets. Imagine we feed tons of content present on the internet to the algorithms. By learning patterns and relationships between the words and the sentences, the grammar used, syntax, and semantics, they can create human-like responses. These models, such as OpenAI's GPT or Google's BERT, are very powerful for drafting emails with correct language and grammar, creating detailed reports, writing code modules in a language like Java/C++, and many other tasks. Using this power, content creators, writers and copyrighters, brand managers and marketers, and business owners can produce high-quality text in a much more scalable and efficient manner.

Despite its amazing potential, GenAI still has some areas in need of improvement. Sometimes it generates inaccurate information, also known as hallucinations. Ensuring that the output remains unbiased and ethical is another hurdle, as models can inadvertently reflect societal biases present in the data they were trained on. AI-generated text is increasingly being used in customer service, automating responses while still maintaining a personal tone. Researchers are also exploring its use in the healthcare and legal fields, where it can help with documentation and drafting. While GenAI is revolutionizing the way text is produced, the need for human oversight remains critical to ensure quality, accuracy, and fairness.

7.18 Concluding thoughts

Text data is one of the most useful datasets. A lot of intelligence is hidden in the texts: logs, blogs, reviews, posts, tweets, complaints, comments, articles, and so on—the sources of text data are many. Organizations are investing in setting up the infrastructure for accessing text data and storing it. Analyzing text data requires better processing powers and better machines than our standard laptops. It requires special skill sets and a deeper understanding of the concepts. NLP is an evolving field, and a lot of research is underway. At the same time, we cannot ignore the importance of sound business acumen and knowledge.

Data analysis and machine learning are not easy. We have to understand a lot of concepts around data cleaning, exploration, representation, and modeling. But analyzing unstructured data might be even more complex than analyzing structured datasets. We worked on an images dataset in the last chapter, and in the current chapter, we worked on text data.

Text data is one of the most difficult datasets to analyze. There are so many permutations and combinations for text data. Cleaning the text data is a difficult and complex task. In this chapter, we discussed a few important techniques to clean text data. We also covered some methods to represent text data in vector forms. You are advised to practice each of these methods and compare the performances by applying each of the techniques. We also introduced the concept of GenAI for text data.

With this, we come to the end of chapter 7. This also marks an end to part 2. In the next part, the complexity increases. We will be studying even deeper concepts of unsupervised learning algorithms.

7.19 *Practical next steps and suggested readings*

The following provides suggestions for what to do next and offers some helpful reading:

- Get the datasets from the following link. You will find a lot of text datasets here. You are advised to implement clustering and dimensionality reduction solutions:
  - 50 Free Machine Learning Datasets: Natural Language Processing: https://mng.bz/ZljO

- You will find a lot of useful datasets at Kaggle as well: https://www.kaggle.com/datasets?search=text
- Go through the following research papers:
  - Mikolov, T., Chen, K., Corrado, G., and Dean, J. (2013). Efficient Estimation of Word Representations in Vector Space. https://arxiv.org/pdf/1301.3781.pdf
  - Pennington, J., Socher, R., and Manning, C. D. (2014). GloVe: Global Vectors for Word Representation. https://nlp.stanford.edu/pubs/glove.pdf
  - Das, B., and Chakraborty, S. (2018). An Improved Text Sentiment Classification Model Using TF-IDF and Next Word Negation. https://arxiv.org/pdf/1806.06407.pdf

- Consider these widely quoted papers:
  - Blum, A., and Mitchell, T. (1998). Combining labeled and unlabeled data with co-training. https://dl.acm.org/doi/10.1145/279943.279962
  - Knight, K. (2009). Bayesian Inference with Tears. https://mng.bz/RVp0
  - Hofmann, T. (1999). Probabilistic latent semantic indexing. https://dl.acm.org/doi/10.1145/312624.312649
  - Hindle, D., and Rooth, M. (1993). Structural Ambiguity and Lexical Relations. https://aclanthology.org/J93-1005.pdf

       – Collins and Singer. (1999). Unsupervised Models for Named Entity Classification. https://aclanthology.org/W99-0613.pdf

- See the comprehensive study on TF-IDF feature weighting: Das, M., Selvakumar, K., and Alphonse, J. P. A. (2023). A Comparative Study on TF-IDF Feature Weighting Method and its Analysis using Unstructured Dataset. https://arxiv.org/abs/2308.04037

Summary

- Text data's omnipresence in blogs, social media, surveys, and more, and its capacity to express emotions, emphasizes the importance of this form of data.
- Applications of text analysis include sentiment analysis, document categorization, language translation, spam filtering, and named-entity recognition.
- Challenges in text data include handling junk characters, multiple languages, evolving language, synonyms, and context-based meanings.
- Data preprocessing and cleaning involves removing stop words and unwanted characters and normalizing text through stemming and lemmatization.
- Within text representation techniques, one-hot encoding is basic but not scalable; advanced techniques consider frequency and context.
- Tokenization involves breaking down text into tokens and is fundamental for creating analysis-ready datasets.
- The BOW approach is a fast, frequency-based method that ignores word order and context.
- TF-IDF weighs words based on importance over mere frequency, offering more insightful analysis than BOW.
- Language models and n-grams use word sequences for probabilistic predictions, with variations like unigrams, bigrams, and trigrams.
- Python for text parsing illustrates cleaning and preprocessing text data using Python libraries like `nltk`.
- Techniques like Word2Vec and GloVe maintain contextual relationships between words for better semantic understanding.
- Word2Vec is prediction based, while GloVe is frequency based; both create compact and meaningful word representations.
- LLMs have revolutionized the entire landscape for text datasets.

Part 3

Advanced concepts

Welcome to the final part of the book.

You've completed the first two parts of the book: you've built programs, solved case studies, and navigated the foundational challenges of unsupervised learning solutions. But machine learning, like any other discipline, art, or sport, has no finish line. It's a constantly evolving field wherein constant upgradation is required, and to truly be a master, you must adapt and improve, innovate and learn, and push the boundaries of what you know.

In this final part of the book, we'll dive into the more nuanced aspects of unsupervised learning. We will cover much more advanced topics that separate good data scientists from great ones: deep learning, autoencoders, generative AI, and patterns that scale across large applications. We will also cover the end-to-end lifecycle of a machine learning project, including deployment and maintenance.

But don't be fooled—this part isn't about quick Python codes that you can cut and paste. These advanced techniques are about developing a much more sophisticated system that can be used for datasets like text, images, and videos. It's about making more bespoke solutions that are customizable as well as scalable. These solutions don't just work today but will work tomorrow too.

Are you ready to take your skills to the next level? Let's dig deeper.

Deep learning: The foundational concepts

The art of simplicity is a puzzle of complexity.

—Douglas Horton

Welcome to the third part of the book. So far, you have covered a lot of concepts and case studies and Python code. From this chapter onward, the level of complexity will be even higher.

In the first two parts of the book, we covered various unsupervised learning algorithms like clustering, dimensionality reduction, etc. We discussed both simpler and advanced algorithms. We also covered working on text data in the second part of the book. Starting from this third part of the book, we will start our journey on deep learning.

Deep learning and neural networks have changed the world and the business domains. You have probably heard about deep learning and neural networks. Their implementations and sophistication result in better cancer detection, autonomous driving cars, improved disaster management systems, better pollution control systems, reduced fraud in transactions, and so on.

In the third part of the book, we will explore unsupervised learning using deep learning. We will study what deep learning is and the basics of neural networks, as well as the layers in a neural network, activation functions, the process of deep learning, and various libraries. Then we will move to autoencoders and generative adversarial networks (GANs) and generative AI (GenAI). The topics are indeed complex and sometimes quite mathematically heavy. We will use different kinds of datasets for working on the problems, but primarily the datasets will be unstructured in nature. As always, Python will be used to generate the solutions. We also share a lot of external resources to complement the concepts. Please note that these are advanced topics, and a lot of research is still ongoing for these topics.

We have divided the third part of the book into four chapters. This chapter covers the foundational concepts of deep learning and neural networks. The next two chapters focus on autoencoders, GAN and GenAI. The final chapter of the book talks about the deployment of these models.

In this chapter, we discuss the concepts of neural networks and deep learning. We discuss what a neural network is, its activation functions, different optimization functions, the neural network training process, etc. The concepts covered in this chapter form the base of neural networks and deep learning and subsequent learning in the next two chapters. Hence, it is vital that you are clear about these concepts. The best external resources to learn these concepts in more detail are given at the end of the chapter.

Welcome to the eighth chapter, and all the very best!

8.1   Technical toolkit

We will continue to use the same version of Python and Jupyter Notebook as we have used so far. The codes and datasets used in this chapter have been checked in at the same GitHub location. You will need to install a couple of Python libraries in this chapter: `tensorflow` and `keras`.

8.1.1   Deep learning: What is it? What does it do?

Deep learning has gathered a lot of momentum in the past few years. Neural networks are pushing the boundaries of machine learning solutions. Deep learning is machine learning only. Deep learning is based on neural networks. It utilizes a similar concept—that is, using historical data and understanding the attributes and the intelligence gathered to find patterns or predict the future, albeit deep learning is more complex than the algorithms we have covered so far.

Recall chapter 1, where we covered the concepts of structured and unstructured datasets. Unstructured datasets include text, images, audio, video, etc. Figure 8.1 describes the major sources of text, images, audio, and video datasets.

Figure 8.1   **Unstructured datasets like text, audio, images, and video can be analyzed using deep learning. There are multiple sources of such datasets.**

While deep learning can be implemented for structured datasets too, it is mostly working wonders on unstructured datasets. One of the prime reasons is that the classical machine learning algorithms are sometimes not that effective on unstructured datasets like that of images, text, audio, and video. A few of the path-breaking solutions delivered by deep learning across various domains are as follows:

- *The medical field and pharmaceuticals*—Deep learning sees application in areas such as the identification of bones and joint problems or in determining if there are any clots in arteries or veins. In the pharmaceutical field, it expedites clinical trials and helps to reach the target drug faster.
- *The banking and financial sector*—Deep learning-based algorithms are used to detect potential fraud in transactions. Using image recognition-based algorithms, we can also distinguish fake signatures on checks.
- *The automobile sector*—You have probably heard about autonomous driving (aka self-driving) cars. Using deep learning, the algorithms can detect traffic signals, pedestrians, other vehicles on the road, their respective distances, and so on.
- *Retail*—In the retail sector, using deep learning-based algorithms, humans can improve customer targeting and develop advanced and customized marketing tactics. The recommended models to provide next-best products to the customers have been improved using deep learning. We can get better returns on investments and improve cross-sell and upsell strategies.

In addition, automatic speech recognition is possible with deep learning. Using sophisticated neural networks, humans can create speech recognition algorithms. These solutions are being used across Siri, Alexa, Translator, Baidu, etc.

Image recognition is also advancing. Neural networks are improving image recognition techniques. This can be done using convolutional neural networks, which are improving computer vision. Use cases include the following:

- Deep learning is quite effective for differentiation between cancerous cells and benign cells. Differentiation can be achieved by using the images of cancerous cells and benign cells.

- An automated number plate reading system has been developed using neural networks.
- Object detection methods and monitor sensing and tracking systems can be developed using deep learning.
- In disaster management systems, deep learning can detect the presence of humans in affected areas. Just imagine how, during rescue operations, human lives can be saved using better detection.

GenAI is changing the world rapidly. Use cases include automating content creation, such as writing articles, essays, and social media posts and generating images and videos. It improves customer service and customer experience by providing chatbots that provide instant, personalized responses to the queries of the customers. It can be implemented in any industry. In data-heavy industries, it creates ripples by summarizing complex and long documents and generating insights from dashboards and reports. These reports can be Power BI/Tableau dashboards, PowerPoints, or pdf files, for example. It has also helped software developers in code generation and debugging and has improved software development efficiency. The use cases are many, ranging from retail; telecommunications; healthcare; R&D; banking, finance, and insurance, etc., in improving sales, reducing costs, saving time, and improving accuracy.

The use cases listed are certainly not exhaustive. Using deep learning, we can improve natural language processing solutions used to measure customers' sentiments, language translation, text classification, named-entity recognition, etc. Across use cases in bioinformatics, the military, mobile advertising, technology, the supply chain, and so on, deep learning is paving the path for the future.

8.2   Building blocks of a neural network

Artificial neural networks (ANNs) are said to be inspired by the way the human brain works. The human brain is the best machine we currently have access to. When we see a picture or a face or hear a tune, we associate a label or a name with it. That allows us to train our brain and senses to recognize a picture or a face or a tune when we see/hear it again. ANNs learn to perform similar tasks by learning or getting trained.

Exercise 8.1
Answer these questions to check your understanding:
1 What is the meaning of deep learning?
2 Neural networks cannot be used for unsupervised learning. True or False?
3 Explore more use cases for deep learning in nonconventional business domains.

8.2.1   Neural networks for solutions

In deep learning, too, the concepts of supervised and unsupervised learning are applicable. We cover both types of training of the network: supervised and unsupervised.

This will give you a complete picture. At the same time, to fully appreciate unsupervised deep learning, you should be clear on the supervised deep learning process.

Let's understand the deep learning process by using an example. Consider this: we wish to create a solution that can identify faces—a solution that can distinguish faces and identify the person by allocating a name to the face. For training the model, we will use a dataset that will have images of people's faces and corresponding names. The ANN will start with no prior understanding of the image's dataset or the attributes. During the process of training, it will learn the attributes and the identification characteristics from the training data. These learned attributes are then used to distinguish between faces. At this moment, we are only covering the process at a high level; we will cover this process in much more detail in subsequent sections. Figure 8.2 shows a representation of a neural network.

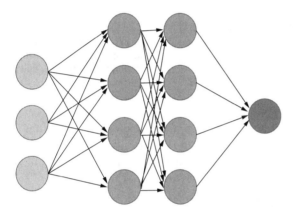

Figure 8.2 A typical neural network with neurons and various layers

The process in a neural network is quite complex. We will first cover all the building blocks of a neural network, like neurons, activation functions, weights, bias terms, etc., and then move on to the process followed in a neural network. Let's start with the protagonist: a neuron.

8.2.2 *Artificial neurons and perceptrons*

The human brain contains billions of neurons. The neurons are interconnected cells in our brains. These neurons receive signals, process them, and generate results. Artificial neurons are based on biological neurons only and can be considered simplified computational models of biological neurons.

In 1943, researchers Warren McCullock and Walter Pitts proposed the concept of a simplified brain cell called the McCullock-Pitts neuron. It can be thought of as a simple logic gate with binary outputs.

The working methodology for artificial neurons is similar to that of biological neurons, albeit artificial neurons are far simpler than biological neurons. A perceptron is a mathematical model of a biological neuron. In the actual biological neurons, dendrites receive electrical signals from the axons of other neurons. In a perceptron, these electrical signals are represented as numerical values.

The artificial neuron receives inputs from the previous neurons or can receive the input data. It then processes that input information and shares an output. The input can be the raw data or processed information from a preceding neuron. The neuron then combines the input with its own internal state, weighs them separately, and passes the output received through a nonlinear function to generate output. These nonlinear functions are also called activation functions (we will cover them later). You can think of an activation function as a mathematical function. A neuron can be represented as shown in figure 8.3.

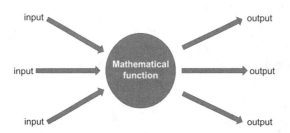

Figure 8.3   A neuron gets the inputs, processes them using mathematical functions, and then generates the output.

In simpler terms, a neuron can be termed as a mathematical function that computes the weighted average of its input datasets; then this sum is passed through activation functions. The output of the neuron can then be the input to the next neuron, which will again process the input received. Let's go a bit deeper.

In a perceptron, each input value is multiplied by a factor called the *weight*. Biological neurons fire once the total strength of the input signals exceeds a certain threshold. A similar format is followed in a perceptron. In a perceptron, a weighted sum of the inputs is calculated to get the total strength of the input data, and then an activation function is applied to each of the outputs. Each output can then be fed to the next layer of perceptron.

Let's assume that there are two input values, a and b, for a perceptron X, which for the sake of simplicity has only one output. Let the respective weights for a and b be P and Q. So the weighted sum can be calculated as $P * X + Q * b$. The perceptron will fire or will have a nonzero output only if the weighted sum exceeds a certain threshold. Let's call the threshold C. So, we can say the following:

The output of X will be 0 if $P * X + Q * y <= C$.

The output of X will be 1 if $P * S + Q * y > C$.

If we generalize this understanding, we can represent it as follows. Representing a perceptron as a function maps input x as the function:

$$f(x) = \begin{cases} 1 \text{ if } w \times x + b > 0 \\ 0 \text{ otherwise} \end{cases}$$

where x is the vector of input values, w represents the vector of weights, and b is the bias term. We explain the bias and the weight terms next.

Recall the linear equation: $y = mx + c$ where m is the slope of the straight line and c is the constant term. Both bias and weight can be defined using the same linear equation.

The role of weight is similar to the slope of the line in a linear equation. It defines the change in the value of $f(x)$ by a unit change in the value of x.

The role of the bias is similar to the role of a constant in a linear function. In case there is no bias, the input to the activation function is x multiplied by the weight.

> **NOTE** Weights and bias terms are the parameters that get trained in a network.

The output of the function will depend on the activation function used. We will cover various types of activation functions in the next section after we have covered different layers in a network.

8.2.3 *Different layers in a network*

A simple and effective way of organizing neurons is the following. Rather than allowing arbitrary neurons connected with arbitrary others, neurons are organized in layers. A neuron in a layer has all its inputs coming only from the previous layer and all its output going only to the next. There are no other connections, for example, between neurons of the same layer or between neurons in neurons belonging to distant layers (with a small exception for specialized cases, which is beyond the scope of this book).

We know that information flows through a neural network. That information is processed and passed on from one layer to another layer in a network. There are three layers in a neural network, as shown in figure 8.4.

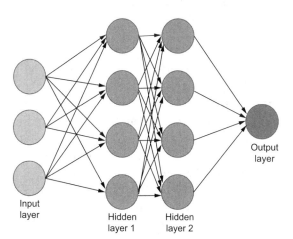

Input layer

Hidden layer 1

Hidden layer 2

Output layer

Figure 8.4 A typical neural network with neurons and input, hidden, and output layers

The neural network shown in figure 8.4 has three input units and two hidden layers with four neurons each and one final output layer:

- *Input layer*—As the name signifies, this receives the input data and shares it with the hidden layers.
- *Hidden layer*—This is the heart and soul of the network. The number of hidden layers depends on the problem at hand; the number of layers can range from a few to hundreds. All the processing, feature extraction, and learning of the attributes is done in these layers. In the hidden layers, all the input raw data is broken into attributes and features. This learning is useful for decision-making at a later stage.
- *Output layer*—This is the decision layer and final piece in a network. It accepts the outputs from the preceding hidden layers and then makes a prediction.

For example, the input training data may have raw images or processed images. These images will be fed to the input layer. The data then travels to the hidden layers where all the calculations are done. These calculations are done by neurons in each layer. The output is the task that needs to be accomplished—for example, identification of an object or classification of an image, etc.

The ANN consists of various connections. Each of the connections aims to receive the input and provide the output to the next neuron. This output to the next neuron will serve as an input to it. Also, as discussed earlier, each connection is assigned a weight, which is representative of its respective importance. It is important to note that a neuron can have multiple input and output connections, which means it can receive inputs and deliver multiple outputs.

Exercise 8.2

Answer these questions to check your understanding:

1 The input data is fed to the hidden layers in a neural network. True or False?
2 A bias term is similar to the slope of a linear equation. True or False?
3 Find and explore the deepest neural network ever trained.

So what is the role of a layer? A layer receives inputs, processes them, and passes the output to the next layer. Technically, it is imperative that the transformation implemented by a layer is parameterized by its weights, which are also referred to as parameters of a layer. In simple terms, to ensure a neural network is "trained" to a specific task, something must be changed in the network. It turns out that changing the architecture of the network (i.e., how neurons are connected) has only a small effect. On the other hand, as we will see later in this chapter, changing the weights is the key to the "learning" process.

We now move to the very important topic of activation functions.

8.2.4 *Activation functions*

We have already mentioned activation functions. The primary role of an activation function is to decide whether a neuron/perceptron should fire or not. These functions play a central role in the training of the network at a later stage. They are sometimes referred to as *transfer functions*. It is also important to know why we need nonlinear activation functions. If we use only linear activation functions, the output will also be linear. At the same time, the derivative of a linear function will be constant. Hence, there will not be much learning possible. Thus, we prefer to have nonlinear activation functions. We study the most common activation functions next.

SIGMOID FUNCTION

A sigmoid is a bounded monotonic mathematical function. It always increases its output value when the input values increase. Its output value is always between –1 and 1.

A sigmoid is a differentiable function with an S-shaped curve, and its first derivative function is bell-shaped. It has a nonnegative derivative function and is defined for all real input values. The sigmoid function is used if the output value of a neuron is between 0 and 1.

Mathematically, a sigmoid function can be represented by equation 8.1:

$$S(x) = \frac{1}{1 + e^{-x}} \qquad \textbf{(8.1)}$$

Figure 8.5 shows a graph of a sigmoid function. The sigmoid function finds its applications in complex learning systems. It is usually used for binary classification and in the final output layer of the network.

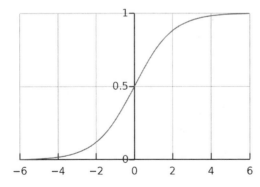

Figure 8.5 A sigmoid function. Note the shape of the function and the min/max values.

TANH FUNCTION

In mathematics, the tangent hyperbolic (TANH) function is a differentiable hyperbolic function. It is a smooth function, and its input values are in the range of –1 to +1.

A TANH function is written as equation 8.2:

$$TANH = \frac{e^x - e^{-x}}{e^x + e^{-x}}$$ (8.2)

A graphical representation of TANH is shown in figure 8.6. It is a scaled version of the sigmoid function, and hence a TANH function can be derived from a sigmoid function and vice versa.

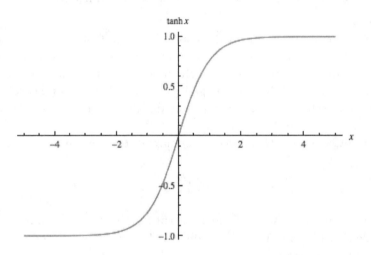

Figure 8.6   A TAHN function, which is a scaled version of a sigmoid function

A TANH function is generally used in the hidden layers. It makes the mean closer to zero, which makes the training easier for the next layer in the network. This is also referred to as centering the data.

RECTIFIED LINEAR UNIT

A rectified linear unit (ReLU) is an activation function that defines the positives of an argument. Equation 8.3 shows the ReLU function. Note that the value is 0 even for the negative values, and from 0 the value starts to incline.

$$F(x) = \max (0, x)$$ (8.3)

It will give the output as x if positive, else 0.

The ReLU is a simple function and hence less expensive to compute and much faster. It is unbounded and not centered at zero. It can be differentiated at all places except zero. Since the ReLU function is less complex, it is computationally less expensive and, hence, is widely used in the hidden layers to train the networks faster. Figure 8.7 is a graphical representation of a ReLU function.

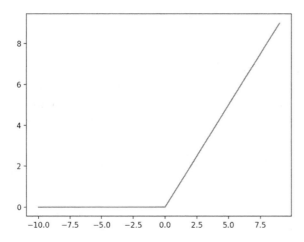

Figure 8.7 A ReLU function. It is one of the favored activation functions in the hidden layers of a neural network. A ReLU is simple to use and less expensive to train.

SOFTMAX FUNCTION

The softmax function is used in the final layer of the neural network to generate the output from the network. It is an activation function that is useful for multiclass classification problems and forces the neural network to output the sum of 1.

As an example, say the distinct classes for an image are cars, bikes, or trucks. The softmax function will generate three probabilities for each category. The category that has received the highest probability will be the predicted category.

There are other activation functions too, like ELU, PeLU, etc., which are beyond the scope of this book. We provide a summary of various activation functions at the end of this chapter.

We next cover hyperparameters, which are the control levers we have while the network is trained.

8.2.5 Hyperparameters

During training a network, the algorithm is constantly learning the attributes of the raw input data. At the same time, the network cannot learn everything itself; there are a few parameters for which initial settings must be provided. These are the variables that determine the structure of the neural network and the respective variables that are useful to train the network.

A few examples of hyperparameters are the number of hidden layers in a network, the number of neurons in each layer, the activation functions used in layers, weight initialization, etc. We have to pick the best values of the hyperparameters. To do so, we select some reasonable values for the hyperparameters, train the network, measure the performance of the network, tweak the hyperparameters and retrain the network, reevaluate and retweak, and so on.

> **NOTE** Hyperparameters are controlled by us, as we input hyperparameters to improve the performance.

We now move to the next important component in a neural network: optimization functions.

8.2.6 *Optimization functions*

In deep learning, optimizers play a critical role. They minimize the loss function by adjusting the model parameters, which are weights and biases. The optimizers facilitate faster convergence and improve the overall performance of the network. Some of the most commonly used optimization functions are discussed next.

BATCH GRADIENT DESCENT, STOCHASTIC GRADIENT DESCENT, AND MINI-BATCH STOCHASTIC GRADIENT DESCENT

In any prediction-based solution, we want to predict as best as we can; or, in other words, we want to reduce the error as much as possible. Error is the difference between the actual values and the predicted values. The purpose of a machine learning solution is to find the optimum value for our functions. We want to decrease the error or maximize the accuracy. Gradient descent can help to achieve this purpose.

The batch gradient descent technique is an optimization technique used to find the global minima of a function. We proceed in the direction of the steepest descent iteratively, which is defined by the negative of the gradient.

But batch gradient descent can be slow to run on very large datasets or datasets with a very high number of dimensions. This is due to the fact that one iteration of the gradient descent algorithm predicts for every instance in the training dataset. Hence, it is obvious that it will take a lot of time if we have thousands of records. For such a situation, we have stochastic gradient descent (SGD).

In SGD, rather than at the end of the batch of the data, the coefficients are updated for each training instance, and hence it takes less time.

Figure 8.8 shows the way gradient descent works. Notice how we can progress downward toward the global minimum.

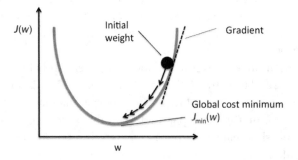

Figure 8.8   The concept of gradient descent. It is the mechanism to minimize the loss function.

Mini-batch gradient descent batches gradient descent and SGD by using small subsets of data. They are called mini-batches. In this fashion, it can balance both speed and accuracy. At the same time, it adds a hyperparameter, and we have to carefully tune the batch size. Generally, it is kept in the power of 2 (32, 64, 128, 256, etc.).

ADAPTIVE OPTIMIZATION ALGORITHMS

Researchers have observed that there is a need for optimization algorithms for more complex tasks like image, text, video, or audio analysis. Hence, adaptive optimization solutions like momentum, Nesterov accelerated gradient (NAG), Adagrad, etc., have been developed. We provide a brief summary of these solutions:

- *Momentum*—This optimizer adds a fraction of the previous gradient to the current gradient. The idea is to give more weight to the most recent update as compared to the previous updates. It accelerates the convergence and achieves better accuracy

$$V(t) = \gamma . V(t-1) + \frac{\alpha . \partial(J(\theta))}{\partial \theta}$$

and hence the weights are updated by $\theta = \theta - V(t)$.

Generally, the value of the momentum term (γ) is set to 0.9. With momentum, the convergence is faster, but at the same time, we must compute one more variable for each update.

- *NAG*—This is an improvement over momentum. In momentum, if the value becomes too large, the optimizer might miss the local minima. Hence, NAG was developed. It is a look-ahead method wherein the weights are modified to determine the future location.

Next, we discuss the most widely used optimization algorithms in the industry.

LEARNING AND LEARNING RATE

For a network, we take various steps to improve the performance of the solution: learning rate is one of them. The learning rate will define the size of the corrective steps that a model takes to reduce the errors. Learning rate defines the amount by which we should adjust the values of weights of the network with respect to the loss gradients (more on this process later). If we have a higher learning rate, the accuracy will be lower. If we have a very low learning rate, the training time will increase.

Exercise 8.3

Answer these questions to check your understanding:

1. Compare and contrast the sigmoid and TANH functions.
2. ReLU is generally used in the output layer of the network. True or False?
3. Gradient descent is an optimization technique. True or False?

We have examined the main concepts of deep learning. Now let us study how a neural network works. You will learn how the various layers interact with each other and how information is passed from one layer to another.

8.3   *How does deep learning work in a supervised manner?*

We have covered the major components of a neural network. It is the time for all the pieces to come together and orchestrate the entire learning process. The training of a neural network is quite a complex process and can be examined in a step-by-step fashion.

You might be wondering what is meant by "learning" of a neural network. Learning is a process to find the best and most optimized values for weights and bias for all the layers of the network so that we can achieve the best accuracy. As deep neural networks can have practically infinite possibilities for weights and bias terms, we have to find the optimum value for all the parameters. This seems like a herculean task considering that changing one value affects the other values, and indeed, it is a process where the various parameters of the networks are changing.

Recall in the first chapter we covered the basics of supervised learning. We will refresh that understanding here. The reason is to ensure that you are fully able to appreciate the process of training the neural network.

8.3.1   *Supervised learning algorithms*

Supervised learning algorithms have a "guidance" or "supervision" to direct toward the business goal of making predictions for the future. Formally put, supervised models are statistical models that use both the input data and the desired output to predict the future. The output is the value we wish to predict and is referred to as the *target variable,* and the data used to make that prediction is called the *training data.* The target variable is sometimes referred to as the *label.* The various attributes or variables present in the data are called *independent variables.* Each of the historical data points or *training examples* contain these independent variables and corresponding target variables. Supervised learning algorithms make a prediction for the unseen future data. The accuracy of the solution depends on the training done and patterns learned from the labeled historical data.

> **NOTE**   Most deep learning solutions are based on supervised learning. Unsupervised deep learning is rapidly gaining traction, however, as unlabeled datasets are far more abundant than labeled ones.

Supervised learning problems are used in demand prediction, credit card fraud detection, customer churn prediction, premium estimation, etc. They are heavily used across retail, telecom, banking and finance, aviation, insurance, and other fields.

We have now refreshed the concepts of supervised learning. We now move on to the first step in the training of the neural network: feed-forward propagation.

8.3.2   *Step 1: Feed-forward propagation*

Let us start the process that occurs in a neural network (see figure 8.9). This is the basic skeleton of a network we have created to explain the process. Let's say we have some input data points and the input data layer, which will consume the input data. The information flows from the input layer to the data transformation layers (hidden layers). In the hidden layers, the data is processed using the activation functions and based on the weights and bias terms. Then a prediction is made on the dataset. This is called *feed-forward propagation,* as during this process, the input variables are calculated in a sequence from the input layer to the output layer.

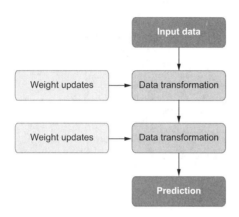

Figure 8.9   The basic skeleton of a neural network training process. We have the input layers and data transformation layers.

For example, say we wish to create a solution that can identify the faces of people. In this case, we will have the training data, which is different images of people's faces from various angles, and a target variable, which is the name of the person.

This training dataset can be fed to the algorithm. The algorithm will then understand the attributes of various faces or, in other words, *learn* the various attributes. Based on the training done, the algorithm can then make a prediction on the faces. The prediction will be a probability score if the face belongs to Mr. X. If the probability is high enough, we can safely say that the face belongs to Mr. X.

8.3.3   Step 2: Adding the loss function

The output is generated in step 1. Now we have to gauge the accuracy of this network. We want our network to have the best possible accuracy in identifying the faces. Using the prediction made by the algorithm, we will control and improve the accuracy of the network.

Accuracy measurement in the network can be achieved by the loss function, also called the *objective function.* The loss function compares the actual values and the predicted values. The loss function computes the difference score and hence is able to measure how well the network has done and what the error rates are. Let's update the diagram we created in step 1 by adding a loss function and corresponding loss score, used to measure the accuracy of the network, as shown in figure 8.10.

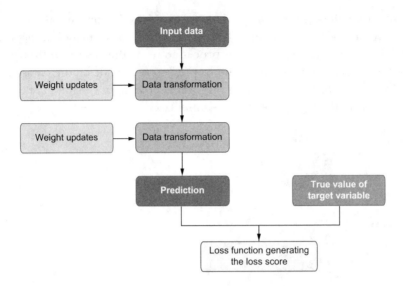

Figure 8.10   A loss function has been added to measure the accuracy.

8.3.4   Step 3: Calculating the error

We generated the predictions in step 1 of the network. In step 2, we compared the output with the actual values to get the error in prediction. The objective of our solution is to minimize this error, which is the same as maximizing the accuracy.

To constantly lower the error, the loss score (Predictions – Actual) is then used as feedback to adjust the value of the weights. This task is done by the backpropagation algorithm.

8.4   Backpropagation

In step 3 of the last section, we said we use an optimizer to constantly update the weights to reduce the error. While the learning rate defines the size of the corrective steps to reduce the error, backpropagation is used to adjust the connection weights. These weights are updated backward based on the error. Following this, the errors are recalculated, the gradient descent is calculated, and the respective weights are adjusted. Hence, backpropagation is sometimes called the central algorithm in deep learning.

Backpropagation was originally suggested in the 1970s. Then, in 1986, David Rumelhartm, Geoffrey Hinton, and Ronald Williams's paper received a lot of appreciation. Nowadays, backpropagation is the backbone of deep learning solutions.

Figure 8.11 shows the process for backpropagation, where the information flows from the output layer back to the hidden layers. Note that the flow of information is backward as compared to forward propagation, where the information flows from left to right.

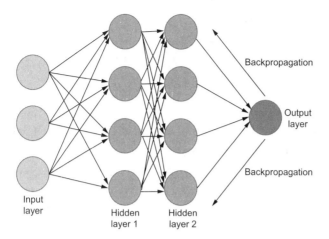

Figure 8.11   Backpropagation as a process: the information flows from the final layers to the initial layers

First, we describe the process at a very high level. Remember that in step 1, at the start of the training process, some random values were assigned to the weights. Using these random values, an initial output is generated. Since this is the first attempt, the output received can be quite different from the real values and the loss score is accordingly very high. But this is going to improve. While training the neural network, the weights (and biases) are adjusted a little in the correct direction, and subsequently, the loss score decreases. We iterate this training loop many times, and it results in the optimum weight values that minimize the loss function.

> **NOTE** Backpropagation allows us to iteratively reduce the error during the network training process.

The following section is mathematically heavy. If you are not keen to understand the mathematics behind the process, you can skip it.

8.4.1 *The mathematics behind backpropagation*

When we train a neural network, we calculate a loss function. The loss function tells us how different the predictions from the actual values are. Backpropagation calculates the gradient of the loss function with respect to each of the weights. With this information, each weight can be updated individually over iterations, which reduces the loss gradually.

In backpropagation, the gradient is calculated backward—that is, from the last layer of the network through the hidden layers to the very first layer. The gradients of all the layers are combined using the calculus chain rule to get the gradient of any particular layer.

We go into more details of the process next. First, let's denote a few mathematical symbols:

- $h^{(i)}$—output of the hidden layer i
- $g^{(i)}$—activation function of hidden layer i
- $w^{(i)}$—hidden weights matrix in the layer i
- $b^{(i)}$—bias in layer i
- x—input vector
- N—total number of layers in the network
- $W^{(i)}{}_{jk}$—weight of the network from node j in layer $(i-1)$ to node k in layer i
- $\delta A / \delta B$—partial derivative of A with respect to B

During the training of the network, the input x is fed to the network, and it passes through the layers to generate an output $\hat{y}$. The expected output is y. Hence, the cost function or the loss function to compare y and $\hat{y}$ is $C(y, \hat{y})$. Also, the output for any hidden layer of the network can be represented as equation 8.4

$$h^{(i)} = g^{(i)} \left(W^{(i)T} x + b^{(i)} \right)$$

(8.4)

where i (index) can be any layer in the network.

The final layer's output is

$$y(x) = W^{(N)T} h^{(N-1)} + b^{(N)}$$

(8.5)

During the training of the network, we adjust the network's weights so that C is reduced. Hence, we calculate the derivative of C with respect to every weight in the network. The following is the derivative of C with respect to every weight in the network:

$$\frac{\partial c}{\partial W(i)jk}$$

Now we know that a neural network has many layers. The backpropagation algorithm starts at calculating the derivatives at the last layer of the network, which is the Nth layer. Then these derivatives are fed backward. So the derivatives at the Nth layers will be fed to the $(N-1)$ layer of the network and so on.

Each component of the derivatives of C is calculated individually using the calculus chain rule. As per the chain rule, for a function c depending on b, where b depends on a, the derivative of c with respect to a can be written as equation 8.6:

$$\frac{dc}{da} = \frac{dc}{db}\frac{db}{da}$$

(8.6)

Hence, in backpropagation the derivatives of the layer N are used in the layer $(N-1)$ so that they are saved and again used in the $(N-2)$ layer. We start with the last layer of the network, through all the layers to the first layer, and each time, we use the derivatives of the last calculations made to get the derivatives of the current layers. Hence, backpropagation turns out to be extremely efficient compared to a normal approach where we would have calculated each weight in the network individually.

Once we have calculated the gradients, we update all the weights in the network. The objective is to minimize the cost function. We have already studied methods like gradient descent in the last section. We now continue to the next step in the neural network training process.

8.4.2   Step 4: Optimization

Backpropagation allows us to optimize our network and achieve the best accuracy (see figure 8.12). Notice the optimizer, which provides regular and continuous feedback to reach the best solution.

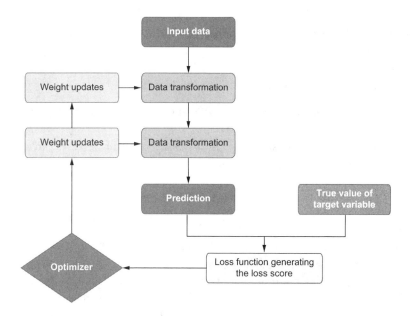

Figure 8.12   Optimization is the process to minimize the loss function.

Once we have achieved the best values of the weights and biases for our network, we say that our network is trained. We can now use it to make predictions on an unseen dataset that has not been used for training the network.

8.5   How deep learning works in an unsupervised manner

We know that unsupervised learning solutions work on unlabeled datasets; thus, for deep learning in unsupervised settings, the training dataset is unlabeled.

As compared to supervised datasets where we have tags, unsupervised methods have to self-organize themselves to get densities, probabilities' distributions, preferences, and groupings. We can solve a similar problem using supervised and unsupervised methods. For example, a supervised deep learning method can be used to identify dogs versus cats while an unsupervised deep learning method might be used to cluster the pictures of dogs and cats into different groups. In machine learning, a lot of solutions that were initially conceived as supervised learning ones, over a period of time, employed unsupervised learning methods to enrich the data and hence improve the supervised learning solution.

During the learning phase in unsupervised deep learning, it is expected that the network will mimic the data and then improve itself based on the errors. In the supervised learning algorithm, other methods play the same part as the backpropagation algorithm. These include, among others,

- Boltzmann learning rule
- Contrastive divergence
- Maximum likelihood
- Hopfield learning rule
- GAN
- Deep belief network (DBN)

In this book, we cover autoencoders and GAN in depth in separate chapters. The rest of the methods are covered in this chapter.

Next, we study the two most widely used types of neural networks in supervised learning settings: the convolutional neural network (CNN) and the recurrent neural network (RNN).

Exercise 8.4

Answer these questions to check your understanding:
1. Write in a simple form the major steps in a backpropagation technique.
2. Backpropagation is preferred in unsupervised learning. True or False?
3. The objective of deep learning is to maximize the loss function. True or False?

8.6   Convolutional neural networks

CNNs are a class of deep learning models that are primarily used for image and video processing tasks. They have become a powerful tool in the field of computer vision due to their ability to automatically detect and learn the pattern from raw images and, hence, are used for several use cases across multiple domains and functions. We provide only a brief overview, as there can be an entire book on different types of CNN solutions.

8.6.1   Key concepts of CNN

The following are the key concepts of CNN:

- *Input layer*—The input to the CNN is generally a tensor representing an image. As we know, an image is made up of pixels, and each pixel is made up of RGB channels. An image is represented by a 3D matrix, which is a width × height channel.

- *Convolution layer*—This is the core building layer of a CNN. It applies a filter to the input data, which scans over the image to detect patterns like lines, curves, texture, edges, etc. The filter size is generally small and usually 3 × 3 or 5 × 5. As the kernel slides over the input, it performs an element-wise multiplication and sum, creating a feature map. Multiple filters can be applied to learn different features, generating multiple feature maps. The entire process is illustrated in figure 8.13.

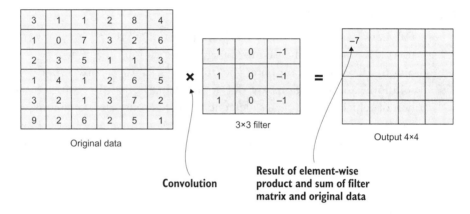

Figure 8.13   CNN process. The original data is 6 × 6, and the filter applied is 3 × 3, which results in a 4 × 4 output.

- *ReLU activation function*—This is applied to add nonlinearity. It helps the network to understand and model more complex and difficult patterns that are present in the data.
- *Polling layer*—This is used to reduce the spatial dimensions of images while preserving the most significant details. The most common type of pulling is called max pulling. It takes the maximum value from a region of input. The major function of the pooling layer is to reduce the computation load and also reduce overfitting by providing a form of translation in variance.
- *Output*—After we have created several convolutional and pooling layers, we receive the output. It is generally flattened into a 1D vector and the output is then passed to the fully connected layer. The main task of the fully connected layer is to perform high-level classification of the image based on the features extracted by the previous layers.
- *Output layer*—If the solution is for classification of data points, the output layer would contain a function like softmax. The softmax function gives respective

probabilities for different classes. For example, if you are trying to predict that a given picture is a cat or a dog, the softmax function will give the probability of the picture being a dog or a cat.

In CNNs, the same filter is applied across different regions of the image. Thus the number of parameters is reduced as compared to a traditional fully connected network. Each neuron in the convolutional layer is connected only to a small region of the input, and so the complexity of the network is also reduced. The network also automatically trains and learns to detect low-level patterns. An example of a low-level pattern is edges. The network subsequently progresses to learn more complex patterns like shapes in the deeper layers.

8.6.2 Use of CNN

Call networks are fundamental and foundational to the modern-day competition solutions. They are heavily used for image classification, image processing, speech recognition, developing computer board games, and various other video processing solutions. Many solutions are developed using CNN—for example, automatic detection of vehicle license plates, detection of cancerous cells from scans, detection of broken bones from x-rays, facial recognition solutions, automatic entry handwriting, recognition solutions, and many other solutions that are having an amazing affect across our lives.

There are quite a few CNN architectures available, like Inception, ResNet, LeNet, VGG-16, etc., that are useful for creating computer vision solutions. We now move on to the second common type of neural network: RNN.

8.7 Recurrent neural networks

RNNs are quite a popular class of networks that are designed to recognize patterns in a sequence of data—for example, time service data or videos, natural languages, or any other kind of data with this sequence of information. Here RNNs are very useful. The most significant feature of RNNs is their ability to maintain a memory about the previous input, which they capture using temporal dependencies and the order in the dataset. This augments their capability to recognize patterns in the sequential datasets, and hence RNN has been found to be a parting solution in multiple domains.

8.7.1 Key concepts of RNN

RNNs are especially designed for sequential datasets, and here the order of the input display plays a pivotal role. Hence, RNNs are the go-to solution for sequential data handling.

Unlike a regular neural network, which is also known as a feed-forward neural network, RNNs have recurrent connections. This means that the output from one time step is fed back as the input to the next time step. This information is persistent across the sequence. At the same time, the same weight is used across different time steps.

This makes them very efficient in terms of the number of parameters, as the same network can be applied to every time step of the input sequence.

RNNs work in the following fashion:

- The input data is processed sequentially. At each time step t, the network receives an input x_t, which is then combined with a hidden state h_{t-1}. This hidden state is the output from the previous time step and serves as a memory that carries information from one time step to the next time step.
- The hidden state h_t is then updated using a nonlinear function:

$$h_t = f\left(W.x_t + U.h_{t-1} + b\right)$$

- The final output at each of the time steps can be calculated and used either for each individual time step or only at the final time step.

Figure 8.14 illustrates the RNN process.

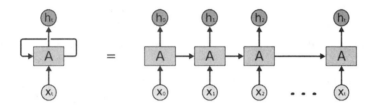

Figure 8.14 The RNN process. RNNs have internal memory, which allows them to use information from the previous inputs to influence the current input and outputs.

The most basic version of an RNN is a simple recurrent network, but it struggles with a long-term dependency because the gradient can either vanish or explode, making it hard for the network to remember information from far back in the sequence; hence, it cannot be used for a solution like a chatbot. Long short-term memory (LSTM) is much more useful here. LSTM is a special type of network designed to mitigate the vanishing gradient problem and handle long-term dependencies better than plain vanilla RNNs. They achieve this feat by introducing gates. There are three types of gates: input, forget, and output gates. These gates regulate the flow of information through the network and allow it to maintain important information over longer periods of time. Gated recurrent units are another type of RNN, but LSTM and gated recurrent units are beyond the scope of this book.

RNNs are very powerful for processing sequences, and their ability to model time dependencies makes them indispensable in the fields of natural language processing and time-series analysis. Their use has been pathbreaking for many innovative solutions—for example, predicting the next word in a sentence; translating text from one language to another; processing sequences of video frames to understand behaviors over time; modeling temporal dependencies like audio signals, which can be used to recognize speech patterns over time; and many more. RNNs are the power engines behind GenAI solutions.

8.8 Boltzmann learning rule

The Boltzmann learning rule is an unsupervised learning rule used in neural networks. It is based on the principle of statistical mechanics of physical systems. It is seldom used in the context of Boltzmann machines. It adjusts the weights of a neural network with an objective to minimize the energy of the system, thereby ensuring the network reaches a stable state.

8.8.1 Concepts of the Boltzmann learning rule

The following are the key concepts of the Boltzmann learning rule:

- It is a type of probabilistic RNN where neurons are connected in a fully connected graph.
- The neurons in the Boltzmann machine are stochastic units that fire as per a probability distribution. Thus we can use the Boltzmann learning rule for dimensionality reduction, pattern recognition, feature extraction, and optimization tasks.
- A Boltzmann machine has an energy function $E(v,h)$ where v is the input visible unit while h is the hidden unit. The energy function determines the cost of a given state of the network. During the training of the network, we aim to adjust the weights in such a manner so that the energy of the system is minimized.
- The network models the probability of a particular state (v,h) using a Boltzmann distribution. It depends on the energy of the state, which is given by equation 8.7:

$$P(s) = \frac{e^{-E(s)}}{Z} \qquad (8.7)$$

Here, Z is the partition function, which ensures that the sum of probabilities = 1.

- The rule seeks to adjust the weights to keep on decreasing the energy of the system during the training of the network, and it happens over time. The weights are updated by a rule derived from gradient of the energy function with respect to the weights. The weight update rule is given in equation 8.8:

$$\Delta w_{ij} = \eta \left(\langle v_i v_j \rangle_{\text{positive}} - \langle v_i v_j \rangle_{\text{negative}} \right) \qquad (8.8)$$

Here, η is the learning rate, and $(v_i h_j)_{\text{data}}$ is the correction between the visible unit v_i and hidden unit h_j. It is computed from the data distribution. It represents how often they are active together in the hidden unit. $(v_i h_j)_{\text{model}}$ is the correction computed from the model distribution. It represents how often the visible unit v_i and hidden unit h_j are active together in the state generated by the network.

During the training of the model, a learning rule is followed, which is to make the data distribution match the model distribution. Hence, it reduces the energy of the system and thereby increases the overall performance.

8.8.2 Key points

There are certain key points we should bear in mind. Energy-based models like the Boltzmann machine use the Boltzmann learning rule to minimize an energy function by adjusting the network's weights:

- The network strives to model the probability distribution over its inputs. The core objective here is to associate the higher energy with less likely configurations. Similarly, the lower energy is associated with more like configurations.
- Boltzmann learning is an unsupervised and probabilistic method. It works on the concept of contrasting the model distribution and data distribution.
- The rule is computationally expensive in its basic form; hence, to increase the training speed, sometimes we utilize methods like contrastive divergence. We cover contrastive divergence in the next section.
- The Boltzmann learning rule is primarily used for unsupervised learning tasks such as dimensionality reduction, feature extraction, and generative modeling.
- The model training is sometimes slower than expected.

In summary, the Boltzmann learning rule is a probabilistic approach to training neural networks by adjusting weights based on minimizing an energy function, and it provides a foundation for generative models like Boltzmann machines. However, due to computational challenges, approximations such as contrastive divergence are often used to make it practical for real-world applications.

8.9 Deep belief networks

A DBN is a type of GAN made up of multiple layers of stochastic, binary latent variables (hidden units), where each layer is a restricted Boltzmann machine (RBM) or a variant of it. DBNs were popularized by Geoffrey Hinton (who was awarded the Nobel Prize in Physics in 2024, shared with John Hopfield) and his collaborators in the mid-2000s for pretraining deep networks in an unsupervised way.

8.9.1 Key points of DBN

The key points of a DBN are as follows:

- RBM
  - A DBN consists of several layers of RBMs. A RBM contains a visible layer and a hidden layer. The visible layer represents the observed data while the hidden layer captures the hidden features.

- Each DBN is trained independently with an objective to model the underlying structure of the data.

- The objective of the training in DBN is to optimize the log-likelihood of the data under the network's generative model. For each layer, the contrastive divergence algorithm is used to approximate the gradient of the log-likelihood with respect to the weights. This allows the network to learn a good set of weights for each layer.

- The contrastive divergence algorithm is a stochastic approximation method used to estimate the gradient of the log-likelihood of the model. The algorithm starts with a sample from the visible layer and then performs Gibbs sampling to update the hidden layer and visible layer iteratively. Contrastive divergence ensures that the network learns to model the input data distribution efficiently.

- Layer-based pretraining:

  - DBNs are typically trained in a layer-wise manner, where each layer is pretrained as an RBM. The first RBM has an objective to learn to capture low-level features from the data.

  - Based on this knowledge, each subsequent RBM then learns increasingly complex, abstract features from the representations learned by the previous layers. In this manner, the cycle continues.

  - This phase involves training each RBM individually using contrastive divergence.

  - This process tunes the weights to capture relevant patterns and features in the input data, without the need for labeled data.

  - Since each layer learns features at increasing levels of abstraction and complexity, it makes the overall solution good enough for complex tasks like image or speech recognition.

- Supervised fine-tuning:

  - Once the pretraining is done, the entire network is fine-tuned. It is done in a supervised fashion using methods like backpropagation or a labeled dataset with an objective to optimize the network.

  - The supervised system adjusts the network weights to minimize the prediction error such as what is done in classification or regression tasks.

  - The unsupervised pretraining phase helps initialize the weights in such a way that the network is less likely to overfit during supervised fine-tuning, as it starts with a better understanding of the data.

  - They are computationally expensive and time-consuming, particularly when dealing with large datasets or deep architectures.

  - Pretraining using RBMs is useful, but fine-tuning the entire DBN can sometimes be difficult, especially if we are dealing with a very deep neural network. It may necessitate meticulous hyperparameter training and lots of labeled datasets.

– Similar to other deep learning architectures, DBNs are also prone to the vanishing gradient problem, where gradients diminish as they are propagated backward through many layers. This further complicates the entire training process.

DBNs are typically used for unsupervised learning, dimensionality reduction, and feature learning, but they can also be fine-tuned for supervised tasks such as classification. DBNs are used to improve the performance of speech recognition systems by learning representations of sound features that are invariant to noise and other distortions. As generative models, DBNs can be used to create new data instances that resemble the training data. For example, DBNs have been used in generative art, where new images are created that resemble a set of input images.

DBNs are a significant milestone in the development of deep learning techniques. They combine the strengths of generative models like RBMs with deep learning principles to create a powerful method for learning complex representations of data. While newer architectures have emerged and gained prominence, DBNs remain a key historical and theoretical component of modern AI, influencing the development of many advanced models. By utilizing unsupervised learning, DBNs can be highly effective for tasks like dimensionality reduction, generative modeling, and classification. However, challenges related to training complexity and fine-tuning remain significant hurdles for widespread adoption.

8.10 *Popular deep learning libraries*

Over the last few chapters, we have used a lot of libraries and packages for implementing solutions. There are quite a few libraries available in the industry for deep learning. These packages expedite the solution building and reduce the efforts as most of the heavy lifting is done by these libraries.

The most popular deep learning libraries are

- *TensorFlow (TF)*—Developed by Google, this is arguably one of the most popular and widely used deep learning frameworks. It was launched in 2015 and since has been used by a number of businesses and brands across the globe.

    Python is mostly used for TF but C++, Java, C#, Javascript, and Julia can also be used. You have to install the TF library on your system and import the library.

NOTE Go to www.tensorflow.org/install and follow the instructions to install TF.

TF is one of the most popular libraries and can work on mobile devices like iOS and Android.

- *Keras*—Keras is a mature API-driven solution and quite easy to use. It is one of the best choices for starters and is among the best for prototyping simple concepts in an easy and fast manner. Keras was initially released in 2015 and is one of the most recommended libraries.

NOTE Go to https://keras.io and follow the instructions to install Keras. Tf.keras can be used as an API.

Serialization/deserialization APIs, call-backs, and data streaming using Python generators are very mature. Massive models in Keras are reduced to single-line functions, which makes it a less configurable environment and hence very convenient and easy to use.

- *PyTorch*—Facebook's brainchild PyTorch was released in 2016 and is another popular framework. PyTorch operates with dynamically updated graphs and allows data parallelism and distributed learning models. There are debuggers like pdb or PyCharm available in PyTorch. For small projects and prototyping, PyTorch can be a good choice.
- *Sonnet*—DeepMind's Sonnet is developed using and on top of TF. Sonnet is designed for complex neural network applications and architectures. It works by creating primary Python objects corresponding to a particular part of the neural network. Then these Python objects are independently connected to the computational TF graph. Because of this separation (creating Python objects and associating them to a graph), the design is simplified.

NOTE Having high-level object-oriented libraries is very helpful, as the abstraction is allowed when we develop machine learning solutions.

- *MXNet*—Apache's MXNet is a highly scalable deep learning tool that is easy to use and has detailed documentation. A large number of languages like C ++, Python, R, Julia, JavaScript, Scala, Go, and Perl are supported by MXNet.

There are other frameworks too, like Swift, Gluon, Chainer, DL4J, etc.; however, we only discuss the popular ones here. We now examine a short code in TF and Keras. It is just to test that you have installed these libraries correctly. You can learn more about TF at https://www.tensorflow.org and Keras at https://keras.io.

8.10.1 *Python code for Keras and TF*

We implement a very simple code in TF. We simply import the TF library and print "hello". We also check the version of TF:

```
import tensorflow as tf
hello = tf.constant('Hello, TensorFlow!')
sess = tf.Session()
print(sess.run(hello))
print("TensorFlow version:", tf.__version__)
```

If this code runs for you and prints the version of TF, it means that you have installed `tensorflow` correctly:

```
from tensorflow import keras
from keras import models
```

If this code runs for you and prints the version of Keras, it means that you have installed `keras` correctly.

8.11 Concluding thoughts

Deep learning is changing the world we live in. It is enabling us to train and create really complex solutions that were a mere thought earlier. The effect of deep learning can be witnessed across multiple domains and industries. Perhaps there are no industries that have been left unaffected by the marvels of deep learning.

Deep learning is one of the most-sought-after fields for research and development. Every year, many journals and papers are published on deep learning. Researchers across prominent institutions and universities (like Oxford, Stanford, etc.) of the world are engrossed in finding improved neural network architectures. At the same time, professionals and engineers in reputed organizations (like Google, Facebook, etc.) are working hard to create sophisticated architectures to improve performance.

Deep learning is making our systems and machines able to solve problems typically assumed to be in the realm of humans only. We have improved the clinical trials process for the pharma sector, fraud detection software, automatic speech detection systems, and various image recognition solutions; and created more robust natural language processing solutions, targeted marketing solutions that improve customer relationship management and recommendation systems, better safety processes, and so on. The list is quite long and growing day by day.

At the same time, there are still a few challenges. The expectations from deep learning continue to increase. Deep learning is not a silver bullet or a magic wand to resolve all problems. It is surely one of the more sophisticated solutions, but it is certainly not the 100% solution to all business problems. The dataset we need to feed the algorithms is not always available. There is a dearth of good-quality datasets that are representative of business problems. Often, big organizations like Google, Meta, or Amazon can afford to collect such massive datasets. But many times we do find a lot of quality problems in the data. Having the processing power to train these complex algorithms is also a challenge. With the advent of cloud computing, though, this problem has been resolved to a certain extent.

In this chapter, we explored the basics of neural networks and deep learning. We covered the details around neurons, activation function, different layers of a network, and loss function. We also covered in detail the backpropagation algorithm—the central algorithm used to train a supervised deep learning solution. Then we briefly went through unsupervised deep learning algorithms. We will cover these unsupervised deep learning solutions in greater detail in the later chapters. Figure 8.15 shows the major activation functions.

Name	Plot	Equation	Derivative
Identity		$f(x) = x$	$f'(x) = 1$
Binary step		$f(x) = \begin{cases} 0 & \text{for } x < 0 \\ 1 & \text{for } x \geq 0 \end{cases}$	$f'(x) = \begin{cases} 0 & \text{for } x \neq 0 \\ ? & \text{for } x = 0 \end{cases}$
Logistic (aka Soft step)		$f(x) = \dfrac{1}{1 + e^{-x}}$	$f'(x) = f(x)(1 - f(x))$
TanH		$f(x) = \tanh(x) = \dfrac{2}{1 + e^{-2x}} - 1$	$f'(x) = 1 - f(x)^2$
ArcTan		$f(x) = \tan^{-1}(x)$	$f'(x) = \dfrac{1}{x^2 + 1}$
Rectified Linear Unit (ReLU)		$f(x) = \begin{cases} 0 & \text{for } x < 0 \\ x & \text{for } x \geq 0 \end{cases}$	$f'(x) = \begin{cases} 0 & \text{for } x < 0 \\ 1 & \text{for } x \geq 0 \end{cases}$
Parameteric Rectified Linear Unit (PReLU)		$f(x) = \begin{cases} \alpha x & \text{for } x < 0 \\ x & \text{for } x \geq 0 \end{cases}$	$f'(x) = \begin{cases} \alpha & \text{for } x < 0 \\ 1 & \text{for } x \geq 0 \end{cases}$
Exponential Linear Unit (ELU)		$f(x) = \begin{cases} \alpha(e^x - 1) & \text{for } x < 0 \\ x & \text{for } x \geq 0 \end{cases}$	$f'(x) = \begin{cases} f(x) + \alpha & \text{for } x < 0 \\ 1 & \text{for } x \geq 0 \end{cases}$
SoftPlus		$f(x) = \log_e(1 + e^x)$	$f'(x) = \dfrac{1}{1 + e^{-x}}$

Figure 8.15   Major activation functions at a glance (Source: towardsdatascience)

8.12   *Practical next steps and suggested readings*

The following provides suggestions for what to do next and offers some helpful reading:

- The book *Deep Learning with Python* by François Chollet is one of the best resources to clarify the concepts of deep learning. It covers all the concepts of deep learning and neural networks and is written by the creator of Keras.
- Read the following research papers:

– Hinton, G., Vinyals, O., and Dean, J. (2015). Distilling the Knowledge in a Neural Network. https://arxiv.org/pdf/1503.02531.pdf

– Srivastava, R., Greff, K., and Schmidhuber, J. (2015). Training Very Deep Networks. https://arxiv.org/pdf/1507.06228

– Mikolov, T., Sutskever, I., Chen, K., Corrado, G., and Dean, J. (2013). Distributed Representations of Words and Phrases and their Compositionality. https://arxiv.org/abs/1310.4546

– Goodfellow, I. J., Pouget-Abadie, J., Mirza, M., et al. (2014). Generative Adversarial Networks. https://arxiv.org/abs/1406.2661

– He, K., Zhang, X., Ren, S., and Sun, J. (2015). Deep Residual Learning for Image Recognition. https://arxiv.org/abs/1512.03385

Summary

- Deep learning is an advanced form of machine learning based on neural networks, and it's particularly effective with unstructured data like text, images, audio, and video.

- Deep learning finds applications across various sectors, such as
  - *The medical field and pharmaceuticals*—Used for diagnosing medical conditions and expediting drug development
  - *Banking and finance*—Detects fraud and distinguishes fake signatures
  - *The automobile sector*—Powers autonomous driving by recognizing traffic elements
  - *Speech and image recognition*—Enables technologies like Siri and image-based systems for medical diagnostics and security

- Key concepts for neural networks include
  - *Artificial neurons (perceptrons)*—Simplified models of biological neurons. Weights and biases play crucial roles in the function of a perceptron.
  - *Layers*—Networks are structured with input, hidden, and output layers. Hidden layers extract and learn features critical for decision-making.
  - *Activation functions*—Critical for neural network performance and include sigmoid, TANH, LeLU, and softmax.

- Training neural networks involves processes like feed-forward propagation, calculating loss, and employing backpropagation for weight adjustments to maximize prediction accuracy.

- While unsupervised learning relies on unlabeled data, techniques like Boltzmann learning and DBNs are central to improving data organization in such settings.

- CNNs are primarily used in image and video processing. CNNs excel in recognizing patterns due to their architecture, featuring layers like convolutional and polling layers for feature extraction.

- RNNs are suitable for sequential data. RNNs maintain information across inputs and are enhanced by LSTMs for long-term dependency challenges. They are key in natural language processing and time-series analysis.
- The Boltzmann learning rule is an unsupervised, probabilistic method used in neural networks to adjust weights by minimizing an energy function, often aiding in tasks like dimensionality reduction and feature extraction, but computational challenges require approximations like contrastive divergence.
- DBNs are GANs consisting of layers of RBMs, utilizing unsupervised pretraining to learn complex data representations and supervised fine-tuning for tasks like classification, yet they face challenges, including computational expense and potential overfitting.
- DBNs use layer-wise pretraining to capture abstract features, making them suitable for complex applications like image or speech recognition; however, problems like the vanishing gradient problem and intricate fine-tuning processes can impede performance.
- Despite newer deep learning architectures gaining popularity, DBNs remain integral to the evolution of AI, playing a critical role in the development of models for tasks including dimensionality reduction, generative modeling, and classification, although training complexity continues to be a barrier.

Autoencoders

9

This chapter covers

- Introducing autoencoders
- Training of autoencoders
- Types of autoencoders
- Python code using TensorFlow and Keras

Out of intense complexities, intense simplicities emerge.

—Winston Churchill

In the preceding chapter, we explored the concepts of deep learning. In this chapter, we start with unsupervised deep learning. Autoencoders are the very first topic. We will first cover the basics of autoencoders, what are they, and how we train them. We then get into the different types of autoencoders followed by a Python code on the implementation. Welcome to the ninth chapter, and all the very best!

9.1   *Technical toolkit*

We will continue to use the same version of Python and Jupyter Notebook as we have used so far. The codes and datasets used in this chapter have been checked in at the GitHub location. You need to install a couple of Python libraries in this chapter: `tensorflow` and `keras`.

9.2   *Feature learning*

Predictive modeling is quite an interesting topic. Across various domains and business functions, predictive modeling is used for various purposes like predicting the sales for a business in the next year, the amount of rainfall expected, whether the incoming credit card transaction is fraud or not, whether the customer will make a purchase or not, and so on. The use cases are many, and all the aforementioned use cases fall under supervised learning algorithms.

> **NOTE** The datasets that we use have variables or attributes. They are also called characteristics or features.

While we wish to create these predictive models, we are also interested in understanding the variables that are useful for making the prediction. Let's consider a case where a bank wants to predict if an incoming transaction is fraudulent or not. In such a scenario, the bank will wish to know which factors are significant to identify an incoming transaction as fraud. Factors that might be considered include the amount of the transaction, the time of the transaction, the origin/source of the transaction, etc. The variables that are important for making a prediction are called *significant variables*.

To create a machine learning–based predictive model, *feature engineering* is used. Feature engineering, otherwise known as feature extraction, is the process of extracting features from the raw data to improve the overall quality of the model and enhance the accuracy as compared to a model where only raw data is fed to the machine learning model.

Feature engineering can be done using domain understanding, various manual methods, and a few automated methods too. One such method is known as feature learning. Feature learning is the set of techniques that help a solution automatically discover the representations required for feature detection. With the help of feature learning, manual feature engineering is not required. The effect of feature learning is much more relevant for datasets where images, text, audio, and video are being used.

Feature learning can be both supervised and unsupervised. For supervised feature learning, neural networks are the best example. For unsupervised feature learning, we have examples like matrix factorization, clustering algorithms, and autoencoders. We have already covered clustering and matrix factorization. In this chapter, we start with an introduction to autoencoders.

9.3   *Introducing autoencoders*

When we start with any data science problem, data plays the most significant role. A dataset that has a lot of noise is one of the biggest challenges in data science and machine learning. There are quite a few solutions available now, and autoencoders are one of them.

Simply put, an autoencoder is a type of artificial neural network, and it is used to learn the data encodings. Autoencoders are typically used for dimensionality reduction methods. They can also be used as generative models, which can create synthetic data that is like the old data. For example, if we do not have a good amount of data to train machine learning, we can use generated synthetic data to train the models.

Autoencoders are feed-forward neural networks, and they compress the input into a lower dimensional code and then try to reconstruct the output from this representation. The objective of an autoencoder is to learn the lower dimensional representation (also sometimes known as encoding) for a high-dimensional dataset. Recall from the previous chapters principal component analysis (PCA). Autoencoders can be thought of as a generalization for PCA. PCA is a linear method whereas autoencoders can learn nonlinear relationships as well. Hence, autoencoders are required for dimensionality reduction solutions wherein they capture the most significant attributes from the input data.

9.4   Components of autoencoders

The architecture of an autoencoder is quite simple to understand. An autoencoder consists of three parts: an encoder, a bottleneck or a code, and a decoder, as shown in figure 9.1. In simple terms, an encoder compresses the input data, a bottleneck or code contains this compressed information, and the decoder decompresses the knowledge and hence reconstructs this data back to its original form. Once the decompression has been done and the data has been reconstructed to its encoded form, the input and output can be compared.

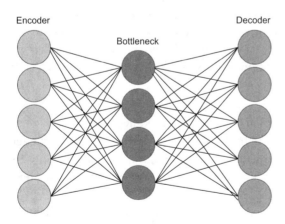

Figure 9.1   Structure of an autoencoder with an encoder, a bottleneck, and a decoder

Let's study these components in more detail:

- *Encoder*—The input data passes through the encoder. An encoder is nothing but a fully connected artificial neural network. It compresses the input data into an encoded representation, and in the process the output generated is reduced in size. An encoder compresses the input data into a compressed module known as a bottleneck.

- *Bottleneck*—The bottleneck can be considered the brain of the encoder. It contains the compressed information representations, and it is the job of the bottleneck to allow only the most important information to pass through.
- *Decoder*—The information received from the bottleneck is decompressed by a decoder. It re-creates the data back to its original or encoded form. Once the job of the decoder is done, the actual values are compared with the decompressed values created by the decoder.

There are a few important points about autoencoders to consider:

- There is a loss of information in autoencoders when the decompression is done as compared to the original inputs. So when the compressed data is decompressed, there is a loss as compared to the original data.
- Autoencoders are specific to datasets. This means that an algorithm that is trained on images of flowers will not work on images of traffic signals and vice versa. This is because the features the autoencoder learned will be specific to flowers only. So we can say that autoencoders are only able to compress the data similar to the one used for training.
- It is relatively easier to train specialized instances of algorithms to perform well on specific types of inputs. We just need representative training datasets to train the autoencoder.

9.5   *Training of autoencoders*

It is important to note that if there is no correlation between the variables in the data, then it is really difficult to compress and subsequently decompress the input data. For us to create a meaningful solution, there should be some level of relationship or correlation between the variables in the input data. To create an autoencoder, we require an encoding method, a decoding method, and a loss function to compare the actual versus decompressed values.

The process is as follows:

1 The input data passes through the encoder module.
2 The encoder compresses the input of a model into a compact bottleneck.
3 The bottleneck restricts the flow of information and allows only important information to pass through; hence, a bottleneck is sometimes referred to as *knowledge-representation*.
4 The decoder decompresses the information and re-creates the data back to its original or encoded form. This encoder-decoder architecture is quite efficient in getting the most significant attributes from the input data.

The objective of the solution is to generate an output identical to the input. Generally, the decoder architecture is a mirror image of the coder architecture. This is not mandatory but is generally followed. We ensure that the dimensionality of the input and outputs are the same.

NOTE If you do not know the meaning of hyperparameter, refer to the appendix.

We need to define four hyperparameters for training an autoencoder:

- *Code size*—This is perhaps the most significant hyperparameter. It represents the number of nodes in the middle layer. This decides the compression of the data and can also act as a regularization term. The less the value of code size, the more compressed the data.
- *Parameter*—This denotes the depth of the autoencoder. A model that has more depth is obviously more complex and will have a longer processing time.
- *Number of nodes per layer*—This is the weight used per layer. It generally decreases with every subsequent layer as the input becomes smaller across the layers. It increases back in the decoder.
- *Loss function used*—If the input values are in the [0,1] range, binary cross-entropy is preferred; otherwise, mean squared error is used.

We have covered the hyperparameters used in training autoencoders. The training process is similar to backpropagation, which we have already covered.

9.6   *Application of autoencoders*

Autoencoders are capable of solving a number of problems inherent to unsupervised learning. Major applications for autoencoders include

- *Dimensionality reduction*—Sometimes autoencoders can learn more complex data projections than PCA and other techniques.
- *Anomaly detection*—The error or the reconstruction error (error between the actual data and the reconstructed data) can be used to detect the anomalies.
- *Data compression*—It is difficult to beat the basic solutions like JPEG by training the algorithm. Moreover, since autoencoders are data specific, they can use only the types of datasets they have been trained upon. If we wish to enhance the capacity to include more data types and make it more general, then the amount of the training data required will be too high, and obviously, the time required will be high too.
- *Other applications*—These include drug discovery, machine translation, image denoising, etc.

There are still not a lot of practical implementations of autoencoders in the real world. This is due to a multitude of reasons like the nonavailability of datasets, infrastructure, readiness of various systems, etc.

9.7   *Types of autoencoders*

There are five main types of autoencoders. A brief description of the different types of encoders is given next. We have kept the section mathematically light and skipped the math behind the scenes as it is quite complex to understand. For curious readers, the papers listed in section 9.10 can explain the mathematics:

- *Undercomplete autoencoders*—An undercomplete autoencoder is the simplest form of an autoencoder. It simply takes an input dataset and then reconstructs the same dataset again from the compressed bottleneck region. By penalizing the neural network as per the reconstruction error, the model will learn the most significant attributes of the data. By learning the most important attributes, the model will be able to reconstruct the original data from the compressed state. As we know, there is a loss when the compressed data is reconstructed; this loss is called *reconstruction* loss.

Undercomplete autoencoders are unsupervised in nature as they do not have any target label to train. Such types of autoencoders are used for dimensionality reduction. Recall in chapter 2 we discussed dimensionality reduction (PCA), and in chapter 6, we discussed the advanced dimensionality reduction algorithms (t-distributed stochastic neighbor embedding and multidimensional scaling). See figure 9.2.

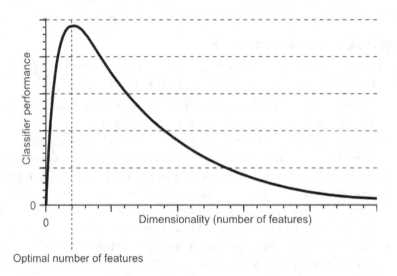

Figure 9.2   The performance starts to improve with more dimensions but decreases after some time. The curse of dimensionality is a real problem when it comes to creating sound data science solutions.

Dimensionality reduction is possible using undercomplete autoencoders as the bottleneck is created, which is the compressed form of the input data. This compressed data can be decompressed back with the aid of the network. Recall in chapter 3 we explained that PCA provides a linear combination of the input variables. For more details and to refresh your memory on PCA, please refer to chapter 3. We know that PCA tries to get a low-dimensional hyperplane to describe the original dataset; undercomplete autoencoders can also learn non-linear relationships. The difference is shown in figure 9.3.

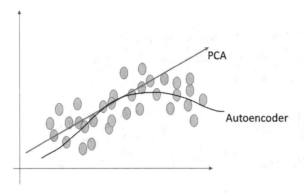

Figure 9.3 PCA is linear in nature while autoencoders are nonlinear. This is the core difference between the two algorithms.

Interestingly, if all the nonlinear activation functions are removed from the undercomplete autoencoder and only linear layers are used, the autoencoder is equivalent to a PCA only. To make the autoencoder generalize and not memorize the training data, an undercomplete autoencoder is regulated and fine-tuned by the size of the bottleneck. It allows the solution to not memorize the training data and generalize very well.

NOTE If a machine learning model works very well on the training data but does not work on the unseen test data, it is called overfitting.

- *Sparse autoencoders*—Sparse autoencoders are similar to undercomplete autoencoders except they use a different methodology to tackle overfitting. Conceptually, a sparse autoencoder changes the number of nodes at each of the hidden layer and keeps it flexible. Since it is not possible to have a neural network capable of a flexible number of neurons, the loss function is customized for it. In the loss function, a term is introduced that captures the number of activated neurons. The penalty term is proportional to the number of activated neurons. The higher the number of activated neurons, the higher the penalty. This penalty is called the *sparsity function*. Using the penalty, it is possible to reduce the number of activated neurons; hence the penalty is lower, and the network is able to tackle the problem of overfitting.
- *Contractive autoencoders*—Contractive autoencoders work on a similar concept as other autoencoders. They consider that the inputs that are quite similar should be encoded the same. Hence, they should have the same latent space representation. It means that there should not be much difference between the input data and the latent space.

- *Denoizing autoencoders*—Denoizing means removing the noise, and that is the precise task of denoizing autoencoders. They do not take an image as an input; instead they take a noisy version of an image as an input as shown in figure 9.4.

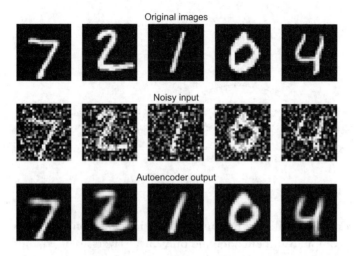

Figure 9.4   An original image, noisy output, and the outputs from the autoencoder

The process of denoizing the autoencoder is depicted in figure 9.5. The original image is changed by adding noise to it. This noisy image is fed to the encoder-decoder architecture and the output received is compared to the original image. The autoencoder learns the representation of the image, which is used to remove the noise; this is achieved by mapping the input image into a lower dimensional manifold.

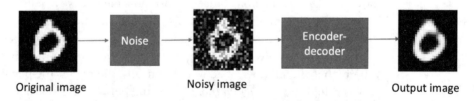

Figure 9.5   The process of denoizing in an autoencoder. It starts with the original image; noise is added, which results in a noisy image, and then it is fed to the autoencoder.

We can use denoizing autoencoders for nonlinear dimensionality reduction.

- *Variational autoencoders*—A standard autoencoder model represents the input in a compressed form using the bottleneck. A variation is probabilistic generative models (usually Gaussian) over latent variables, which only need neural networks as a part of their overall structure. They are trained using expectation-maximization meta-algorithms. The mathematical details are beyond the scope of this book.

9.8 *Python implementation of autoencoders*

Let's create two versions of an autoencoder. The code has been taken from the official source at the Keras website (https://blog.keras.io/building-autoencoders-in-keras.html) and has been modified for our usage. The steps are as follows:

1 Import the necessary libraries:

```
import keras
from keras import layers
```

2 Create our network architecture:

```
# This is the size of our encoded representations
encoding_dim = 32  # 32 floats -> compression of factor 24.5, assuming
the input is 784 floats

# This is our input image
input_img = keras.Input(shape=(784,))
# "encoded" is the encoded representation of the input
encoded = layers.Dense(encoding_dim, activation='relu')(input_img)
# "decoded" is the lossy reconstruction of the input
decoded = layers.Dense(784, activation='sigmoid')(encoded)

# This model maps an input to its reconstruction
autoencoder = keras.Model(input_img, decoded)
```

3 Add more details to the model:

```
# This model maps an input to its encoded representation
encoder = keras.Model(input_img, encoded)

# This is our encoded (32-dimensional) input
encoded_input = keras.Input(shape=(encoding_dim,))
# Retrieve the last layer of the autoencoder model
decoder_layer = autoencoder.layers[-1]
# Create the decoder model
decoder = keras.Model(encoded_input, decoder_layer(encoded_input))

autoencoder.compile(optimizer='adam', loss='binary_crossentropy')
```

4 Load the datasets:

```
(x_train, _), (x_test, _) = mnist.load_data()
```

5 Create the train and test the datasets:

```
x_train = x_train.astype('float32') / 255.
x_test = x_test.astype('float32') / 255.
```

```
x_train = x_train.reshape((len(x_train), np.prod(x_train.shape[1:])))
x_test = x_test.reshape((len(x_test), np.prod(x_test.shape[1:])))
print(x_train.shape)
print(x_test.shape)
```

6 Fit the model (see figure 9.6):

```
autoencoder.fit(x_train, x_train,
                epochs=5,
                batch_size=128,
                shuffle=True,
                validation_data=(x_test, x_test))
```

```
In [9]:   1   autoencoder.fit(x_train, x_train,
          2                   epochs=5,
          3                   batch_size=128,
          4                   shuffle=True,
          5                   validation_data=(x_test, x_test))
```
```
WARNING:tensorflow:From /Users/vaibhavverdhan/anaconda3/lib/python3.6/site-packages/tensorflow/
python/ops/math_ops.py:3066: to_int32 (from tensorflow.python.ops.math_ops)is deprecated and
will be removed in a future version.
Instructions for updating:
Use tf.cast instead.
Train on 6000 samples, validate on 1000 samples
Epoch 1/5
60000/60000 [==============================] - 2s 32us/step - loss: 0.2271 - val - loss: 0.1579
Epoch 2/5
60000/60000 [==============================] - 2s 26us/step - loss: 0.1409 - val - loss: 0.1252
Epoch 3/5
60000/60000 [==============================] - 1s 24us/step - loss: 0.1184 - val - loss: 0.1103
Epoch 4/5
60000/60000 [==============================] - 1s 24us/step - loss: 0.1072 - val - loss: 0.1025
Epoch 5/5
60000/60000 [==============================] - 1s 25us/step - loss: 0.1009 - val - loss: 0.0974
```
```
Out[9]: <keras.callbacks.History at 0x7f852e2bfd30>
```

Figure 9.6   Fitting the model

7 Test it on the test dataset:

```
# Encode and decode some digits
# Note that we take them from the *test* set
encoded_imgs = encoder.predict(x_test)
decoded_imgs = decoder.predict(encoded_imgs)
```

8 Plot the results. You can see the original image and final output (see figure 9.7):

```
# Use Matplotlib (don't ask)
import matplotlib.pyplot as plt

n = 10  # How many digits we will display
plt.figure(figsize=(20, 4))
for i in range(n):
```

```
# Display original
ax = plt.subplot(2, n, i + 1)
plt.imshow(x_test[i].reshape(28, 28))
plt.gray()
ax.get_xaxis().set_visible(False)
ax.get_yaxis().set_visible(False)

# Display reconstruction
ax = plt.subplot(2, n, i + 1 + n)
plt.imshow(decoded_imgs[i].reshape(28, 28))
plt.gray()
ax.get_xaxis().set_visible(False)
ax.get_yaxis().set_visible(False)
plt.show()
```

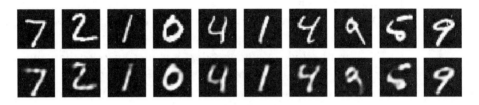

Figure 9.7   The original image (bottom) and the final outcome (top)

9.9   Concluding thoughts

Deep learning is a powerful tool. With a sound business problem and a quality dataset, we can create a lot of innovative solutions. Autoencoders are only one type of such solutions.

In this chapter, we started with feature engineering, which allows us to extract the most significant features from a dataset. Then we moved to autoencoders. Autoencoders are a type of neural network only used to learn efficient coding of unlabeled datasets. Autoencoders can be applied to many business problems like facial recognition, anomaly detection, image recognition, drug discovery, machine translation, and so on.

9.10   Practical next steps and suggested readings

The following provides suggestions for what to do next and offers some helpful reading:

- Read the blog at https://mng.bz/qxaw.
- Study the following papers:
  - Hinton, G. E., Krizhevsky, A., and Wang, S. D. (2011). Transforming Autoencoders. https://mng.bz/7p99
  - Bank, D., Koenigstein, N., and Giryes, R. (2020). Autoencoders. https://arxiv.org/abs/2003.05991
  - Michelucci, U. (2020). An Introduction to Autoencoders. https://arxiv.org/abs/2201.03898

- See the good code and dataset available on the TensorFlow official page. https://mng.bz/mGQr.

Summary

- Predictive modeling is used in various domains to make future predictions using supervised learning algorithms.
- Key aspects of predictive modeling involve identifying significant variables or features for accurate predictions.
- Feature engineering enhances model accuracy by extracting useful features from raw data.
- Feature learning automates feature detection, suitable for datasets like images, text, and audio.
- Autoencoders are a type of neural network used for data encoding, dimensionality reduction, and generating synthetic data.
- The architecture of autoencoders includes encoder, bottleneck, and decoder components for data compression and reconstruction.
- Autoencoders face information loss, are dataset-specific, and are suitable for precise applications.
- Training autoencoders requires encoding, decoding, and defining hyperparameters such as code size and loss function.
- Major applications include dimensionality reduction, anomaly detection, and data compression, among others.
- Types of autoencoders include undercomplete, sparse, contractive, denoizing, and variational.
- Sparse and contractive autoencoders address overfitting using different methodologies.
- A Python implementation of basic autoencoder architecture involves the Keras library for encoding and decoding data.

10

Generative adversarial networks, generative AI, and ChatGPT

Reality is created by mind. We can change our reality by changing our mind.

—Plato

In the last chapter, we discussed autoencoders. We now move to the some of the most revolutionary technical advancements in recent times. You have probably heard the terms generative adversarial networks (GANs), generative AI (GenAI), and ChatGPT in the news. These are certainly game-changers for the industry. In this penultimate chapter of the book, we discuss these innovations. Welcome to the tenth chapter, and all the very best!

10.1 AI: A transformation

AI is a transformative field in computer science. It aims to create machines and solutions that can mimic human intelligence. AI has indeed come a long way since its birth and is changing our lives in multiple ways.

The concept of AI can be traced back to the mid-20th century. In 1956, John McCarthy, Marvin Minsky, Nathaniel Rochester, and Claude Shannon organized the Darmouth Workshop, which is often credited for the birth of AI, as during this workshop the term "artificial intelligence" was coined. The researchers wanted to see how machines can mimic human intelligence and be used for everyday life. In the initial years, the researchers focused on symbolic AI. This approach involved using symbols and logic to represent the knowledge and solve the problems. The progress in AI slowed down during 1970s and 1980s when the funding was reduced. The late 20th century and the early 21st century saw the resurgence of AI, thanks to the development of machine learning techniques like neural networks and deep learning. The new enabled AI systems started to make predictions and decisions by learning from the historical data. With the availability of cloud computing, better service, and more processing power, the training of algorithms was faster, easier, and cheaper, and there was a shift from rule-driven to data-driven algorithms. With the launch of libraries like TensorFlow and Keras, creating deep learning networks became something that anyone with an internet connection could do.

AI has had a significant effect on day-to-day life. For example, we have virtual assistants like Siri and Alexa to make recommendations on streaming platforms and e-commerce websites. AI has been applied in finance, retail, aviation, life sciences, manufacturing, and many other industries and business functions, improving efficiency and decision-making processes, increasing customer satisfaction, and decreasing costs. The integration of AI with robotics has resulted in auto-driving cars, drones, automation, and digital twins. We now have very intelligent robotic systems that have the capability to perform very complex tasks. AI has thus far been a boon to the human race, and with responsible use, it can provide great benefits.

AI continues to grow, and that growth presents a unique set of opportunities and challenges. There are biases and ethical concerns in AI systems; many activists have also raised concerns about potential job displacements due to automation. Policymakers and the government along with researchers are working tirelessly to make sure that AI technologies are used responsibly and developed to serve humans, not work against them.

10.2   *GenAI and its significance*

GenAI is a transformative field within the broader domains of AI. It is a testament to one of the remarkable achievements we have made in the field of machine learning, resulting in improvements in computer processing and generation of new content. You have no doubt seen the examples of Generative Pre-trained Transformer 3 (GPT-3) and its advanced versions, which are being used in multiple industries and functions.

The significant difference between traditional AI and GenAI is that GenAI solutions can produce data while traditional AI systems perform tasks like predictions, recommendations, or classifications. GenAI solutions are generally based on

GANs—autoregressive models like the transformer architecture, which empowers solutions like GPT.

GenAI is useful for multiple business domains and functions. A few of them are as follows:

- Natural language processing-based solutions have immensely benefitted from GenAI models. GenAI has enabled the development of intelligent chatbots, virtual assistants, summarization of text, query engines, and customized content. These solutions have been helpful for branding and marketing purposes, customer services, research and development, optimizations, and academics. The use of GenAI for natural language processing (NLP) is huge and is expanding and improving every day.

- The life sciences and healthcare industry has been revolutionized through GenAI tools. With these tools, the discovery of new drugs, generation of medical reports, simulation of medical scenarios, training of healthcare professionals, search of medical journals, and the overall medical research profession has improved significantly. For example, AI can identify existing drugs that could be repurposed for new therapeutic uses. By analyzing large datasets, AI can discover connections between drugs and diseases that were not previously recognized. AI-driven virtual screening can predict the binding affinity of small molecules to target proteins. This saves time and resources by reducing the number of compounds that need to be synthesized and tested in the lab. The use of GenAI within the healthcare industry is immensely beneficial for humans.

- Machine learning and data analysis is completely dependent on the quantity and quality of data available. Many times, there is a scarcity of good-quality datasets. GenAI is playing a valuable role in the creation of synthetic data to augment and expand smaller datasets. This process improves the overall quality of the training dataset and hence improves the performance of the model. Using the synthetic data, the model becomes less generic, and the risk of overfitting is reduced.

- Using GenAI, customer experiences are improving. With GenAI algorithms, a business is able to create customized recommendations, experiences, content, and solutions. With this enhanced experience, overall user engagement is improved, and the customer becomes more satisfied, leading to higher customer lifetime value. Certainly, GenAI has been changing the personalization experience of customers. It can be extended to any business domain like retail, finance, telecom, or aviation.

- GenAI's ability to create content like art, music, text, videos, and images is very useful. It helps professionals in the creative fields by automating multiple steps of their work. Authors now can use GenAI for innovative ideas, image designers can use it to create designs, and music directors can use it to create a piece of music.

- In the field of research and science, GenAI is helping scientists and researchers in the simulation of experiments. It can simulate multiple scenarios, model very complex physical systems, and predict the outcome of the experiments. Certainly, it decreases the amount of time and cost involved in the overall experiment. Researchers and scientists can reach results much faster now.

These are only a few examples of the significance of GenAI; the possibilities are immense. GenAI is certainly a game-changer with futuristic applications.

Next we compare discriminative and generative models. We have discussed discriminative models throughout the book. Now we will clarify the differences between discriminative models and GenAI ones.

10.3 *Discriminative models and GenAI*

In the realm of machine learning and AI, discriminative models and generative models are two fundamental approaches. Both can be used for classification, estimation, and generation purposes. There are similarities and differences.

Discriminative models create the boundary that separates different classes or categories of datasets. These types of models are generally helpful for making predictions and for data classification solutions. Some of the attributes of discriminative models are as follows:

- Discriminative models are generally used in supervised learning solutions. As you know, supervised learning is for labeled datasets, where we have a target variable to train an algorithm. Using supervised learning solutions for categorical variables, we can predict the probability for an event to happen or not—for example, if the customer will churn or not, whether the incoming credit card transaction is fraud or genuine, and so on. Similarly, using supervised learning solutions for numeric variables, we can predict an estimated value for a numeric variable—for example, what the sales of a store next month will be or the number of calls a call center can expect in the next week. Discriminative models predict the conditional probability for an output given an input value, and hence they are a great solution for any kind of classification task.
- The most common examples of discriminative models are logistic regression, decision trees, random forests, support vector machines, and deep learning–based networks used for image and text classification. There are many discriminative models at our disposable.

For generative models, our purpose is to capture the underlying distribution of the data they are trained on. They seek to learn how the data is generated and how they can use that intelligence to generate new data points that are similar to the training dataset. Some of the salient attributes of the generative models are as follows:

- Generative models provide a probability distribution over the entire data space; they can generate new data points that are similar to the training data. It makes them very helpful for solutions like synthetic text and image generation.
- Generative models are very helpful for unsupervised learning solutions like dimensionality reduction and clustering. This is because they do not rely on the presence of explicit labels, and hence they can reveal the underlying patterns

present in the dataset. A few examples are hidden Markov models, GANs, and variational autoencoders.

If we compare discriminative and generative models, we will find the following:

- Generative models generally require a bigger dataset for training as they have to learn the entire data distribution. Discriminative models, however, can work with smaller labeled datasets too.
- Generative models are typically much more complex than discriminative models. Generative models use the underlying structure of the data and require more computational time and resources to achieve the solution.
- Generative models have been used for content generation and the estimation of density; discriminative models, on the other hand, are designed for broader classifications and predictions. Hence, in current scenarios you will find discriminative models are more popular than generative models.
- Discriminative models are more efficient and require less computation cost and memory. Thus they are more popular in the present scenarios for industry.

Both generative and discriminative models have their own set of pros and cons. The choice depends on the business problem at hand and the dataset available. While discriminative models are much more effective and efficient in classification and prediction, generative models are more versatile and useful for data generation and exploration. As users, we require an in-depth understanding of these models and their characteristics. Only then can we choose the right solution for the business problem at hand.

10.4 Generative adversarial networks

GANs represent a revolutionary deep learning architecture that has made significant contributions to the field of generative modeling. GANs were introduced by Ian Goodfellow and his colleagues in 2014 and have since become a cornerstone in various applications, including image generation, style transfer, data augmentation, and more.

At their core, GANs consist of two neural networks: the generator and the discriminator. The generator is responsible for creating synthetic data, such as images or text, while the discriminator's role is to distinguish between real data and data produced by the generator. In our in-depth explanation, we dissect the GAN architecture, providing a detailed understanding of its key components, training process, and practical applications.

10.4.1 The generator network

The generator network is the creative force behind GANs. Its primary role is to produce synthetic data, mimicking real data as closely as possible. The generator network takes random noise as input, often sampled from a simple distribution like a Gaussian or uniform distribution. This noise vector is then passed through a series of layers, typically consisting of convolutional or transposed convolutional layers in the case of image generation or recurrent layers for text generation. The generator's purpose is to transform the input noise into data that closely resembles the real data distribution. See figure 10.1.

Let's take a closer look at how the generator network operates:

- *Input noise*—The generator initiates the process with an input noise vector. This noise vector serves as the seed for generating data. The noise vector is typically drawn from a simple probability distribution, such as a Gaussian distribution.
- *Transformations*—The input noise is passed through a series of layers within the generator. Each layer transforms the input in a way that makes it increasingly resemble the real data distribution. These transformations are learned through the training process.
- *Generation*—As the input noise progresses through the network, it gradually takes on the characteristics of the target data. This transformation process continues until the data produced by the generator is presented as the final output.
- *Loss function*—The quality of the generated data is measured using a loss function, which quantifies how similar the generated data is to the real data. The goal of the generator is to minimize this loss, thereby creating data that is as realistic as possible.

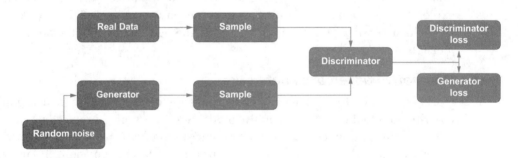

Figure 10.1   Representation of a GAN

The generator's ultimate objective is to produce data that is virtually indistinguishable from authentic data. However, achieving this level of realism is a complex task, and it relies heavily on the adversarial relationship with the discriminator network.

We now move to the counterpart of the generative network, which is the discriminator network.

10.4.2 The discriminator network

The discriminator network, as the counterpart of the generator, plays a crucial role in GANs. Its purpose is to differentiate between real data and fake data. The discriminator is a binary classifier, trained to assign high probabilities (close to 1) to real data and low probabilities (close to 0) to fake data.

Let's explore the discriminator network in more detail:

- *Training data*—Usually, the discriminator network is exposed to a dataset comprising real data. This dataset is primarily used to clean the discriminator, which allows it to distinguish the authentic data from the synthetic data.
- *Discrimination*—When the discriminator has been trained, we can use it to evaluate the datasets. It takes both real data from the training dataset used and the synthetic data produced by the generator as an input.
- *Loss calculation*—Now the discriminator computes a loss. This loss or error is based on the ability of the discriminator to distinguish real data from the synthetic data. If the discriminator correctly identifies real data as real and synthetic data as synthetic, it means the performance is good, and hence the loss is minimized. However, if the discriminator makes some errors, the loss would increase.
- *Parameters updates*—The discriminator's parameters are adjusted to minimize the computed loss. These updates are helpful for the discriminator to increase its accuracy.

With an understanding of the underlying structure behind GANs, we now move to the heart of the entire process: the training of the network.

10.4.3 *Adversarial training*

The adversarial training process is the heart of the GAN architectures. The overall training process is as follows:

1 Initially, both the generator and the discriminator start with random weights.
2 The generator produces synthetic data from the random noise and presents it to the discriminator along with the real dataset.
3 The discriminator analyzes, assesses, and assigns probabilities to each input. This is an attempt to correctly distinguish real data from the synthetic data.
4 The generator is updated based on the feedback from the discriminator. The objective is to generate data that becomes indistinguishable from the real data by the discriminator.
5 The discriminator is updated to improve its ability to differentiate between real and synthetic data.
6 This process is continued iteratively. The generator and the discriminator keep on improving their capabilities. The generator becomes increasingly adept at producing a realistic dataset while the discriminator becomes more skilled at the identification process. This iterative and interesting competition drives the overall solution to a point where the generated data is virtually indistinguishable from the authentic dataset.

The overall training process relies on two key loss functions:

- *Generator loss*—This function aims to minimize the discriminator's ability to distinguish between real and synthetic datasets. Commonly used loss function examples are binary cross entropy loss, which allows the generator to produce data that the discriminator is more likely to classify as real.

- *Discriminator loss*—The discriminator loss function's purpose is to maximize its ability to distinguish real datasets from the synthetic or fake datasets. It aims to minimize the binary cross-entropy loss while assessing real data and maximizes when working on generated or synthetic datasets.

GANs are quite remarkable with this training process. We now move to a few variants of GAN and some applications.

10.4.4 *Variants and applications of GANs*

GANS are useful for specific challenges and problems. This has also led to some of the prominent variants that follow:

- *Conditional GAN*—These models take additional information (e.g., class labels) as input to control the generated data's attributes.
- *Deep convolutional GANs*—Optimized for image generation, deep convolutional GANs use convolutional layers to generate high-quality images.
- *CycleGANs*—Used for style transfer and image-to-image translation, these models learn to map images from one domain to another.
- *BigGAN and StyleGAN*—These models produce high-resolution images and offer advanced control over image styles and attributes.

Next, we briefly cover the latest technological solutions available—for example, Bidirectional Encoder Representations from Transformers (BERT), GPT-3, and others.

10.4.5 *BERT, GPT-3, and others*

BERT, GPT-3, and other models are prominent examples of advanced NLP techniques that have revolutionized the field of AI. These models have made significant strides in understanding and generating human-like text and enabling various applications in language understanding, translation, text generation, and more.

Developed by Google in 2018, BERT is a transformer-based model designed for understanding the context of words in a sentence. Unlike previous models, which read text sequentially, BERT can consider the context of each word by processing text bidirectionally. BERT is pretrained on a massive amount of text data and can be fine-tuned for specific NLP tasks like sentiment analysis, question answering, and named entity recognition. BERT's pretraining has significantly improved the performance of many NLP tasks, making it a foundational model in the field.

GPT-3, developed by OpenAI, is one of the most famous language models. It was released in 2020 and is the third iteration of the GPT series. GPT-3 is a generative model capable of producing human-like text. It is pretrained on a massive corpus of text data and can generate coherent and contextually relevant text when given a prompt. It can also perform a wide range of NLP tasks, including text completion, language translation, and text summarization and can even engage in text-based conversations.

Text-to-Text Transfer Transformer (T5) is another transformer-based model, developed by Google in 2019. It is unique because it frames all NLP tasks as a text-to-text problem. T5 is pretrained on a variety of text data and can be fine-tuned for various NLP tasks, including text classification, translation, and summarization, making it a versatile model for NLP tasks.

XLNet was developed as a successor to BERT and introduced a permutation-based training approach. It considers all possible permutations of words in a sentence during training, enabling it to model complex language dependencies more effectively. XLNet has shown strong performance on various NLP benchmarks and tasks.

RoBERTa is another model that builds upon BERT's architecture, developed by Facebook AI in 2019. It optimizes BERT's pretraining methodology and achieves state-of-the-art results on multiple NLP benchmarks.

The transformer architecture, originally introduced in the paper "Attention Is All You Need" by Vaswani et al. (https://arxiv.org/abs/1706.03762), forms the foundation of many of these models. It relies on self-attention mechanisms to process and generate text data.

10.5 ChatGPT and its details

ChatGPT is an advanced AI model designed to engage in natural and dynamic conversations with users, making it a pivotal development in the field of AI. Developed by OpenAI, ChatGPT is built upon the GPT-3.5 architecture, which is known for its capacity to understand and generate human-like text.

10.5.1 Key features of ChatGPT

The key features of ChatGPT are as follows:

- *Natural language understanding*—ChatGPT comprehends and generates text in a manner that closely resembles human communication, making interactions with it feel more intuitive and engaging.
- *Contextual awareness*—The model can maintain context throughout a conversation, remembering previous messages and providing coherent responses, enabling more meaningful and flowing dialogues.
- *Multilingual capabilities*—ChatGPT can communicate in multiple languages, expanding its utility and accessibility to a global audience.
- *Customization*—It can also be fine-tuned to perform specific tasks, such as drafting emails, answering FAQs, or offering tutoring, making it versatile for various applications.

10.5.2 Applications of ChatGPT

Applications of ChatGPT include the following:

- *Customer support*—ChatGPT can be used to provide 24/7 customer support, answering queries, troubleshooting problems, and ensuring a high level of user satisfaction. It can be hence used as a chatbot and can serve as a virtual assistant, helping users with scheduling, reminders, and information retrieval.

- *Research and development*—Researchers can employ ChatGPT to sift through vast amounts of data and generate reports or summaries, saving time and effort.
- *Content generation*—It can assist content creators by generating blog posts, marketing materials, or creative writing prompts.
- *Education*—It can also offer personalized tutoring and answer students' questions, enhancing the learning experience.

While there are many applications of ChatGPT, there is an ethical consideration too. The use of ChatGPT must prioritize user privacy, with measures in place to protect sensitive information shared during conversations. Monitoring and supervising ChatGPT's interactions may be necessary to ensure responsible usage. Developers must work diligently to reduce biases and the potential to generate false or harmful information in responses. Developers, organizations, and users should collectively hold ChatGPT accountable for its actions and output.

Next we discuss the integration of GenAI in some real-world business applications. This will give you a view on how you can employ these technologies in the pragmatic business world.

10.6   *Integration of GenAI*

Integrating GenAI into real-world business involves a systematic process that requires careful planning and consideration. Consider the following step-by-step guide on how to integrate GenAI effectively:

1 *Set the objectives and business problem definition.* First, we should define the specific objectives and use cases for GenAI within our business priorities. This requires determining where it can provide the most value—whether that's customer support and solutions, data analysis/visualizations, personalization, content generation, or others.

2 *Evaluate the data available and the infrastructure.* Next, we should check the data available and assess its quality and quantity. High-quality data is essential for training and maintaining GenAI models. We also must ensure that our IT infrastructure can support the integration of AI systems.

3 *Select the model.* We then choose to develop a custom GenAI model or to use an existing pretrained model. If we decide to build a custom model, we will have to consider working with AI development teams or external vendors with expertise in the field. This is a vital step, as we should choose teams that have the required skills to develop the models. It is better to take recommendations from the experts in the field.

4 *Perform data collation, preprocessing, and preparation.* Data is the protagonist here, and the next step is to gather and preprocess the data necessary to train the GenAI model. This may involve cleaning, labeling, and structuring the data for training. Data preprocessing is a critical step for model accuracy. The data should be representative of the business problem at hand.

5 *Train the model.* We next train the GenAI model using the preprocessed data. This process may require powerful hardware and deep learning expertise. There might be some iterations to the model to align with our specific business requirements. This step can take a lot of time, depending on the quantity of the data, the quality of the infrastructure, and the complexity of the solution.

6 *Test, validate, and tweak.* We then test the GenAI system to ensure that it functions as expected. This will involve validating its performance on real-world data and use cases. A few variables to keep in mind are accuracy, response times, and user experience.

7 *Perform user education and training.* GenAI will be used by employees, customers, or other stakeholders; hence, we have to provide training and educational materials on how to use the AI system effectively.

8 *Consider compliance and privacy.* It is vital to develop guidelines and policies for the responsible use of GenAI, addressing problems like privacy, bias, and compliance with relevant regulations. We have to ensure that the AI system aligns with our organization's ethical standards.

9 *Perform maintenance.* As our business grows, the demand on GenAI may increase. We have to regularly update the model with fresh data to keep it accurate and effective. We should always plan for scalability and ongoing maintenance. It is important to implement monitoring systems to track GenAI's performance and user feedback. This information can help us in making continuous improvements and address any problems that arise.

10 *Adapt, innovate, and improve.* We should continuously evaluate the return on investment of this GenAI integration by determining whether the expected benefits are being realized and adjust as needed. It is important that we stay abreast of advancements in AI technology and continually adapt and innovate our GenAI integration to remain competitive and efficient.

Integrating GenAI into your business is a complex process that involves multiple steps and ongoing efforts. Successful integration requires a clear strategy, a commitment to responsible AI use, and a focus on delivering value to our organization and its stakeholders.

10.7 Concluding thoughts

GenAI is an exciting and ambitious frontier in AI research. While it represents a long-term goal, the pursuit of creating highly adaptable and versatile AI systems has the potential to revolutionize the way we interact with technology and address a wide range of challenges. However, it also comes with ethical and societal responsibilities that need careful consideration and regulation as we move forward in AI development.

ChatGPT is a remarkable AI model with the potential to revolutionize human-computer interactions. As it continues to evolve, the responsible use and development of ChatGPT will be essential to harness its full potential while addressing ethical and practical concerns. Whether it's in customer service, content generation, education, or research, ChatGPT is poised to transform the way we engage with AI, bringing us closer to more intuitive and seamless communication with machines.

10.8   *Practical next steps and suggested readings*

The following provides suggestions for what to do next and offers some helpful reading:

- See the first paper on GANs: Goodfellow, I., Pouget-Abadie, J., Mirza, M., et al. (2014). Generative Adversarial Networks. https://arxiv.org/abs/1406.2661
- Study the following papers:
  - Kingma, D. P., and Welling, M. (2013). Auto-Encoding Variational Bayes. https://arxiv.org/abs/1312.6114
  - Arici, T., and Celikyilmax, A. (2016). Associative Adversarial Networks. https://arxiv.org/abs/1611.06953
- If you want to study Bayesian GAN, see Saatchi, Y., and Wilson, A. J. (2014). Bayesian GAN. https://arxiv.org/abs/1705.09558.

Summary

- AI seeks to emulate human intelligence and has evolved significantly since the 1956 Dartmouth Workshop, where the term "artificial intelligence" was coined.
- Initially focused on symbolic AI, the field slowed during the 1970s and 1980s but was revitalized in the late 20th century with machine learning advances.
- The rise of cloud computing and libraries like TensorFlow shifted AI from rule-driven to data-driven algorithms, enhancing its accessibility.
- AI affects various sectors including finance, aviation, and manufacturing, improving efficiency, decision-making, and cost reduction.
- GenAI distinguishes itself by generating data, underpinning technologies like GPT, and benefitting domains like NLP and healthcare.
- GenAI creates synthetic data, enhancing machine learning models by expanding dataset quality and reducing overfitting risks.
- Discriminative models are data classifiers, while generative models learn data distribution to create new, similar data points.
- GANs, featuring generator and discriminator networks, progressively improve data realism through adversarial training.
- GAN variants, such as CycleGAN and StyleGAN, address tasks like style transfer and high-resolution image generation.
- Natural language models like BERT and GPT-3 have advanced NLP capabilities, offering solutions for translation and conversational AI.
- ChatGPT, based on GPT-3.5, excels in generating human-like conversational text, finding use in customer support and content generation.
- Integrating generative AI into business requires careful planning, data preparation, model training, and continual evaluation for success.

End-to-end model
deployment

11

This chapter covers

- The end-to-end model deployment process
- Maintenance of the model postdeployment
- Python codes for each of the steps

> *The journey is the destination.*
>
> —Dan Eldon

The path to learning never ends. It takes a lot of courage, patience, and hard work to learn something. We have to be persistent, resourceful, and always looking for opportunities to learn and excel.

Across all of the chapters so far, you have covered a lot of concepts, techniques, and algorithms. In this last chapter of the book, we are going to discuss the end-to-end model deployment process. We will cover various aspects ranging from a business problem definition, data cleaning, and exploratory data analysis (EDA) to model deployment and maintenance. This end-to-end journey is crucial for you to appreciate the entire process. We will discuss Python codes at all the relevant places.

Welcome to this last chapter, and all the very best!

11.1   *The machine learning modeling process*

Recall in chapter 1 we briefly discussed end-to-end model development. In this section, we cover each of the respective steps in detail and the most common problems we face with each of them and how to tackle them. It will finally lead to the model deployment phase. Figure 11.1 shows the model development process we follow.

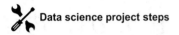

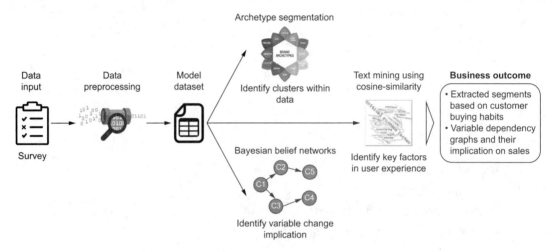

Figure 11.1   The complete machine learning modeling process

The steps in the model development process are as follows:

1 Business problem definition
2 Data discovery and feasibility analysis
3 Data cleaning and prepreparation
4 Exploratory data analysis
5 Modeling process and business approval
6 Model deployment
7 Model documentation
8 Model maintenance and model refresh

Throughout this chapter, we will cover each of these processes in much more detail. These are all relevant to the modeling process.

11.2   *Business problem definition*

Your business problem definition is the very first step. It is vital that the business problem is concise, clear, measurable, and achievable. Many times, in practice, the business problem is vaguely defined, such as "decrease the costs or increase the revenue," which often leads to poor results throughout the rest of the process. A good business problem is defined clearly with key performance indicators (KPIs) and parameters that can be used to measure the effect. A good business problem ensures there is no ambiguity, the goal is clear, and we can achieve it with the available resources and within the timeframe.

Some of the most important considerations regarding a business problem are as follows:

- If a business problem is vaguely defined, it is going to cause problems and should be avoided. For example, all of the businesses and various functions would want to increase their revenue and profits, reduce costs, optimize various processes, and so forth. With a vague business problem, we will not have clarity on the process, which will lead to ambiguity.

- The business purpose should be practically achievable. Unrealistic goals like doubling the revenue or halving the cost should not be set. Unrealistic goals mean that good results might get rejected, as they do not meet the business targets.

- The business problem should be measurable if possible. If the business problem is only qualitative, then it will be of limited help. We won't be able to understand the real effect of the machine learning model created.

- Scope creep is one of the problems we face sometimes. Scope creep happens when at the start of the project, during project building, the scope is changed drastically, changing the requirements and time needs of the project without changing resources and deadlines accordingly.

An effective business problem is defined correctly, completely, and in discussion with the business teams. It is concise with measurable KPIs and is achievable within a given timeframe.

NOTE   Business stakeholders and subject matter experts should be involved in defining the business problems. They should be a part of the team from the start and own the overall process.

A few examples of a good business problem are as follows:

- The marketing team in an organization aims to optimize the various costs and maximize the return on investments. They want to identify the optimal combinations of marketing efforts (email, calls, TV advertising, and meetings) to increase the return on investment by 1.5% in the next six months.

- A manufacturing team faces an increase in the number of defects in the last three months. The business problem can be to identify all the potential reasons for such an increase in defects. The team also wishes to know if there is a trend or pattern. The business goal may be to shortlist the most significant reasons for defects and reduce them by 2.5% in the next six months.

We have described the attributes of a business problem. We now move to the next phase, which is data discovery and feasibility.

11.3   *Data discovery and feasibility analysis*

The data discovery phase is one of the most important steps in the entire model building process. If there is not enough data, both quantitatively and qualitatively, it might be very difficult to create the solution we desire. At the same time, having access to this data is of paramount importance.

During this process, we also do the feasibility analysis for the project:

1   The data is the protagonist. The very first step is the identification of the datasets required for the business problem use case and mechanisms for its access by all the stakeholders. For this reason, it is advisable that

  – The dataset is available from servers or clouds and relevant permissions are set correctly to the people who need access. The servers can access the data from a database such as SQL/MySQL/NoSQL/MongoDB.
  – If the data is in Excel/.csv/text files, it will be useful to make it available on the server. In recent times, cloud servers like AWS, Azure, Google Cloud, etc., are used for storing the data.

2   It is imperative to check that the dataset is complete and relevant to the business problem. The dataset should be representative enough of the business problem at hand and capture all the variability in the business. The time and duration of the data is another important dimension we should bear in mind. For example, if we wish to analyze the business of a telecom operator or a retail company, we should have enough data (for at least the last year so that we capture seasonality as well) and variables around sales, transactions, discounts, products/services purchased, marketing behaviors, historical behaviors, offline/online purchases, etc.

3   It is prudent to plan the data refresh at this stage. After all, once the model is built, we will have to maintain it and refresh it.

During this phase, the most common problems we can face are as follows:

  ▪ We might find that there are certain missing values, outliers, etc., in the dataset. We will cover that in detail in the next section.
  ▪ We must also ensure that correct business rules are applied on the dataset. The steps to ensure it are

  – Get the relevant dataset for the business problem.
  – Make some basic analyses like total sales, number of customers, month-wise trends, discounts, etc.
  – Get these KPIs verified by the business stakeholders. If the numbers are wrong, the business rules are refined.

Only once the data is correct and the numbers are accurate can we move on to the feasibility analysis for the use case. For the feasibility analysis, we do the following:

1   Check the data quality in detail. We cover the various aspects in the next section.

2 Analyze the data for any patterns, such as seasonality, etc. We also check if there are any correlations present among various variables to ensure which variables are related to each other.

3 Check for relationships between the business problem and the dataset. This is followed by an exploratory analysis to identify if there is any significant difference between various customer groups.

After this step, we go to the data cleaning, preprocessing, and data preparation step. This is one of the most time-consuming steps we have to do.

11.4 Data cleaning and prepreparation

In the last step, we shortlisted the data for the business problem. Now we will go to the data cleaning and preprocessing phase of the modeling process.

Data in its original form might not be usable enough to be fed to the machine learning model. We have to create a few additional variables and treat some others. In the real business world, the dataset is generally "dirty." There can be many problems that can be present in the data, which are as follows:

- Duplicate values
- Categorical variables (may cause some problem for certain algorithms)
- Missing values, NULL, or not a number (NaN), etc.
- Outliers
- Other problems (as described in previous chapters)

Let's deal with each of these things in turn. The code for this chapter has been checked in at https://mng.bz/vKY7. You can access the code and datasets there. We will now work on how to deal with duplicate values in a dataset.

11.5 Duplicate values in the data

Duplicates are often a problem in datasets. If there are two rows in the dataset that are a complete copy of each other, they are duplicates in nature. This problem might occur during data-capturing time. The problem with duplicates is that the statistics will be affected—for example, by making some events appear to be more frequent than they are. When removing duplicates, one needs to pay attention to not removing genuine data of events that happened twice—for example, a customer purchasing an item twice at two different times or a customer purchasing two identical items at the same time versus the transaction of the purchase being recorded twice.

The following are the steps of a simple Python program to remove duplicates (see figure 11.2):

1 Import `numpy` and `pandas`.
2 Define a dataframe with some dummy variables.
3 Print the dataframe.
4 There is an inbuilt method: `drop_duplicates()`. Use it to drop the duplicates.
5 Print the dataframe and find that the duplicate rows have been dropped.

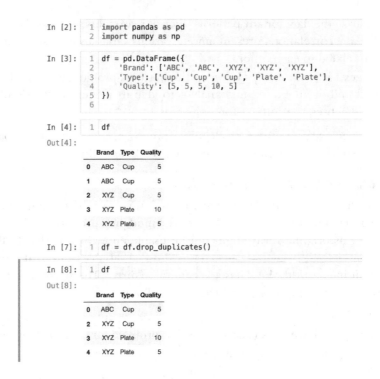

```
In [2]:    1  import pandas as pd
           2  import numpy as np

In [3]:    1  df = pd.DataFrame({
           2      'Brand': ['ABC', 'ABC', 'XYZ', 'XYZ', 'XYZ'],
           3      'Type': ['Cup', 'Cup', 'Cup', 'Plate', 'Plate'],
           4      'Quality': [5, 5, 5, 10, 5]
           5  })
           6

In [4]:    1  df

Out[4]:
```

	Brand	Type	Quality
0	ABC	Cup	5
1	ABC	Cup	5
2	XYZ	Cup	5
3	XYZ	Plate	10
4	XYZ	Plate	5

```
In [7]:    1  df = df.drop_duplicates()

In [8]:    1  df

Out[8]:
```

	Brand	Type	Quality
0	ABC	Cup	5
2	XYZ	Cup	5
3	XYZ	Plate	10
4	XYZ	Plate	5

Figure 11.2   Removing duplicates in a simple Python program

11.6   *Categorical variables*

The next step is treating the categorical variable. Let's revisit the definition of categorical variables. Variables like gender, city, product categories, zip codes, etc., are examples of categorical variables. Categorical variables may not strictly be a problem in the data, but they can create problems for certain algorithms like k-means clustering. Recall that for k-means clustering, the distance needs to be calculated between the data points.

In certain datasets, a categorical variable can have nearly all values as the same. For example, if the whole dataset is for the UK and a variable is "city," since a significant percentage of the population lives in London, then this variable might be of limited benefit. It will not create any variation in the dataset and will not be useful. Similarly, a categorical variable like "zip code" can have all the values as distinct and will not add much to the analysis.

Perhaps the most common method to deal with categorical variables is using one-hot encoding. In one-hot encoding, as shown in the Python code book, the variable gets transformed:

1   Use the same dataset we used in the last code.
2   There is a built-in method in pandas, `get_dummies()`, which can be used for converting categorical variables to numeric ones. See figure 11.3.

```
In [8]:   1  df
Out[8]:
```

	Brand	Type	Quality
0	ABC	Cup	5
2	XYZ	Cup	5
3	XYZ	Plate	10
4	XYZ	Plate	5

```
In [9]:   1  one_hot_encoded_data = pd.get_dummies(df, columns = ['Type'])
          2
```

```
In [10]:  1  one_hot_encoded_data
Out[10]:
```

	Brand	Quality	Type_Cup	Type_Plate
0	ABC	5	1	0
2	XYZ	5	1	0
3	XYZ	10	0	1
4	XYZ	5	0	1

Figure 11.3   The output of the code when executed

11.7   *Missing values in dataset*

One of the most common challenges in real-world datasets is missing values, which might be blank, NULL, NaN, etc. It might be due to a data capturing problem or data transformation. Missing values should be treated to ensure a robust solution. There can be a few reasons for missing values:

- The values were not recorded properly during data capturing. This can be due to faulty equipment or a manual error when recording the data.
- Many times, nonmandatory fields are not entered. For example, a customer might not enter age while filling out a retail loyalty form.
- Survey responses might not be completely filled out—for example, salary details.

To mitigate the missing values, there are a few options:

- First, we should check if the data is missing by design and whether it is a problem that needs to be addressed. For example, it is possible for a sensor to not record any temperature values above a certain pressure range. In that case, having missing values of temperature is correct.
- We should also check if there are any patterns in the missing values with respect to the other independent variables and with respect to the target variable. For example, in the dataset used in the next example we can deduce that whenever the value of temperature is NULL, then the equipment has failed. In such a case, there is a clear pattern in this data between temperature and the failed equipment. Hence, it will be the wrong step to delete the temperature or treat the temperature variable.

- Perhaps the easiest approach to deal with missing values is to delete the rows that have missing values. Though this is simple and fast, it reduces the size of the population and can delete very important pieces of information, as described earlier, or, for example, if a person has a legitimate last name that is not available. Hence, we should be careful deleting rows.
- We can impute the missing values by the mean, median, or mode values. Mean or median are only possible for continuous variables. Mode can be used for both continuous and categorical variables.
- There are also other popular methods for imputing the missing values like using k-nearest neighbor and multivariate imputation by chained equation.

We now use Python to impute missing values. We will use the built-in method `SimpleImputer` and impute the missing values with the mean. The second solution is for the categorical variables, where the mode is used to replace the missing values. See figure 11.4.

```
:   1  import numpy as np
    2  from sklearn.impute import SimpleImputer
    3  df = SimpleImputer(missing_values=np.nan, strategy='mean')
    4  df.fit([[3, 4], [np.nan, 5], [7, 8]])
    5  SimpleImputer()
    6  a = [[np.nan, 4], [5, np.nan], [7, 6]]
    7  print(df.transform(a))

    [[5.          4.        ]
     [5.          5.66666667]
     [7.          6.        ]]
```

```
In [2]:  1  import pandas as pd
         2  df = pd.DataFrame([["q", "w"], [np.nan, "e"], ["q", np.nan], ["a", "w"]], dtype="category")
         3  imputer = SimpleImputer(strategy="most_frequent")
         4  print(imputer.fit_transform(df))
         5

         [['q' 'w']
          ['q' 'e']
          ['q' 'w']
          ['a' 'w']]
```

```
3]:  1  import numpy as np
     2  from sklearn.experimental import enable_iterative_imputer
     3  from sklearn.impute import IterativeImputer
     4  imputer = IterativeImputer(max_iter=9, random_state=5)
     5  imputer.fit([[2, 3], [4, 5], [5, 6], [np.nan, 4], [6, np.nan]])
     6  IterativeImputer(random_state=5)
     7  x = [[np.nan, 2], [6, np.nan], [np.nan, 6]]
     8
     9  print(np.round(imputer.transform(x)))
    10

     [[1. 2.]
      [6. 7.]
      [5. 6.]]
```

```
In [4]:  1  import numpy as np
         2  from sklearn.impute import KNNImputer
         3  nan = np.nan
         4  X = [[1, 2, nan], [3, 4, 3], [nan, 6, 5], [8, 8, 7]]
         5  imputer = KNNImputer(n_neighbors=2, weights="uniform")
         6  imputer.fit_transform(X)
         7

Out[4]: array([[1. , 2. , 4. ],
               [3. , 4. , 3. ],
               [5.5, 6. , 5. ],
               [8. , 8. , 7. ]])
```

Figure 11.4   The output of the code when executed

In the next solutions, we will use `IterativeImputer` and the k-nearest neighbor algorithm.

11.8   Outliers present in the data

Outliers can be a big problem in the data. Consider this: let's assume that average rainfall for a city is 50 cm. But one particular year, due to heavy rains, the average rainfall is 100 cm. This data point would be an outlier and will completely change the analysis results should it be included. In the example, depending on whether the year of heavy precipitation is included or not in the statistical analysis, the results (say, of likely insurance claims) would be very different.

Therefore, like missing values, outliers may not necessarily be an error. We should apply business acumen to infer if the data points are really outliers for the problem under study.

We can detect outliers in the following ways:

- If a data point lies beyond the 5th percentile and 95th percentile or 1st percentile and 99th percentile, it can be considered an outlier.
- A value that is beyond $-1.5 \times$ interquartile range (IQR) and $+1.5 \times$ IQR can also be considered an outlier. Here IQR is given by (value at 75th percentile) − (value at 25th percentile).
- Values beyond one, two, or three standard deviations from the mean can be termed outliers.

We can create charts and visualize outliers. We can treat outliers by using the following methods:

- A data point beyond the 5th percentile and 95th percentile can be capped at the 5th percentile and 95th percentile, respectively. Or a data point beyond the 1st percentile and 99th percentile can be capped at the 1st percentile and 99th percentile, respectively.
- Replacement by mean, median, or mode is also used sometimes.
- Sometimes taking a natural log of the variable reduces the effect of outliers. But since a natural log will change the actual values, we should use sound mathematical models for the problem under investigation to make sure it's appropriate.

Outliers pose a big challenge to our datasets. They skew the insights we have generated from the data. Sometimes this skew is appropriate (e.g., the insurance claims of an outlier heavy precipitation year, which the insurance company needs to take into account). In any case, it becomes important that we at least highlight outliers in the dataset and sometimes modify them.

11.9   Exploratory data analysis

EDA is one of the most crucial steps before we start modeling. Using EDA, we generate insights that are quite useful for the business. The insights generated from the EDA conform to the modeling outputs too.

In EDA, we examine all the variables and understand their patterns, interdependencies, relationships, and trends. During the EDA phase, we come to know how the data is expected to behave. We uncover insights and recommendations from the data at this stage. A strong visualization complements the complete EDA.

> **NOTE**   EDA is the key to success; many times, a good EDA can solve the business problem.

Next we perform a detailed EDA on a dataset using Python. The entire code is quite big for a book; hence, the Python notebook has been checked in to the GitHub repository (https://mng.bz/vKY7) with full explanations and comments.

11.10 *Model development and business approval*

We have already covered the modeling process in detail throughout the book. This includes creating the first version of the model and then iterating with different hyperparameters and with different algorithms.

Throughout the book, we have covered a lot of algorithms on clustering and dimensionality reduction methods. We also covered modeling for the text datasets. During the model development phase, based on the business problem and dataset at hand, we choose the candidate algorithms. We always strive to select the best algorithm based on the accuracy measurement parameters we have discussed in earlier chapters.

The output of the modeling process is the final algorithm that delivers the best output for the business problem at hand. After a model with satisfactory performance is found, we should have a discussion with the business stakeholders for their final feedback. There might be a few iterations required to further improve the model.

Now, you have a model that is statistically significant, useful, and approved by the business stakeholders. We can move on to the model deployment stage.

11.11 *Model deployment*

A critical stage in the development of AI and machine learning models is model deployment. It is the changeover point between the development and production environments, where the model is used for real-world business purposes. There are many facets to be considered, like infrastructure concerns, deployment methodologies, monitoring, and maintenance. We discuss the challenges and recommended steps related to model deployment, with a methodical and organized strategy to put the models into production.

11.12 *Purpose of model deployment*

Model deployment is a crucial process. The primary reasons for model deployment are given as follows:

- Deployment of a model leads to the transformation of insights into actionable and practical purposes. The model is used for making predictions, optimizations, recommendations, and suggestions.

- The deployed models are integrated with the business processes and workflows. This facilitates the automation of various processes and business functions based on the insights and recommendations made by the model.
- Real-time predictions ensure that the business is responding quickly to the ever-changing business conditions. Real-time predictions are particularly useful for scenarios like credit card fraud detection in transactions, dynamic pricing, etc.
- Optimization and automation are enhanced. Model deployment leads to a decrease in the efforts of the employees by automating the business functions. With the help of deployed models, hardware use is optimized, business functions and processes are made more efficient, and the overall return on investment is increased.
- With deployed models, the versioning of the models can be done. This ensures that the organization can track changes, perform A/B tests, and even perform rollback if required.

In summary, the purpose of model deployment is to translate the potential of machine learning models into practical applications, making them an integral part of business operations and decision-making processes. Deployment enables organizations to harness the power of AI and data science to derive value from their models in real-world scenarios.

11.13 Types of model deployment

There are several types of model deployments. Based on the requirements and the strategic objectives, we can choose between them. The various types of deployment strategies are

- *Batch deployment*—This methodology is used when we have a large dataset that has been collected over a period of time and we need to use the machine learning model to assess this data and make predictions in an offline mode. Generally, the processing is done in large batches. For example, if we want to cluster the customers of a retail store based on k-means clustering, we can take their attributes for the last two years and generate a corresponding cluster for each customer. We can refresh the underlying data after one month, and hence we can reassign these clusters.
- *Real-time deployment*—Consider this: we want to check if the incoming credit card transaction is genuine or fraudulent. In such a scenario, we use a real-time check. The predictions are generated in real time based on the latest information available. Generally, to support real-time predictions, we should employ a multithreaded process so that multiple prediction requests can be handled at the same time. For example, there can be hundreds of credit card requests made simultaneously, which our system needs to classify with very little latency.
- *Edge deployment*—Nowadays, people expect smartphones or Internet of Things devices to have sophisticated features that are a good fit for a machine learning or AI algorithm. In such a scenario, a deployment in the cloud is possible, but

edge deployment is also used when an internet connection is not available. The prerequisite for edge deployment is that the machine learning model should be small in size and require less computation to facilitate running it on the devices with limited resources.

- *Canary deployment*—In canary deployment, we release the model to a subset of users before we make a full-scale deployment for all users. This ensures that an unstable version is not released to all users as we will get the feedback from the test users in the first phase. This is typically done by large companies with a huge number of users providing services through the cloud, such as Google or Facebook.

- *A/B testing*—A/B testing is not actually a model deployment technique, but it can be used as one and that is why it is listed here. In A/B testing, organizations want to test how one solution/service/product compares with another. For example, if the product team wishes to test which of the two offers delivers better profitability, they will use A/B testing. The example of two offers can be "spend $100 and get a 15% discount" or "spend $50 and get a 10% discount." In such a scenario, there can be two similar groups of customers that will receive these offers, and we will check which one delivers better profitability. In A/B testing deployments, two different models (or the same model with different hyperparameters) are tested against each other.

11.14 *Considerations while deploying the model*

There are quite a few factors we should keep in mind while deploying the model to ensure smooth and effective transition from development of the model to deployment:

- *Accuracy monitoring*—We should constantly monitor the performance of the model and improve it if the performance falls below a threshold. We should cover key metrics like accuracy, resource utilizations, time, and accuracy.

- *Scalability*—A solution should be scalable to other departments or brands. Even the volume of the data can increase with time.

- *Security and compliance*—This is one consideration that cannot be compromised at all. Any kind of deployment should be completely secure from any threats and fully compliant with the existing best practices, policies, and requirements.

- *Model drift and data drift*—These should be monitored because the overall business scenario can change. Customers, their preferences, the market, and the overall economy may change. There are events like COVID, war, floods, etc., and hence there is a data drift. It results in a model's performance change too. Hence, we should plan for model drift in advance.

- *Reproducibility*—Reproducibility of the results is an important factor when we deploy the models. We should be able to replicate the results.

- *Continuous integration and continuous deployment*—These pipelines are required to automate the testing and the deployment process. This reduces the risk of errors and ensures smooth deployments.

- *User feedback and successive iterations*—These are very important for a successful project. While planning for the deployment, we should give due diligence to incorporating users' feedback and the iterations in the model.
- *Versioning and rollback*—No model is ever final. There are successive iterations to it. In the infrastructure, there should be a provision to roll back to the previous version if the new version has any problems or if there are reasons based on the business requirements.

With this, we have covered all the considerations in model deployment. We will now deploy a model using Flask. The entire code has been uploaded to the GitHub repository (https://mng.bz/vKY7) with full comments and explanations.

11.15 Documentation

Our model is deployed. Now we ensure that all the code snippets are cleaned, are properly commented, and adhere to best practices. The code files should be checked in and properly documented. Documentation is often (unfortunately) not given enough time, but it is a very important step that should not be ignored. Should priorities be set in writing in the documentation, precedence should be given to the aspects more likely to change and to those that require understanding and interaction with external stakeholders.

There are quite a few tools for version controlling of the code. Git is perhaps the most common one. It is a very good practice to ensure that all of our code is checked in regularly to safeguard ourselves from any potential computer failures. For documentation, we do have a lot of options available in the industry, ranging from Word to PowerPoint to Confluence pages, depending on the industry we work in.

11.16 Model maintenance and refresh

So far, we have covered all the stages of model development and deployment. But once a model is put into production, it needs constant monitoring. We must ensure that the model is always performing at the desired level of accuracy. To achieve this, it is advised to have a dashboard or a monitoring system to gauge the performance of the model regularly. In case of nonavailability of such a system, a monthly or quarterly check-up of the model can be done.

Once the model is deployed, we can do a monthly health check of the model. It means that we compare the performance of the model with the expected accuracy. If the performance is not good, the model requires a refresh. Even though the model might not be deteriorating, it is still a good practice to refresh the model on new data points that are constantly created and saved. The model refresh is generally based on the business problem as well as the business domain for which the model has been built. For example, in the telecom domain, data updates are faster as customers use their mobile phones daily. On the other hand, for retail apparel, we don't expect customers to buy clothes every day. Hence, the model for the telecom domain can be refreshed weekly or biweekly, while for apparel, we can refresh once a quarter or once every six months.

Model refresh is quite an important phenomenon. Our business scenarios are always dynamic in nature. The customers' preferences and lifestyles will change, and there's always some activity being done by the competitor. There are certain scenarios that are beyond our control, like war, COVID, etc. Hence, we always should strive to adjust our models to the latest scenario in our business.

Model refresh means that we are retraining the model based on the new data points we have collected. It ensures that we are capturing the latest trends, backgrounds, and emerging relationships in the data, and hence our models are able to predict, optimize, and expedite the latest data points.

With this we have completed all the steps to design a machine learning system: how to develop it from scratch, how to deploy it, and how to maintain it. It is a long process that is quite tedious and requires teamwork.

11.17 Concluding thoughts

End-to-end machine learning development is quite a time-consuming one. From scratch to maintenance, it requires a lot of planning, teamwork, business knowledge, and effort. In this chapter, we have covered a lot of those steps. There can be other possible solutions too, which are dependent on the business domain and the requirements.

With this we come to the close of this book. We all read and feel that in this new age, data is the new oil, new electricity, new power, and new currency. The field is rapidly growing and making its effect felt across the globe. The pace of enhancements and improvements has opened new job opportunities like data engineers, data scientists, visualization experts, machine learning engineers, MLOps, DevOps, GenAI experts, and so on, with demand increasing day by day. But there is a dearth of professionals who fulfill the rigorous criteria for these job descriptions. The need of the hour is to have *data artists* who can marry business objectives with analytical problems, envision solutions to solve the dynamic business problems, adjust to the ever-changing technical landscape, and yet deliver cost-effective business solutions.

More sophisticated systems are being created every day. We can see examples of self-driving cars, human chatbots, fraud detection systems, facial recognition solutions, object-detection solutions, optimization and monitoring solutions, etc. The use of GenAI has further enhanced the effect.

At the same time, there are some risks too, which we should be aware of. The onus lies on humankind regarding how to harness this power of data. There are instances where (if we believe the claims made) AI has been used for rigging election results or DeepFake has been used for morphing pictures of people or profiling people based on race/color etc. We can use machine learning and AI to spread love or hatred—it is our choice. And like the cliché goes: with great power comes great responsibility!

We sincerely hope you enjoyed the book. Congratulations, and all the very best for your next steps!

11.18 Practical next steps and suggested readings

The following provides suggestions for what to do next and offers some helpful reading:

- Go through these two research papers on model deployment:
  - Paleyes, A., Urma, R-G., and Lawrence, N. D. (2020). Challenges in Deploying Machine Learning: a Survey of Case Studies. https://arxiv.org/abs/2011.09926v2
  - Sculley, D., Holt, G., Golovin, D., et al. (2015). Hidden Technical Debt in Machine Learning Systems. https://mng.bz/4azw
- Use the datasets we have developed in the last few chapters and perform EDA on those datasets.

Summary

- The journey of learning is ongoing, requiring courage, patience, and diligence; understanding the entire process from conceptualization to model deployment is essential for mastering machine learning.
- The end-to-end model deployment process involves key steps such as business problem definition, data cleaning, and EDA and culminating in model deployment and maintenance.
- The machine learning modeling process includes distinct stages such as business problem definition, data discovery and feasibility analysis, data prepreparation, EDA, modeling, deployment, documentation, and maintenance.
- Clear and achievable business problem definition is crucial to align goals effectively, prevent scope creep, and ensure that KPIs are measurable to assess the model's effect.
- Data discovery involves identifying necessary datasets, ensuring access and completeness, and analyzing feasibility, with particular attention to data relevance, quality, and representation.
- Data cleaning and prepreparation address common problems like duplicates, categorical variables, missing data, and outliers, utilizing various techniques to prepare the dataset for effective modeling.
- EDA is key to understanding data patterns and relationships and generating actionable insights, laying the groundwork for successful model development.
- The model development phase uses algorithms suitable for the business problem and requires stakeholder collaboration for refinement.
- Model deployment bridges development and production, necessitating considerations for infrastructure, real-time applications, scaling, security, and continuous integration to optimize model utility.
- Types of model deployment include batch, real-time, edge, canary, and A/B testing, each offering different advantages based on strategic objectives and application contexts.

- Effective deployment involves accuracy monitoring, detecting model and data drift, securing compliance and data, and ensuring reproducibility and scalability.
- Postdeployment, thorough documentation and version control are vital for code integrity and facilitating future iterations or rollbacks when necessary.
- Model maintenance involves regular performance checks and refreshes, adapting to dynamic business environments and ensuring alignment with evolving data trends.
- Data-driven solutions have vast potential but also an equally high duty of responsible use. We wrap up this book by stressing the importance of ethical application.

appendix A
Mathematical foundations

A.1 List of clustering algorithms

A.1.1 Partitioning-based algorithms

- k-means
- k-medoids (PAM)
- CLARA (Clustering Large Applications)
- CLARANS (Clustering Large Applications based on Randomized Search)
- Mini-Batch k-means
- Fuzzy C-Means (FCM)
- k-modes
- k-prototypes

A.1.2 Hierarchical clustering

- Agglomerative Hierarchical Clustering
- Divisive Hierarchical Clustering
- BIRCH (Balanced Iterative Reducing and Clustering using Hierarchies)
- CURE (Clustering Using Representatives)
- Chameleon
- ROCK (Robust Clustering using Links)
- HIERDENC (Hierarchical Density-Based Clustering)
- HAC-S (Hierarchical Agglomerative Clustering with Spatial Constraints)
- EAC (Ensemble Agglomerative Clustering)

A.1.3 Density-based algorithms

- DBSCAN (Density-Based Spatial Clustering of Applications with Noise)
- OPTICS (Ordering Points To Identify the Clustering Structure)

- HDBSCAN (Hierarchical DBSCAN)
- DENCLUE (Density-Based Clustering)
- Mean Shift
- VDBSCAN (Variable Density-Based Spatial Clustering)
- DBCLASD (Distribution-Based Clustering of Large Spatial Databases)
- LDBSCAN (Labeled DBSCAN)

A.1.4   *Grid-based algorithms*

- STING (Statistical Information Grid)
- WaveCluster
- SUBCLU (Subspace Clustering)
- GRIDCLUS (Grid-based Clustering Algorithm)
- OptiGrid
- CLIQUE (Clustering in Quest)

A.1.5   *Model-based algorithms*

- Gaussian Mixture Model (GMM)
- EM (Expectation Maximization) Algorithm
- DBEM (Density-Based EM)
- Bayesian Gaussian Mixture Model
- Hidden Markov Model (HMM) Clustering
- X-Means (Extended k-means)
- G-Means (Gaussian Means)
- MCLUST (Model-based Clustering using EM)
- AUTOCLASS (Bayesian Model-based Clustering)
- Mixmod (Mixture Models for Clustering)

A.1.6   *Spectral clustering*

- Ratio Cut Clustering
- Normalized Cut Clustering
- Multiway Spectral Clustering
- Spectral Biclustering
- Shi-Malik Clustering
- Laplacian Eigenmaps for Clustering

A.1.7   *Graph-based clustering*

- Connected Components Clustering
- Markov Clustering (MCL)
- Girvan-Newman Clustering
- Louvain Method for Community Detection
- Infomap Algorithm

- Walktrap Algorithm
- Edge Betweenness Clustering
- Chinese Whispers Clustering
- SPICi (Speed and Performance In Clustering)
- SCPS (Spectral Clustering on Perona & Shi's graph)

A.1.8   Subspace and high-dimensional clustering

- PROCLUS (Projected Clustering)
- SUBCLU (Subspace Clustering)
- ENCLUS (Entropy-Based Subspace Clustering)
- ORCLUS (Orthogonal Subspace Clustering)
- FSSC (Fast Subspace Clustering)
- P3C (Pattern-based Subspace Clustering)
- FIRES (Frequent Itemset Clustering)
- SNN (Shared Nearest Neighbor Clustering)
- High-Dimensional Spectral Clustering
- LAC (Locally Adaptive Clustering)

A.1.9   Fuzzy and soft clustering

- Fuzzy C-Means
- Gustafson-Kessel Algorithm
- Fuzzy Min-Max Clustering
- Possibilistic C-Means (PCM)
- FCM-GA (Fuzzy C-Means with Genetic Algorithms)
- FCM-SC (Fuzzy C-Means with Spatial Constraints)
- Fuzzy Subspace Clustering
- Fuzzy SOM (Self-Organizing Maps)

A.1.10   Constraint-based clustering

- COP-k-means (Constrained k-means)
- Constrained DBSCAN
- C-DBSCAN (ConstraintBased DBSCAN)
- PCKMeans (Pairwise Constrained k-means)
- Semisupervised k-means
- FCM with Must-Link and Cannot-Link Constraints
- Hard k-means with Constraints

A.1.11   Evolutionary and genetic clustering

- Genetic Algorithm-Based Clustering
- GA-KMeans (Genetic Algorithm with k-means)
- AGCT (Agglomerative Genetic Clustering)

- MEPSO (Multi-Elitist Particle Swarm Optimization for Clustering)
- NSGA-II (Nondominated Sorting Genetic Algorithm-II for Clustering)
- ACO-CLUSTER (Ant Colony Optimization for Clustering)
- GCUK (Genetic Clustering with Unsupervised k-means)

A.1.12 Neural network-based clustering

- Self-Organizing Maps (SOM)
- Neural Gas
- Growing Neural Gas
- Autoencoder-Based Clustering
- Deep Embedded Clustering (DEC)
- Generative Topographic Mapping (GTM)
- DeepCluster (Deep Learning for Clustering)

A.1.13 Other algorithms

- Affinity Propagation
- Bisecting k-means
- Hybrid BIRCH-k-means

A.2   What is a centroid?

A centroid is the central point in a cluster. In geometry, it is the arithmetic mean or the average of all the points in a shape. For example, in a triangle, the centroid is the point where all the medians intersect (see figure A.1). In any other shape, it would be simply an average of all the point coordinates.

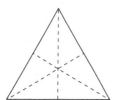 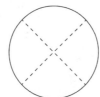 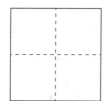

Figure A.1   Examples of centroids

A.3   L1 vs. L2 norm

The L1 norm is the sum of the absolute value of the entries in a vector; on the other hand, the L2 norm is the square root of the sum of the squares of the entries in the vector. It is the core difference between L1 and L2 norm.

A.4   Different scaling techniques used in the industry

The data we get can have different units and values. A dataset can have a variable ranging from 1 to 10 while another variable in the same dataset can range from 1,000 to 100,000. Normalizing the data allows us to normalize it or limit the data between a range. It allows us to fit machine learning better on this normalized dataset.

We normalize a dataset to adjust the values of different variables that are at quite different scales to a common scale. An example is shown in figure A.2.

Distance (miles)	Time (seconds)	Weight (tons)	Price ($)
1.1	20,000	0.01	100,000
1.2	25,000	0.02	400,000
1.3	5,000	0.2	500,000
1.4	10,000	0.2	400,000
1.5	50,000	0.25	500,000

Distance (miles)	Time (seconds)	Weight (tons)	Price ($)
-1.264911064	-0.11	-1.12	-1.70
-0.632455532	0.17	-1.03	0.12
0	-0.97	0.57	0.73
0.632455532	-0.68	0.57	0.12
1.264911064	1.60	1.01	0.73

	Distance (miles)	Time (seconds)	Weight (tons)	Price ($)	Distance (miles)	Time (seconds)	Weight (tons)	Price ($)
Mean	1.3	22000	0.136	380000	0	0	0	0
SD	0.158113883	17535.67792	0.112383273	164316.767	1	1	1	1

Figure A.2 In the first table, we have the mean and standard deviation for each of the variables. Once the data is normalized, then the mean and standard deviation become zero as shown in the second table.

There are different ways to normalize a dataset. The two most popular ones are

- *Standardization*—This involves using the mean and standard deviation for normalizing a dataset. It is also known as *z-transformation*. It standardizes all the variables; the data becomes normally distributed, and all the features become comparable. The equation used is shown in equation A.1:

$$x_{standardized} = \frac{x - \mu}{\sigma}$$ (A.1)

where μ is the mean and σ is the standard deviation.

As we can observe in figure A.2, right, all the variables now have a mean of 0 and a standard deviation of 1.

- *Min-max scaling*—This utilizes the maximum and minimum values of a variable using equation A.2:

$$x_{standardized} = \frac{x - x_{min}}{x_{max} - x_{min}}$$ (A.2)

Normalizing a dataset is one of the important steps followed during the machine learning process.

A.5 Time complexity O(n)

Time complexity is a computational concept used to measure and estimate the amount of time an algorithm will take to complete as a function of the length of the input. Generally expressed using Big O notation, time complexity is used to classify the algorithms as per their worst-case or average-case run-time performance.

Key aspects of time complexity include

- *Constant time [O (1)]*—The algorithm's run time does not change with the size of the input.
- *Logarithmic time [O (log n)]*—The run time grows logarithmically as the input size increases. This often occurs in algorithms that halve the problem size at each step, like binary search.
- *Linear time [O(n)]*—The run time increases linearly with the size of the input.
- *Linearithmic time [O (n log n)]*—This is common in efficient sorting algorithms like mergesort and heapsort.
- *Quadratic time [O (n²)]*—The run time grows quadratically with the input size, often seen in algorithms with nested loops.
- *Exponential time [O (2^n)]*—The run time doubles with each additional element in the input, typical in some recursive algorithms.

Understanding time complexity helps in evaluating the efficiency of algorithms and choosing the right one for a given problem.

A.6   *How to install packages in Python*

In Python, generally the `pip` command is used to install packages. The steps are as follows:

- Open your command-line interface (Terminal, Command Prompt, or Power-Shell). Type `pip install package_name`. For example, if you want to install `numpy`, type `pip install numpy`.
- If you want to install a specific version, use `pip install package_name==version_number`. For example, if you want to install `numpy 1.21.0`, type `pip install numpy==1.21.0`.
- Installing from a requirement file, you can create a `requirements.text` file with all the packages' information and then install it: `pip install -r requirements.text`.
- Sometimes you might have to upgrade a package. Then the command is `pip install –upgrade package_name`. An example is `pip install --upgrade numpy`.

A.7   *Correlation*

Correlation is a statistical and mathematical key performance indicator to measure the extent to which two variables are related. It is used to decipher the relationship between variables, indicating whether an increase in one variable tends to result in an increase (positive correlation) or a decrease (negative correlation) in another.

Key types of correlation are

- *Positive correlation*—As one variable increases, the other also increases. For example, height and weight often show a positive correlation.

- *Negative correlation*—As one variable increases, the other decreases. For example, many times, when the price of an item increases, the demand decreases, and that is a negative correlation.
- *No correlation*—This is when there is no apparent relationship between the two variables. For example, the amount of ice cream sold and the number of TVs sold might show no correlation.

A.7.1 Correlation coefficient

The strength and direction of a correlation are quantified by the correlation coefficient, typically denoted as r. It ranges from -1 to 1:

- $r = 1$—Perfect positive correlation
- $r = -1$—Perfect negative correlation
- $r = 0$—No correlation

Values between -1 and 1 indicate varying degrees of correlation.

A.7.2 Uses of correlation

Correlation is used in many fields, including the following:

- *Data analysis*—Correlation helps analysts identify relationships between variables and helps in further analysis or research.
- *Predictive modeling*—In machine learning and predictive modeling, a model's performance can be improved if we understand the relationship between the variables.
- *Finance*—Investors and financial advisors use correlation analysis to assess the relationships between asset prices, different factors, and reasons to invest, which helps in investment and portfolio diversification strategies.
- *Healthcare*—Researchers in the health sector collect the data on lifestyle factors (like diet, smoking, exercise) and demographics and examine correlations between these factors and health outcomes to identify potential risk factors like heart attack, diabetes, etc.
- *Social sciences*—In fields like psychology and sociology, correlation is used to explore relationships between consumer behaviors, population attitudes, and demographic factors. These studies help uncover relationships in purchasing patterns, reviews, and feedback.

A.7.3 Important considerations

Keep the following ideas in mind when considering correlation:

- Correlation does not imply causation. Just because two variables are correlated does not mean that one causes the other. There might be other factors involved too, or it might be a coincidence. For example, we might find that the sale of ice cream is positively correlated to the number of shark attacks. Hence, we deduce that ice cream sales affect shark attacks—that is absurd. The real reason is ice cream sales increase during the summer season, which is when more people visit beaches.

- There may be outliers. Extreme values can distort correlation coefficients, so it's important to be vigilant on the outliers. Many times if we simply visualize the data with scatter plots, we might get the true relationship.
- There may be nonlinear relationships. Correlation coefficients measure linear relationships. If the true relationship between the two variables is nonlinear, correlation might not capture it.

Understanding correlation is fundamental in various fields and often one of the very first steps. It can be useful to uncover insights that help further drive strategic decisions and the overall path ahead.

A.8   *Time-series analysis*

Time-series analysis involves the study of data points that are collected or recorded at specific time intervals like hourly/daily/weekly/monthly/yearly or others. It is used for examining and understanding trends and behaviors, seasonal patterns and relationships, and cyclical behaviors over time periods, and hence understanding the pattern will be helpful in forecasting. For example, if we want to predict the temperature or rainfall or if we wish to predict the demand for an item, it can involve time-series analysis.

Time-series analysis is commonly used in fields like marketing, finance, environmental studies, and geographic and economic forecasting to predict future values based on historical data. Though there are quite a few techniques, the most common ones are moving averages, exponential smoothing, and ARIMA. Visualization methods, like line graphs, are essential for identifying patterns and anomalies within the data. Overall, time-series analysis is a useful technique for understanding time-based patterns in the data and for making informed predictions and forecasts.

A.9   *Mathematical foundation for data representation*

There are quite a few mathematical terms one must understand to develop a thorough understanding of algorithms. They are useful for understanding the concepts and the mathematical foundation and are imperative for dimensionality reduction methods like principal component analysis and singular value decomposition explored in chapter 3. These mathematical operations are intuitive enough, and you might have covered them in your earlier mathematical courses, but it is important that we refresh the concepts here. The concepts examined are nothing new but are sometimes complex to interpret and comprehend.

> **NOTE** The coding of these concepts in Python can be tricky sometimes. Fortunately, there are quite a few robust libraries and packages that provide easier solutions, and hence we don't have to worry about the implementation of these concepts in Python.

We are trying to reduce the number of dimensions of a dataset. A dataset is nothing but a matrix of values; hence, a lot of the concepts are related to matrix manipulation methods, their geometrical representation, and performing transformations on such matrices. The major concepts are studied next.

A.9.1   Scalar and vector

In simple language, if you walk a distance of 5 km it is scalar; if you walk a distance of 5 km in a direction, say north, it is a vector. So we can say that a vector is a mathematical object that has a magnitude and a direction. Without the direction, it is just a scalar value. We cite a few examples of each in table A.1.

Table A.1   Examples of scalar and vector quantities

Examples of scalar quantities	Examples of vector quantities
Length, width, height, distance	Displacement
Mass, area, density, volume	Weight, force
Pressure, temperature, energy, entropy	Lift, drag, thrust
Speed, time, work, power	Velocity, acceleration, momentum

In plain words, we can conclude that a vector is a scalar with a direction.

A.9.2   Standard deviation and variance

The purpose of standard deviation and variance is to measure how spread the data is. Standard deviation is given by equation A.3

$$\text{Standard deviation } \sigma = \sqrt{\Sigma}(x_i - \mu)\frac{2}{n} \tag{A.3}$$

where x_i is each value from the population, μ the mean of the population, n is the population size or the number of observations, and σ is the standard deviation of the population. And variance is given by equation A.4

$$\text{Variance } S_2 = \Sigma(x_i - xbar)\frac{2}{n-1} \tag{A.4}$$

where x_i is each value from the population, $xbar$ is the mean value of the observations, n is the number of observations, and S_2 is the sample variance.

Suppose we have five children in a class with respective heights of $50, 51, 52, 53$, and 54 inches. The average height is $(50+51+52+53+54)/5 = 52$ inches. See table A.2.

Table A.2   Child height and the calculated difference between the average and height

Child	Height	Difference (Average – Height)
A	50	52 – 50 = 2
B	51	52 – 51 = 1
C	52	52 – 52 = 0

Table A.2   Child height and the calculated difference between the average and height *(continued)*

Child	Height	Difference (Average – Height)
D	53	52 – 53 = –1
E	54	52 – 54 = –2

Note: Variance $\sigma^2 = (2^2 + 1^2 + 0^2 + -1^2 + -2^2)/5 = 10/5 = 2$. Standard deviation $\sigma = \sqrt{(2)} = 1.441$.

A.9.3   *Covariance and correlation*

Covariance and correlation are the measurements of the relationship and mutual dependency between two variables. Covariance is the direction of the linear relationship, while correlation measures the strength and direction of the relationship. See figure A.3.

X	Y
100	1
101	2
102	3
103	4
104	5

X	Y
100	5
101	4
102	3
103	2
104	1

X	Y
100	3
101	4
102	2
103	5
104	1

Figure A.3   If *X* **is increasing, then the value of** *Y* **is also increasing (left). If** *X* **is increasing,** *Y* **is decreasing (middle). There is no observed relationship between** *X* **and** *Y* *(right).*

Figure A.3, left, shows that when *X* decreases, *Y* increases, and vice versa in the middle, while on the right, there seems to be no relationship between the two variables. Here, covariance will simply denote that there is a positive or a negative or no relationship between the variables. The magnitude of covariance will be difficult to comprehend as it is not a normalized result. Correlation, on the other hand, will be able to provide a magnitude of the strength too. Correlation can be calculated by dividing the covariance of the two variables by the product of the standard deviations.

The most popular correlation coefficient is Pearson's correlation coefficient, which only considers the linear relationship between two variables. The other widely used coefficient is Spearman's rank correlation, which is more sensitive to nonlinear relationships. We can visualize correlation as shown in figure A.4.

Correlation does not mean causation. This is the most common mistake made during analysis. For example, consider the statement "There is an increase in sales of shoes, and at the same time there is a decrease in the rate of drowning deaths". If the inference made is that an increase in shoe sales leads to a decrease in drowning deaths, the result is a completely illogical result. This proves that correlation does not mean causation.

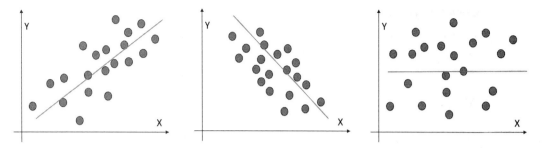

Figure A.4   In the first case, there is a positive correlation between the two variables. In the second case, there is a negative correlation between the two variables. In the third case, there is no observed relationship between the two variables.

The indicators are used to test if there is any relationship between two variables in the datasets. The concept is utilized and referred to in data science quite often. We analyze the strength of the relationship and decide whether a logical trend exists.

A.9.4   *Matrix decomposition, eigenvectors, and eigenvalues*

Sometimes in linear algebra we wish to factorize a matrix into a product of matrices; this process is called *matrix decomposition*. We use matrix decomposition methods if we want to represent a matrix into a product of matrices.

Eigenvectors and eigenvalues are components of matrix decomposition. If we have a square matrix A, then the understanding is as shown in equation A.5

$$A * v = \lambda * v \tag{A.5}$$

where v is the eigenvector and λ is the eigenvalue.

For example, let's say we have a matrix, as shown in figure A.5, and we want to get the eigenvector. Here, -2 is the eigenvalue, and $[1\ -2\ 1]$ is the eigenvector. The eigenvector is a nonzero vector that does not change direction during the transformation. It only scales the original matrix by a factor of λ. The eigenvectors and eigenvalues are utilized for principal component analysis (PCA) implementation.

$$\begin{bmatrix} 3 & 6 & 7 \\ 3 & 3 & 7 \\ 5 & 6 & 5 \end{bmatrix} \begin{bmatrix} 1 \\ -2 \\ 1 \end{bmatrix} = \begin{bmatrix} 3-12+7 \\ 3-6+7 \\ 5-12+5 \end{bmatrix} = \begin{bmatrix} -2 \\ 4 \\ 2 \end{bmatrix}$$

$$-2 \begin{bmatrix} 1 \\ -2 \\ 1 \end{bmatrix} = \begin{bmatrix} -2 \\ 4 \\ 2 \end{bmatrix}$$

Figure A.5   Finding eigenvectors and eigenvalues

A.9.5   *Special matrices*

We next define a few special matrices.

A *diagonal matrix* has all the nondiagonal elements as zero, as shown in figure A.6.

$$\begin{bmatrix} X & 0 & 0 \\ 0 & Y & 0 \\ 0 & 0 & Z \end{bmatrix}$$

Figure A.6   An example of a diagonal matrix

An *orthogonal matrix* is a square matrix that fulfills the following criteria as shown in equation A.6

$$Q^T Q = Q Q^T = I \tag{A.6}$$

where Q is the original matrix, Q^T is its transpose, and I is the identity matrix, represented in figure A.7.

$$\begin{bmatrix} 1 & 0 & 0 \\ 0 & 1 & 0 \\ 0 & 0 & 1 \end{bmatrix}$$

Figure A.7   An example of an orthogonal matrix

A matrix is *symmetric* if its transpose is equal to itself (i.e., $Q^T = Q$).

A.10   *Hyperparameters vs. parameters*

Parameters are the internal values that a model learns from the training of the machine learning model. They are, for example, coefficients in a regression model or weights/biases in a neural network. They are set automatically during the training of the machine learning model.

Hyperparameters, on the other hand, are predefined before the training starts and control the machine learning model. Examples are the number of clusters (k) in k-means clustering or the distance metrics used. They are chosen manually and can be optimized using various techniques like GridSearch CV or Random Search CV.

index